DEEP CREEK

DEEP CREEK

Finding Hope in the High Country

Pam Houston

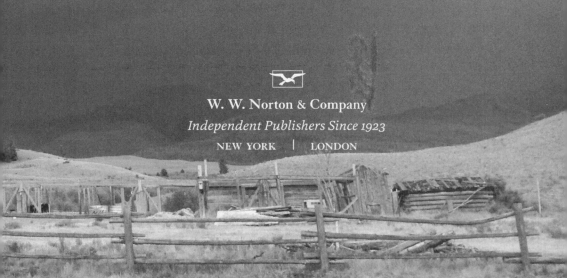

W. W. Norton & Company
Independent Publishers Since 1923
NEW YORK | LONDON

For information about permission to reproduce selections from this book, write to
Permissions, W. W. Norton & Company, Inc., 500 Fifth Avenue, New York, NY 10110

For information about special discounts for bulk purchases, please contact
W. W. Norton Special Sales at specialsales@wwnorton.com or 800-233-4830

Manufacturing by LSC Communications, Harrisonburg
Book design by Fearn Cutler de Vicq
Production manager: Beth Steidle

Library of Congress Cataloging-in-Publication Data

Names: Houston, Pam, author.
Title: Deep Creek : finding hope in the high country / Pam Houston.
Description: First edition. | New York : W. W. Norton & Company, [2019]
Identifiers: LCCN 2018037969 | ISBN 9780393241020 (hardcover)
Classification: LCC PS3558.O8725 A6 2019 | DDC 814/.54—dc23
LC record available at https://lccn.loc.gov/2018037969

W. W. Norton & Company, Inc., 500 Fifth Avenue, New York, N.Y. 10110
www.wwnorton.com

W. W. Norton & Company Ltd., 15 Carlisle Street, London W1D 3BS

1 2 3 4 5 6 7 8 9 0

For

Emma, Kyle, Becky, Dustin, Meghan,

Jessica, Kyle (#2) and Maggie,

who tended the ranch while I was away,

and who let themselves be mothered.

And for Mike Blakeman,

who has given me one more big beautiful reason to come home.

None of the single original claims was capable
of providing a living for a family, but land is fascinating and
more or less magnetic and has always had a value and probably
always will. It is a feeling of stability and security to own
a piece of land. You always feel like you have a home,
no matter how humble.

—John LaFont,
The Homesteaders of the Upper Rio Grande

What elegy is, not loss but opposition.

—C. D. Wright

Contents

PART THREE | DIARY OF A FIRE

PART FOUR | ELSEWHERE

PART FIVE | DEEP CREEK

DEEP CREEK

Introduction:
Some Kind of Calling

When I look out my kitchen window, I see a horseshoe of snow-covered peaks, all of them higher than 12,000 feet above sea level. I see my old barn—old enough to have started to lean a little—and the low-ceilinged homesteaders' cabin, which has so much space between the logs now that the mice don't even have to duck to crawl through. I see the big stand of aspen ready to leaf out at the back of the property, ringing the small but reliable wetland, and the pasture, greening in earnest, and the bluebirds, just returned, flitting from post to post. I see Isaac and Simon, my bonded pair of young donkey jacks pulling on opposite ends of a tricolor lead rope I got from a gaucho in Patagonia. I see Jordan and Natasha, my Icelandic ewes nibbling on the grass inside the goose pen, keeping their eyes on Lance and L.C., this year's lambs. I see two elderly horses glad for the warm spring day, glad to have made it through another winter of 30 below zero, and whiteout blizzards, of 60 mph winds, of short days and long frozen nights and coyotes made fearless by hunger. Deseo is twenty-seven and Roany's over thirty, and one of the things *that* means is I have been here a very long time.

It's hard for anybody to put their finger on the moment when life changes from being something that is nearly all in front of you to something that happened while your attention was elsewhere. I bought this ranch in 1993. I was thirty-one years old, and it seems to me now I knew practically nothing about anything. My first book, *Cowboys Are My Weakness,* had just come out, and for the first time ever I had a little bit of money. It was $21,000—more money than I had ever imagined having—and when my agent said, "Don't spend it all on hiking boots," I took her advice as seriously as any I have ever received.

I had no job, no place to live except my North Face VE 24 tent (which was my preferred housing anyhow), nine-tenths of a Ph.D., and all I knew about ownership was it was good if all of your belongings fit into the back of your vehicle, which in my case they did. A lemon yellow Toyota Corolla. Everything, including the dog.

I drove the whole American West that summer, giving readings in small mountain towns and looking for a place to call home. I started in San Francisco and headed north—Point Reyes, Tomales, Elk, Mendocino. I crossed into Oregon and looked at land in Ashland, Eugene and Corvallis. All I knew about real estate was you were supposed to put 20 percent down, which set my spending ceiling at exactly $105,000. I had no idea people often lied to real estate agents about their circumstances, and sometimes the agents lied back. I had $21,000, a book that had been unexpectedly successful, no job and not three pages of a new book to rub together. I understand now that in a certain way, I was as free at that moment as I had ever been, and would ever be again. I came absolutely clean with everybody.

I checked out Bellingham, and all the little towns on the road to Mount Rainier, and then headed over the pass into the Eastern Cascades, where I put a little earnest money down on a place in Winthrop, Washington. Forty-four acres on a gentle hill with an old apple orchard and a small cabin. I worked my way over to Sandpoint, Idaho, and Bozeman, Montana, still looking, still unsure.

But when I drove through Colorado, a place I had ski-bummed between college and grad school, I remembered how much I'd loved it here. In those days I had lived in the Fraser Valley, at a commune of tarpaper shacks and converted school buses called Grandma Miller's New Horizons. I lived for three winters in a sheepherder's trailer named the African Queen. The twenty or so alternatives who lived at Grandma's shared an outhouse, a composting toilet and a bathhouse. From late December to early February it often got down to 35 below. I was working as a tourist bus driver by day and a dishwasher at Fred and Sophie's steakhouse by night. I would collect every strip of steak fat the diners would leave behind on their plates in a giant white Tupperware next to my station. When I got off work, I would go home and feed all that steak fat to my dog, Jackson. If I packed the little woodstove just right, it would burn for exactly two and a half hours. I would don my union suit, my snow pants, my down coat, hat and mittens, and get into my five-below-rated North Face sleeping bag. I would invite Jackson up on top of the pile that had me at the bottom of it, and he would metabolize steak fat all night, emitting not an insignificant number of BTUs.

It was my writer friends Robert Boswell and Antonya Nelson who first told me about Creede. When you drive into town, the sign at the outskirts boasts 586 Nice Folks and 17 Soreheads. It was, and still is, the kind of place where if you happen to be in town for a couple of days poking around, someone will invite you to a wedding. That September, the guy who owned the hardware store was getting ready to marry his longtime sweetheart, and instead of sending out invitations they just put an ad in the weekly *Creede Miner*, so everybody would know to come by.

At the wedding, I met three women who owned their own businesses: Jenny Inge who made jewelry out of silver and horsehair, Victoria Beecher who sold flowers and plants, and Max McClure who had opened a coffee shop and was making Creede residents their very first lattes.

"Creede people wouldn't have even thought the *word* 'flowers' until I showed up," Victoria told me. "But this town supports anyone who has a dream. Nobody goes to dinner without a handful of tulips anymore."

The morning after the wedding, a real estate lady named Kathleen, whom I'd met in the buffet line, showed me an empty lot of approximately five acres and a couple of houses in town that had been built by silver miners using paper and string. She said, "I really ought to take you out to see the Blair Ranch," and I said, "Sure," and she said, "But, it wouldn't be right, a single woman living out there all by herself," and I said, "How far?" and she said, "Twelve miles," and I said, "Maybe I should see it," and she said, "I'm afraid it's out of your price range."

For that I had no argument.

I was sitting in my car, studying the Rand McNally, contemplating the next potential future home . . . Lake City? Gunnison? Ridgway? I was just that close to driving out of Creede forever, when a tall, rodeo-buckle-wearing cowboy named Dale Pizel knocked on the window. "I hear you want to see the Blair Ranch," he said. I got out of my car. "This is Mark Richter," he said, indicating his equally tall, handsome friend. "The property is his listing and he is going to take you out there right now."

If you can't fall in love with the San Juan Mountains during the third week of September, you can't fall in love. The mountainsides are covered with the world's largest aspen forests, and they are changing in vast undulating swathes: yellow, golden, orange, vermilion. The sky is a headstrong break-your-heart blue, the air is so clear you can see a hundred miles on a straight horizon, and the river is cold and crisp and possibly even clearer than the air. The coyotes sing, all night sometimes, and the elk bugle in the misty dawn along the river.

And there was the Blair Ranch, with the best view of it all I had ever seen. One hundred and twenty acres of high mountain meadow in the middle of the larger Antelope Park: 9,000 feet above sea level, with the Upper Rio Grande cutting serpentine turns through the center of it, surrounded on three sides by the 12,000-foot peaks of the Continental Divide, the lower slopes carpeted in Engelmann and blue spruce, Douglas fir, bristlecone pine and aspen. The house was a simple two-bedroom log structure that, rather than being ostentatious, seemed to apologize for itself in the middle of all that beauty. It hunkered down behind a little hill, just enough to miss the worst of the wind and weather. At the top of the hill, Mark told me, the homesteaders, who were called the Pinckleys, were buried in shallow graves. Old Man Pinckley's tiny cabin was still standing behind a weathered fence, along with some outhouses and a pen where he had bred Canada geese. But the real prize was the barn—raised by Pinckley himself in 1920 and built from hand-hewn spruce logs, silhouetted against Red Mountain to the south, and leaning now, just slightly, to the west.

I had no way to imagine, in the first moment of seeing it, that the view out the kitchen window—of the barn and the corral and the Divide behind it—would become the backdrop for the rest of my life. That I would take thousands of photographs of that exact view, in every kind of light, in every kind of weather. That I would write five more books (and counting) sitting at the kitchen table (never at my desk), looking, intermittently, out at the barn. That it would become the solace, for decades, for whatever ailed me, and that whenever it was threatened—and it would be threatened, by fire, flood, cellphone-tower installation, greedy ranchsitters and careless drunks—I would fight for it as though I had cut down the trees and stripped the logs myself.

The price tag was just shy of $400,000. I told Mark the same things I had told every real estate agent from Mendocino to Casper. My $21,000, in terms of the Blair Ranch, would represent just over 5 percent down.

Mark rubbed the back of his hand against his chin for a minute and said, "I believe Dona Blair is going to like *the idea* of you. Dale knows her pretty well and between the two of us. . . . Why don't you give me your five percent down and a signed copy of your book and I will see what I can do." He snapped a picture of me sitting on the split-rail fence like a girl who already owned the place.

Dona Blair sold me the ranch for 5 percent down and a signed hardcover of *Cowboys* because she liked the idea of me, and she carried the note herself because any bank would have laughed in my face. I bought the ranch for its unspeakable beauty, and if I am completely honest, for the adrenaline rush buying it brought on. I nearly killed myself the first few years making the payments. I wrote anything for anyone who would pay me, including an insert for an ant farm, which I turned into a brief Communist ant manifesto I imagined the enlightened but bored parent discovering with pleasure when he helped little Johnny open the box. I wrote an article for a magazine about why Clint Eastwood was my hero (he wasn't). I wrote an article about twenty-something women who were getting plastic surgery to combat signs of aging (who cares?). In the process, I learned how to hustle, and I mean that about myself in only the kindest way.

Dona spends her winters in Texas now and her summers in Creede, and what she's been saying in the coffee shop about me for twenty years is "You know she makes those payments, and on time!"

The people in town, mostly miners and ranchers, didn't understand or much care what I did for a living, but they respected the fact that I had to work hard to keep the place and that I was willing to. I began to get looked out for by the locals who matter: the postmistress, the banker, the judge, the owner of the hardware store, the cops.

There was the night my first winter when Sheriff Phil Leggitt came barreling up my driveway at three in the morning, and ran into my house, yelling "Pam, Pam are you all right?" because, in an attempt to get my apparently dead phone to work, I had dialed 911 and then hung up fast when it began to ring. There was the time the president of the Creede bank intervened to keep one of my early ranchsitters from taking the ranch right out from under my nose in a kind of old-fashioned Wild West land grab. There was the time the postmistress, knowing I was snowed in, brought all my Christmas packages to her house, close enough that I could ski over there and drag them home on a utility sled.

In twenty-five years at the ranch I have learned a few things: to turn the outside water spigots off by mid-September, to have four cords of wood on the porch and two hundred bales of hay in the barn no later than October 1. I've learned not to do more than one load of laundry per week in a drought year, and that if I set the thermostat at sixty and bring the place up to sixty-eight using the woodstove in the living room, the heater doesn't do that horrible banging thing that sounds one tick shy of an explosion. I've learned barn swallows carry bedbugs, and the only way to kill those little suckers is to wait until it is 30 below and drag the mattress out onto the snow and leave it for forty-eight hours. I have learned to hire a cowboy every spring to come out and walk the fence line, because much as I would like to believe I could learn to be handy with a fencing tool, I have proven to myself I cannot. I know eventually the power always comes back on, that *guaranteed overnight* is a euphemism, and for a person who flies a hundred thousand miles most years, choosing a place five hours from the Denver airport was something I might have given a little more thought.

But right from the beginning I've felt responsible to these 120 acres, and for years I've painted myself both savior and protector of this tiny parcel of the American West. And this much is true: as long as I am in charge of it, this land will not turn into condos, it will not be mined or forested, it will not have its water stolen or its trees chopped down. No one will be able to put a cell tower in the middle of my pasture and pay me $3,000 a year for the space. One of the gifts of age, though, is the way it gently dispels all our heroic notions. All that time I thought I was busy taking care of the ranch, the ranch was busy taking care of me.

All my life I've said I am happiest with one plane ticket in my hand and another in my underwear drawer. Motion improves any day for me—the farther the faster the better—on a plane, a boat, a dogsled, a car, the back of a horse, a bus, a pair of skis, in a cabbage wagon, hoofing it down a trail in my well-worn hiking boots. Stillness, on the other hand, makes me very nervous. So what happened to all that wanderlust in the moment I became the first person in my family since my mother's grandfather (who raised pacing horses back in Indiana) to be responsible to a piece of land, to fall in love with a barn and a meadow, to be land rich and money poor for decades?

My parents were travelers too, though they preferred cruise ships to kayaks and beachfront resorts to a North Face tent. Homeownership meant nothing to them, though they grudgingly engaged in it a few times, paying a local kid to mow the lawn and rake the leaves in autumn. My mother had been happiest careening around Europe with the USO in a plane with teeth painted on either side of its nose, and my father often said he'd have been happiest living out his life in his single room at Sloan Simpson's home for bachelors, watching the incessant motion of the Delaware River out the window. I thought this was one way I might be like my parents, until I laid eyes on the ranch.

I have written elsewhere, at possibly too much length, about how unsafe, unwanted and unsettled I felt in the houses where I grew up. One thing I was looking for when I bought the ranch was a place I might be comfortable sitting still. I also wanted something no one could take away from me, but my upbringing left me addicted to danger. So I put a tiny down payment on a property that cost four times more than I could afford, one that required so much maintenance the tasks fell into two categories: things I didn't know how to do, and things I didn't even know I didn't know how to do yet.

That I survived, and that the ranch did, suggests something good about my karma. That when I thought I could go to Denver for New Year's Eve and keep the pipes from bursting by dripping the faucet, it was only the mudroom floor that got flooded. (It got to 38 below zero that night.) That when I thought it would be really cool to paint my propane tank to look like a watermelon, the dark green paint did not, in fact, absorb enough 9,000-foot solar heat to explode. That someone always came along in the nick of time to say "When was the last time you had your chimney swept?" or "How often do you coat your logs with that UV protector?" and then I'd know what I was supposed to have been doing all along.

Because of the short summer tourist season, it's hard for *anyone* to make a living in Creede, even if you don't have 95 percent of a ranch to pay off. Given *my* particular skill set, earning a living always has and always will mean leaving. America loves one or two hermit writers desperately, but the rest of us are encouraged to spend weeks, months and years on the road, giving readings, teaching workshops, hawking books, making sure people don't forget our names. I've spent more nights at the ranch, these two and a half decades, than I've spent any other place; that's certain. Though, a lot of years, between teaching and touring, it doesn't add up to half the year's nights.

I love the ranch differently than someone who goes to bed and wakes up 365 times a year here, someone who was born and raised here, someone whose most regular routine does not involve TSA security and running for connecting flights. You have to be a certain age, I think, to understand longing as scarcely distinguishable from pleasure, and my love affair with the ranch is defined by a thousand leavings and a thousand returns. It's the only place I always miss, no matter how fabulous my temporary circumstance. When the road turns to gravel and bends with the river into Antelope Park, every single part of me takes a deep breath.

It doesn't seem like twenty-five years have gone by since that girl who lived in her VE 24, whose belongings all fit into the back of her Corolla, first sat on the split-rail fence that sits in front of the aging barn, which sits in front of Red Mountain. That girl who dared herself to buy a ranch, dared herself to dig in and care for it, to work hard enough to pay for it, to figure out what other people meant when they used the word "home."

Blink your eyes and that girl is a fifty-six-year-old woman who has lived five times longer than she has ever lived anywhere on a ranch in a high mountain meadow of lupine and fescue, surrounded by granite and spruce. Every penny that has gone toward the mortgage payments I have earned with my writing and that fact matters so much to me that when my father died ten years ago and what was left of his money fell to me, I left it in his brokerage account and pretended it didn't exist.

Sometime in the last twenty-five years, the ranch changed from being the thing I always had to figure out how to pay for, to the place I have spent my life.

And when the chores are all done, the ranch is a meditation in stillness. It says, *Here, sit in this chair. For the rest of the afternoon, let's watch the way the light lays itself across the mountain. Let's be real quiet and see if the three hundred head of elk who live up the mountain come through the pasture on their way to the river to drink.*

In 2013, during the largest fire in southwestern Colorado's history—110,000 acres burning less than a mile from the ranch—treetops exploding into flaming rockets down one arm of the horseshoe of mountains that for twenty years had kept me safe, I drove under an apocalyptic orange sky through lung-searing smoke past two roadblocks the firefighters had set up to take Dona Blair my final ranch payment, my fiction writer's mind unable to decide whether this gesture would make it more or less likely the ranch would be engulfed in flames. When I got to her driveway I saw that all the giant spruce trees her husband had carefully designed the house to fit among had orange flagging tied in their branches. These would be the first ones the Forest Service firefighters would cut if the fire got too close.

We'd been on standby to evacuate for weeks, and I'd decided the only thing I really wanted to save (other than the animals, who were enjoying a smoke-free vacation a hundred miles away in Gunnison) was the barn, which wouldn't fit in the back of my 4Runner. But the summer monsoon came in time to save us, as it always has, right on schedule on Fourth of July weekend—you can set your watch by it—and now it looks as if I will get to spend the rest of my life watching the charred mountainside to the west of me regerminate, revitalize, regrow.

This is the only real home I have ever had—this log cabin with its tilted horse barn, a leaking propane tank and a resident pack rat who has a weakness for raspberry soap. The house isn't plumbed for a clothes dryer, so in the winter I string clotheslines in the kitchen, the mudroom, and around the woodstove in the living room. The fifty-year-old furnace can only keep up with the regular subzero temperatures if the woodstove is burning all the time, and as a result, when I go out into the world in a public way in the winter, I smell as if I have just come from a Grateful Dead concert. All the window screens are frayed because my little coydog, Sally, who came to me from some traumatic puppyhood that landed her in the Flagstaff pound, could predict a lightning storm at fifty miles, and at the first rumble would make a neat little X-shaped slice with her toenail and then power her body through the window and to her place of choice, under the porch.

Sometimes, when I'm driving back out Middle Creek Road after a week teaching writing in Mallorca, Spain, or Ames, Iowa, and I round the corner where Antelope Park stretches out huge and empty and magnificent in front of me, I am openmouthed with astonishment that this is the place I have lived the largest part of my life. It's a full-time job lining up ranchsitters for the significant chunks of time I need to be away, and even if it is someone more competent with a fencing tool than I am, it makes me nervous to leave so often. The ranch and its animal inhabitants sometimes want and need attention of a kind that just can't wait until I'm scheduled to get back, and my life becomes a balancing act I don't always get right. Some days I think I would like to live near the ocean, or a sushi bar, or a movie theater, or my friends, who by and large live vibrant lives in sophisticated cities. But a low-level panic that feels downright primal always stops this kind of thinking in its tracks. A quiet certainty that if I gave up the ranch, there would be no more safe home, no place of refuge, no olly olly oxen free.

And there is one more thing. The summer before I drove all over the West looking for a home was the summer I lost my mother. I am only telling you now because I had never realized the coincidence of it, had never thought about the cause and effect relationship of it—until I began to write the story of the ranch.

I am only a little better at giving in than I used to be, at slowing down, at sitting still. But progress is progress, and any amount of it I have made, I owe entirely to this 120 acres of tall grass and blue sage, with a simple log house, a sagging barn and a couple of equine senior citizens.

How do we become who we are in the world? We ask the world to teach us. But we have to ask with an open heart, with no idea what the answer will be.

It might have been fate, or some kind of calling. It could have been random, but it doesn't *feel* random. Sometimes a few pieces of the puzzle click into place, and the world seems to spin a little more freely. In other words, maybe I didn't choose this ranch at all. Maybe this ranch chose me.

Ranch Almanac: Buying Hay

A farmer named Rick Davie has kept me in hay for twenty-four years. Rick grows both good certified grass hay and alfalfa. I've always bought the grass, because my Paso Fino, Deseo, has a metabolic condition a little like diabetes and can't handle rich forage. But now that the horses are as old as the hills, I have Rick throw in twenty bales of alfalfa for the coldest January mornings.

A few times over the two and a half decades I've lived here, I got talked into buying somebody else's hay, and each time I was sorry. Rot, mildew, sick horses and not enough volume to get me through the winter. Rick's bales are large, dry and heavy, and they keep weight on my guys all winter. When I post a photo on Facebook of my horses eating in the snow, invariably one horsewoman or another will ask "Hey, where did you get that nice-looking hay?"

Each autumn, Rick backs his giant, ancient flatbed through the orange gate—this itself is a thing of beauty, like watching a blind man thread a needle—and swings it around to the front door of my barn. He's stacked a hundred bales on the truck to a height of about twelve feet—a risky proposition considering the fifty-mile drive from his place to mine, but the hay always arrives in perfect condition. Rick climbs up on top of the pile and asks me to position one bale right in the doorway of the barn. He calls it a "bouncer," and sure enough, if he tips each subsequent bale just right every one of them will spring off the bouncer bail and straight into the middle of the barn. From there a couple of Rick's ranch hands and I, and eventually Rick himself, will drag and stack those bales in every available space.

Rick makes fun of me for dragging the bales with my hay hooks. He's sixty-five and strong as a bull and can still pick those suckers up and toss them on top of a stack five bales high. He also makes fun of my fancy ginger ale (Bruce Cost Original with real ginger puree I buy in Denver), but every time he delivers hay he drinks two bottles. Every once in a great while, he'll stay for lunch. He'll come inside and take his cowboy hat off, and, without fail, announce that raising four daughters made all his hair fall out.

All my friends say, upon meeting Rick, Now that's a man, *by which they mean if I would stop—for the love of God—falling in love with poets, I might have some help getting things done around here. I had, for most of a decade, been in a long-distance relationship with the poet Greg Glazner. He lived first in New Mexico, and then in California, and came to the ranch to visit over the holidays and part of every summer. And while Greg did help me with the care and feeding of the animals during the several weeks each year he visited, he would be the first to admit he wouldn't be able to build a birdhouse with a kit.*

Rick, by contrast, built a full-sized basketball court in the loft of his 1915 barn to use as a dance floor because he didn't want his daughters to have to get married on some golf course somewhere.

When he delivers the hay, I see him looking around at all the things that need fixing around here—stuff he could do some morning before breakfast with one hand tied behind his back.

Rick is bringing 250 pair of Gelbvieh Angus cross cattle down off the range tomorrow, but he still makes time to bring me some hay today. I told him I would feel better going back out on the road next week if there were thirty bales of hay in the barn, so he goes ahead and brings me a hundred. My ranchsitters might not use a single bale before I return on the first of November. On the other hand, they could be up to their rumps in snow by the weekend. Rick tells me I don't have to pay him for these hundred bales until he brings the second load, so I go ahead and pay him for all two hundred. These sorts of business deals are one of the best things about living in this place.

PART ONE

Getting Out

The Tinnitus of Truth Telling

My beautiful mother ran away from Spiceland, Indiana, at the end of the eighth grade. Her Aunt Ermie, who had raised her to that point, had bet my mother fifty dollars she could not get straight Cs on her final report card. But she did get straight Cs, took the cash and got on a bus bound for Broadway. There, she got plucked off the streets by two young actors who, thirty years later, became my Uncle Tommy and Uncle Don. Tommy and Don fed my mother, clothed her and bailed her out of most of the teenaged trouble she got herself into. For the next two decades, she danced, sang, told jokes and did cartwheels across stages in countless theaters, nightclubs and cabarets in New York and elsewhere. During World War II, she went overseas with Bob Hope's USO touring show. After that she became Frank Sinatra's opening act in Vegas, then returned to New York and acted in supporting roles, on and off Broadway, with some of the best of the time: Jackie Gleason, Walter Pidgeon, Nancy Walker.

Then, somewhere in the neighborhood of forty-two (she always lied about her age and my father lied in her obituary, so now I will never know for sure), for reasons utterly inexplicable to me, she married my father and got pregnant. In that order—I have checked the dates a hundred times.

At the Bucks County Playhouse in New Hope, Pennsylvania, my father went backstage with a dozen roses and an invitation for the pretty actress to take a spin in his cream-colored Buick convertible. She got so drunk on their first date she threw up all over his milky leather seats, and he said, "You better get your shit together because we are going to get married," and six weeks later they did.

My mother had a big, hearty laugh, which boomed out of her when she was happy, or sometimes angry, or sometimes for not much reason at all. She was so very beautiful. I think of her, more than anywhere else, at her makeup mirror, "putting on her face," her honey hair pulled back in a headband, the eye she was lining super-magnified in the glass. She had gorgeous long legs—dancer's legs, with pretty knees and sturdy calves—which she gave, like a promise, to me. She could do roundoffs and even handsprings down the beach at the Jersey Shore well into her sixties. She could bring people together to put on a show—in the old-fashioned sense—like nobody's business. In Trenton, New Jersey, and then after my father lost his job there, in Bethlehem, Pennsylvania, my mother raised money for the United Way and United Cerebral Palsy by turning amateurs into professional singers and dancers with only a few weeks of rehearsal. And though she would be frustrated by poor lighting, bad sound systems and long-out-of-tune pianos, I believe those hours in the theater made her miss her Broadway days a little less.

"I gave up everything I loved for you," she'd say to me almost daily, to get me to order my salad dressing on the side or use the organic apricot scrub she bought me, or *not* to wear my retainer in front of company. And I would want only to find a way to give it all back, to restore to her the life she'd had before being saddled with the burden of me.

"But *why* did you do that?" I wish I'd had the wherewithal to ask her.

Alcohol addiction notwithstanding, my mother had the strongest will of anyone I have ever known. She barely ate and she never perspired and she did not grow body hair. I am fairly certain if her biological clock had ticked one time she could have willed it silent with her mind or smashed it with her fist.

My father was charming, but she had had forty-two years, plus or minus, to learn to see through his kind of charm. Had thirty years in the ups and downs of show business simply worn her out? Did she marry my father because she saw a future rushing toward her where the fact of her age would make it harder and harder to land roles? Or did some Indianan idea of conventionality sneak up out of the cornfield and grab her from behind, dragging her back to the cul de sac?

If it did, it lied to her about how she would feel once she got there.

My mother's mother died in childbirth with my mother, so it stands to reason my birth would have killed my mother, at least a bit. She lived on until my thirtieth birthday, an honorable life that included her variety shows, devotion to the altar guild, work with the developmentally disabled, good friends and lots of tennis. But it seemed to be only a half-life, a shadow of the thirty years that had preceded it, and when a combination of vodka and Vioxx took her out at seventy, give or take, I was, alongside my sadness, glad that she didn't have to witness herself losing any more than she already had.

My mother liked to say she stopped working after she married my father, but that is not precisely true. For several years she kept doing summer theater. Even after she gave that up, she still landed roles in TV commercials and bit parts on soap operas: the long lost cousin, the visiting aunt. For several years she was Betty of Betty's Roadside Stand in a series of Post Raisin Bran commercials, and she predated Jane Russell as the face of Playtex's "I Can't Believe It's a Girdle." Yet for every day she went off to New York for an audition or shoot and came home glowing and singing, there were ten other days when her task list read: *laundry, dinner, dry cleaning, Pam to dentist, cat to vet.*

And then there is this. Even in the "Betty's Breakfasts" years, when her residual checks added up to more than his income, my mother handed her checks directly over to my father. He gave my mother two hundred dollars household money every two weeks to buy groceries, clothes and every single other thing the family needed, from the time I was born until the time I left for college, with no adjustment for inflation. My father carried more than two hundred dollars in his wallet at all times, bought used Cadillacs and hand-tailored suits while my mother made our clothes on the sewing machine and scoured magazines to find interesting things to do with leftovers. The song that was on continuous repeat in my childhood kitchen was my mother reasoning or flirting or begging for an advance on next week's money, and my father shaming her, no matter what the circumstances, for spending it too fast.

My father was a child of the Depression, which left him and his single mother in such dire circumstances he never recovered emotionally, even though he made a good living all his life. He couldn't stop himself from driving across the state line to New Jersey to buy gas that was a few cents cheaper, from smashing a lamp that had been carelessly left on by my mother or me in an empty room, from putting his finger down on the disconnect button of almost anyone's long-distance phone call. He hated phones in general—even when the call was local, some unspecified meter was running in his head. When forced to speak on the phone, he would say whatever he had to say in as few words as possible and then hang up without saying goodbye.

My father was incapable of organizing the world into anything but profit and loss columns, keeping a running tally in his mind of everything, especially what my mother and I cost. He billed us for his time, not just in dollars but in life energy as well, and made it clear there was nothing we could do that would come close to paying him back.

Now that I am roughly as old as he was when I was born (he lied about his age too, but I did my best to tell the truth in *his* obituary), I can see how my father built himself a prison out of his own stinginess. Not only did he group people in his life by the ways they were trying to "rip him off," he allowed himself to be affronted by every good thing that happened to anyone, even if they were strangers or public figures. He was a golf fan, though not a golfer, and I can remember him boiling with rage when a young Tom Watson won $40,000 in his first Masters victory. Why should Tom Watson have cashed in big for playing seventy-two holes of golf, when my father had had no such opportunity? Why should a tall, talented left-handed pitcher named Steve Carlton command $65,000 to play baseball for his first season with the Philadelphia Phillies, when my father had to work forty hours a week at a job he hated to make far less? When I told my father about the modest—even in those days—advance W. W. Norton paid for *Cowboys*, he shook his head and grimaced. "You know," he said, "Wayne Newton is the highest paid performer in the free world."

I don't have a single memory of my mother seeming to even *like* my father, so it is hard for me to guess what made her fall for him. He was charismatic, but it was an Archie Bunker/Ralph Kramden brand of charisma, if you can imagine either of those two fit and good-looking with a powerful tennis serve and a convertible. He was quick-witted and could be very funny, though the humor was almost always at someone else's expense. The one unqualified positive thing I can say about my father is that he was *game*—for a road trip, a new restaurant, a midnight swim in the ocean, a run on the beach. Into his eighties, he and his teenaged doubles partner, John Speer, won the "100+ combined age" tournament at his beloved tennis club. My father gave me my love of travel, the edgier part of my humor and several IQ points— none of which are small gifts. He also taught me to love baseball, football and hockey, and I remain an embarrassingly enthusiastic sports fan to this day.

My mother was anorexic and did her best to raise me to be too. From earliest memory she'd say to me, "Let's see if we can get all the way to dinner without eating anything." If I got hungry on one of those long, calorie-less days, and I complained about it, she'd say, "Let's try this, then," and her eyes would get that irresistible sparkle they always got on stage. She'd get two pieces of stone ground wheat bread out of the plastic bag on the counter. She'd hand one to me, and then draw me over to the sink where she would run warm water and scrunch up the bread in her palm until it sogged and broke into pieces and ran down into the garbage disposal. "It will give you the illusion of having eaten," she said, beaming, as though she was telling me the very secret of life.

My mother was proud of my straight As and my graduate education and eventually the publication of my first book. But she was never for one moment satisfied with my appearance. No matter how hard I tried, I could never get thin enough to suit her, even in college when I was 5'6½" and weighed 125 pounds. If I could find a way to quantify how much she hated that I parted my hair in the middle, you would think either she was crazy, or that *I* was, for not just going ahead and parting my hair on the side. The truth was, I didn't really part my hair anywhere, and still don't, but it does tend to fall just slightly to the left of center. "Even the Mona Lisa," she would say with a gravity she reserved for such topics, "would not look good with her hair parted in the middle." For all the years I had braces (and there were many), she could hardly stand to look at me, and if I put my rubber bands in, as I had been instructed, it put her over some dangerous edge.

The only reason I was allowed to get braces in the first place was that my orthodontist had an ingenious way of scamming parents. (I heard he was sued over it two years after I finally let one in a long series of white rubber retainers fall into the dishwasher where it melted into a shape that would fit nobody's mouth and declared myself finished with orthodontics.) He would take a photograph of the child, and then, through the wonders of what was at that time brand-new computer technology, age the photos two ways: with braces and without. When he showed my mother the photo of the thirty-year-old me without orthodontia, I looked exactly like a pale-faced, blue-eyed gorilla, and she fainted dead away, right there in his office.

My mother once called my best friend in graduate school (*graduate school!*)—Debra Monroe—to ask her to encourage me to wear lipstick.

"And if you can get her to do *that*," she said, "see if you can't talk her into going with you to Weight Watchers."

On one of my first nights out as a writer, the night the actress Mia Dillon was reading my story "How to Talk to a Hunter" at Symphony Space on Broadway, my mother almost came to blows with my editor, the great Carol Houck Smith. Carol wanted me to look "cowgirl" for the evening, and so I'd chosen a simple black shirt, a long denim skirt, a concha belt and a silver bucking bronco pin. But my mother, who single-handedly kept the world in shoulder pads for at least a decade longer than it needed them, begged me to change into a slimming fire-engine-red Liz Claiborne blazer. No matter that all I would do was stand for a moment in the audience when the master of ceremonies said my name. In the lobby, as the audience filled in around her, my mother waved the hanger holding the red blazer at Carol. "It's a better line! It will brighten her up!" she said, while Carol kept looking over my mother's shoulder, as if for security.

At my mother's funeral, six months later, there was hardly anyone who did not express to me how glad they were she had seen *Cowboys*'s publication, that she had died knowing I had found my way in the world.

"You were her everything," they said, partly to make me feel better, partly to jab at my father. And because my mother had told me daily she had given up all her other everythings for me, I knew, at least in some way, what they said was true.

Years after my mother's death, my lifesaving therapist, Drew L'Oizeaux, asked me to make a list of the things my mother loved, and as usual I obliged him: acting, singing, dancing, tennis, sewing, travel, vodka.

"And how many of those did she actually give up when you were born?"

I had to think about it for a minute. "None of them," I said finally. "She enjoyed every single one of those things right up to her death."

"How about that?" he said. "Turns out the only thing she gave up was . . . what?"

"The condition of childlessness," I said, which I have to grant is no small thing—a state I admit to valuing myself.

In 2011, I was on an 8:00 a.m. breakfast panel at a publishers' trade show in Denver. I arrived with wet hair. The moderator of the panel asked me if I wanted to borrow her lipstick (the damn lipstick again!). The other panelist, who arrived looking like a million dollars, was Cheryl Strayed, who had a book coming out about her grief over her mother's cancer diagnosis, rapid decline and consequent death, which sent Cheryl into a tailspin so deep that, had she not hiked the Pacific Crest Trail and in the process come back to herself, she might have followed her mother to an early grave. Whenever Cheryl tells this story, she mimes how I took the lipstick from the woman and put it on without even looking at the color. She says that is when she knew we would be friends.

In January 2016, we spent a week together on the island of Kaua'i and we talked a lot about mothers. Even then, with her mom having been gone more years of Cheryl's life than she was present, the grief on her face and in her voice when she spoke of her mother was palpable, piercing and so near the surface.

We'd been walking on the beach at Hanalei, the powerful January surf thundering against the sand and rushing up between our feet, threatening to destabilize us.

"Do you miss *your* mother?" Cheryl asked me.

"Yes," I said. And then, "No." And then, "I'm honestly not sure." Another wave pounded against us, the water sluicing up between my knees. That Cheryl's question did not have a clear and immediate answer unnerved me. "I don't miss her, anyway, in the same way you miss yours."

For the moment that was the right answer. But the question

gnawed at me. *Did* I miss my mother? And what exactly did it mean if I did not?

The story I'd been telling for years about my family, to therapists and best girlfriends and prospective lovers, was this: My father broke my femur when I was four years old. I believe he meant to kill me. My mother spent the next decade throwing herself between him and me, trying to make sure he didn't. This is the same story she told her friends. She couldn't leave my father, she always said, because she was afraid of what he might do to her and also afraid she wouldn't be able to make a living on her own.

My mother's version of our story is more or less true—here I am, after all, fifty years later to tell it. But like most truths, it is not uncomplicated. In this version of the story, my mother is sad and little bit heroic. My father *might* have hurt her if she'd tried to leave him, but it seems at least possible—given his rage over having to support us—he might have sighed with relief. Had my mother been freed from picking up my father's dry-cleaned suits and cooking the elaborate dinners he demanded, she might have had more time to turn her substantial talents into income.

"After her funeral," I said to Cheryl, "I found myself reaching for the phone to call her often. I was deeply sad for her that she was not going to get the years she had always imagined at the end of her life without my father—and sad for myself, because I thought maybe if he were gone she could finally relax, maybe we could finally relax together." I could hear how paltry those words sounded in the face of Cheryl's acute, abiding grief.

"My mother loved me a lot," I said, "but she loved vodka more and it ruled her. It made her untrustworthy on an hour-by-hour basis. I think maybe you have a different brand of love for a parent you can't ever trust."

Over the roar of the ocean my ears hummed with the tinnitus of truth telling. Should I go on? Should I, here on this sunny, sea-sprayed beach, tell Cheryl what I'd never told anyone except Drew, my therapist, that my mother *knew* my father was hurting me on a regular basis for more than a decade? That often she was in the next room? That sometimes she was in the *same* room? That the broken femur was only the showiest injury? The one that took the longest to heal? That from a very young age (six? seven?) I had perfected two specific ways of leaving my body, one that worked when he was punching me in the head and another for when he grabbed me by the hair and pulled me with him into the shower? That by the time I turned seventeen, the various objects my father had forced inside me in addition to his dick had created so much scar tissue on my cervix that I had to have hush-hush surgery, performed not by my gynecologist, but by my father's urologist? And that two days after I'd been released from the hospital, when I started to bleed more than any person ought to bleed ever, my mother was too scared of outing my father to take me to the emergency room? That I begged my mother to leave him at least weekly, that I offered to quit school, work full-time, seek sanctuary with my friends' parents, whatever it took?

We were past high tide, and the waves were smaller now, the sets less frequent. I no longer had to raise my voice to speak above them.

"The crime for which my mother was always—whether she knew it or not—atoning, was that her mother died during her birth," I told Cheryl. "I believe it is why she married my father, why she stayed with him, why she drank, why she starved herself, why she let surgeons cut into her face to remove her wrinkles four different times."

We even loaded the car one time, after my father had knocked two teeth out of my mouth with his fist. It was two months after the urologist butchered my cervical surgery, and I told her either we could leave together or I would leave by myself and emancipate. We got as far as Hilton Head Island, of all places, where she spent all weekend flirting with the tennis pro before she lost her nerve and we turned around and went back to my father's house. I had entered first grade early, and would graduate in June and leave for college in September. On the way back from Hilton Head she promised me if I just stuck with her for those final months, she would not try to guilt me out of going to college. I did not emancipate, and she kept her promise.

Cheryl is one of the best listeners I have ever known and she has empathy for miles. But I left a lot out, including the other thing I've only told Drew, which is that insofar as I know, my father never one time hurt my mother. I went to school with bruises so often teachers made inquiries, called social workers in to talk with me, strategized with me about safe houses and exit plans. My mother let surgeons turn her face into a bloody and bruised pile of hamburger meat on a regular basis, but I have no memory of her turning black and blue at my father's hand.

About a decade ago, Drew and I came up with an alternative version of my mother's story. In the new version, my father still plays the villain, but he's no more than an actor, cast into a role by my mother, who wrote, starred in and directed the dark comedy (I refuse to think of it as a tragedy) of my childhood. It was a story that had begun to write itself upon my mother the day she was born, and yet it's been important to me not to have thought either myself or my mother helpless. Maybe that's why Drew's version of the story appeals to me more than the one I had spent decades telling. In the new version my mother is acting out of will instead of fear.

And yet, no amount of reframing will ever convince me my mother didn't love me. She did. And my mother's love, misshapen as it was, had a physical weight and gravitational pull, like a planet, or the sun. I suspect watching my father hurt me physically and abuse me sexually for seventeen years was one more punishment my mother heaped upon herself, one more atonement for the crime of being violently born.

I may not be right about any of this—it is just a grown-up, therapized woman's theory. But I do know when I was born, the designations of victim and criminal got re-sorted somewhere in my mother's emotional architecture. She ceased being my grandmother's killer, and I became the murdering child. In this way, I saved her. And when I look at pictures of myself at one and two and four years old, I can see in my own eyes I knew it even then.

When Cheryl and I reached the end of the beach I lifted my eyes to the mountains that encircle the bay, to the rainbow, that more days than not, reaches out of them and falls into the ocean just offshore. The mountains are steep, but softened by their jungle covering, and Hanalei, even on the days when the sea is the roughest, has always felt to me like a cradle.

When my mother died, I was freed from the terrible hope that she might one day *actually* throw herself between me and my father. As soon as she was no longer my potential protector it was perfectly clear she never had been. My mother's death exploded me out of one story and into another, and I came to understand it had been my job, all along, to protect myself.

Ranch Almanac: Stacking Wood

According to the British Columbia Ministry of Forest and Range Glossary of Forestry Terms, a cord of wood is the amount that, when "racked and well stowed (arranged so pieces are aligned parallel, touching and compact), occupies a volume of 128 cubic feet. This corresponds to a well-stacked woodpile four feet high, eight feet long, and four feet deep; or any other arrangement of linear measurements that yields the same volume."

Karl Kolisch is my wood guy, stoic to the point of near silence, Norwegian, surely, with his broad forehead and those giant hands. He sneaks up my driveway in his beater of a dump truck (it's the loudest truck in the valley yet for some reason in twenty-five years I haven't caught him at it) and dumps a cord of wood in front of the garage. I know he'll be back with another cord in an hour or a day, and then another, and another. I begin every winter with four cords, and wait and see what happens from there.

When the wood arrives, it's my job to move one cord off the

*driveway, around the house, and up on to the wood porch, and
to stack the other three cords along the house's west side. The
first winter I was here I stacked all four cords on the wood porch
four layers deep and by the time spring came my porch had as
much give as a moderately tight trampoline, so now I bring the
cords up in stages. My body prefers it when I move and stack the
wood for two hours a day over a several-day period—unless Karl
drops the wood off on a day before a predicted blizzard, and then
I try to knock it all out before dark. I find moving and stacking
this amount of wood both mind-numbingly tedious and deeply
satisfying. When I was a kid, I used to love cutting the lawn
for similar reasons. As a teenager, when I worked at Long John
Silver's, I loved refilling each table's condiment bottles at the end
of every shift. There is something so pleasingly pure about having
a task to be accomplished and then accomplishing it. It is the exact
opposite of writing, and pretty close to the opposite of teaching. In
both writing and teaching, nothing is ever finished, only finished
enough to let go.*

*Karl brings the wood with the big rounds already split, which
means the only splitting I have to do is to make enough kindling,
every night, to get the fire going. You would think with twenty-
five years of practice I would be among the best wood splitters in
America, but in truth I am not. I am still likely to miss the log and
wrench my back, or drop the maul on my toe, or split a piece of
wood in such a way that a splinter jumps up and stabs me in the eye.*

*Visitors, especially urban visitors, love to split wood, for a
variety of reasons. It makes them feel primal, or it reminds them
of visiting their grandparents' house when they were children, or
they like to pretend each log is their ex-wife or -husband's face. I
encourage the passion, whatever its source. Last November my
friend Dixon came out from Sausalito and got so into the splitting
I still have a cardboard box full of kindling he cut hiding under
my bed for nights when I just can't face it.*

Every time I split wood, I picture the cover of the book Chop Wood, Carry Water: A Guide to Finding Spiritual Fulfillment in Everyday Life, *which came out in 1984 and was a big hit at the commune where I lived then, and whose advice I apparently took both seriously and literally. For the first fifteen years on the ranch I had to carry water too. Once the creek froze for the year, every drop the animals drank had to be carried to the trough from the mudroom in five-gallon plastic containers. Ten years ago I invested in two frost-free pumps, one at the edge of the pasture and one in the corral.*

Frost-free pumps have an old-fashioned pump handle on top of a ten-foot pole that connects to a water line laid from the house at a six-foot depth. They work pretty well most of the winter, but I can tell whoever named them never tested them at 9,000 feet above sea level in a valley with temperatures that dip to 40 below zero and winds that crank up to fifty miles per hour. Luckily, when we sank the water lines, we sank an electric line too, so I can wrap the poles in heat tape for the winter and plug in. Sometimes, though, even the heat tape isn't enough to stop the pumps from freezing.

Four Christmases ago they froze solid, and my friend Steph and I went out there on a 10 below afternoon with a pry bar, a crème brûlée torch, two space heaters and a bunch of space blankets, made a kind of tent around us, and chipped and clawed our way a foot down into the frozen soil trying to defrost the pipe. After three hours, Greg came out with two cups of hot chocolate and the message that, in case we hadn't noticed, it was getting dark. We worked on into the night with headlamps, warming the dirt before we replaced it and packing it tight around the pole, making sure no stones or clods were leaving frigid air pockets. But every time we tried the pump, we got nothing.

Eventually we gave up, came inside, and took turns in the clawfoot tub thawing our frostbitten toes and fingers. But the next morning, a sunny one, where the 10:00 a.m. temp climbed above zero for the first time in a week, we went out to test the pump and after a few noisy sputters water began flowing. Some combination of the crème brûlée torch and the space-heater-warmed dirt we repacked around the pipe must have been just enough to give the heat tape a chance to catch up overnight. Steph and I high-fived and all but did the bump we were so excited. It was almost as satisfying as the time I took my cell phone apart and fixed it with a steak knife.

Retethering

In my first semester in a Ph.D. program in creative writing at the University of Utah, a professor had laid out the rules for stories turned in to his workshop: "No trees, no snow, no mountains, no skiing, no eyes, no tears, and no female bodily excretions."

If you have read *Cowboys Are My Weakness*, you might conclude I wrote it as an act of defiance, and, knowing me, I probably did. But it's also true I both avoided and survived the hip parade of graduate school by working as a river, hunting and skiing guide simultaneously. I rowed rubber rafts down all the rivers of the Colorado Plateau: the Colorado, the Green, the San Juan and the Yampa; as well as the Salmon, the Middle Fork and the Selway in Idaho. I guided for whitetail deer in Montana's Little Snowy Mountains and for Dall sheep in the Alaska Range and the Brooks Range in the far north. I worked as a ski instructor and backcountry ski guide in Park City. My daily life was full of trees, snow, mountains, skiing, eyes, tears and female bodily excretions, and so were my stories. They were the ones I had to tell.

But my professors at Utah didn't like my work and did not receive news of the book's success warmly. One accused me of glorifying an archaic form of masculinity. Another had written on my evaluation, "Pam should find something else to do with her hands."

Two months after publication, I waited outside the graduate studies director's office door a full hour after our appointment time. I needed him to sign my tuition waiver for what would be the final quarter of my Ph.D. It was not uncommon, in our department, for the creative writers to be treated like the poor cousins of the literature students, especially by this man who we had nicknamed "Our Advocate." But this was a simple piece of paperwork, imaginary money passed from one imaginary entity to another within the university's bureaucracy. I didn't anticipate trouble.

Eventually My Advocate waived me in but did not invite me to sit.

"Fiction or poetry?" he asked, by way of a greeting.

"Fiction," I said.

"And you are ABD, or what?"

"My dissertation is finished." I took a small breath. "And published."

He narrowed his eyes. "That must be nice for you," he said.

"It is," I said.

He moved a few papers around on his desk and sighed. "I can't sign this today," he said, "You'll have to come back tomorrow."

I was living in Park City. "Coming back tomorrow" would involve a two-hour round-trip drive and we were supposed to get snow. My Advocate picked up his office phone and started dialing. I rose to leave. Somewhere between the office chair I had not been asked to sit in and the little hallway that connected us to the main English office, the idea of walking out of Orson Spenser Hall forever sprang up in my mind, and once it had lodged there I could not shake it free. By the time I passed the copy machine, where the guy who had said I should find something else to do with my hands and the guy who disallowed female bodily excretions were having a conversation about whether it was better to be an imminent writer or an eminent writer, leaving felt more like a promise I had already made myself. I walked down the hall gaining speed, flushed, almost giddy with this thing I was about to do.

In the two and a half months since my book had come out I'd been on tour, spending time with real writers, who, generally speaking, cared more for life and one another than those who populated that building. I banged out the front door of Orson Spenser Hall and never went back—not for my books or my coat. I've not been back to this day. I never told anyone I was leaving, and no one ever asked if I would return.

My book tour rolled on, taking me all over the country as well as to England, Scotland, Ireland and France. I didn't have much time to worry about what I'd given up. My lease in Park City ended on June 30 and I hadn't even begun to think about where I'd next call home when one morning my father called me, shock so thick in his voice it was almost unrecognizable. The night before, my mother had told him she didn't feel well. He asked her if she wanted to go to the hospital and she said no. When he woke up that morning next to her, she was dead. He said, "I keep asking the paramedics why they can't bring that machine in here and do that thing they do on TV."

What I remember most about the funeral is being scared. Of my mother's friends who would shame me for moving to the other side of the country and leaving her to suffer my father's anger alone. Of the void that would open up now that my lifelong occupation—keeping my mother from despair—was no longer required. Mostly, though, I was afraid of my father, of how we would face each other without my mother always finessing and controlling that neutral space between us.

My father had been hypercritical of my mother for the thirty years I had been on the planet, but the day she died she became the most wonderful woman in the world. Without her, would he even be able to clothe and feed himself? Two nights after the funeral I found him standing in the kitchen, contemplating the dishwasher. "I discovered," he said, "if you put the glasses in there right side up, they get all full of water." I barely had time to teach him how to push the buttons on the microwave before I was back on the road to writers' conferences and summer workshops.

For the first time in my life there was no back to school, there was no back to anything, only forward. I rented, on a month-to-month basis, a bedroom in the Oakland Hills, where I knew virtually no one. I spent mornings working on my second book, and cultivated a macchiato addiction in the late afternoon. Predictably sleepless, I drove the three bridges in circles half the night. Bay Bridge—Golden Gate—Richmond and back home again, listening to Tori Amos's "Little Earthquakes," singing along to "Silent All These Years" at the top of my voice.

The next six months went by in an instant, and in January the paperback of *Cowboys* came out, marking the start of another long tour. Those months are blurry now, but I do remember, with perfect clarity, after a reading at the King's English Bookshop in Salt Lake City, my friend Terry Tempest Williams taking my face in both of her hands and saying, "Now you are untethered. There is nothing holding you, anymore, to this earth."

All these years later, it's impossible for me to say whether I remember so little of 1992–93 because I was in shock over my mother's death, or because all of my dreams were coming true to an extent I had no way to contextualize. It was probably a little of both.

It was the summer of 1993 when I embarked upon the aforementioned western-states reading and real estate tour. In early September, I found myself in Steamboat Springs, where I met a pair of writer sisters who invited me to Denver for a couple of days. They had tickets to Monday Night Football, Broncos-Raiders as well as a Rockies make-up doubleheader against the Houston Astros on Tuesday afternoon. My years in Colorado between college and grad school had turned me into a Broncos fan, and as of that season, Denver had gotten the baseball team they'd been vying for for years.

The Rockies were playing at gigantic Mile High Stadium—Coors Field had yet to be built—and were on track to break the all-time MLB season attendance record. Never mind both teams were in last place in their division and Houston had played most of their home games that dismal season in front of fewer than a thousand people. I remember the look of astonishment on the Houston players' faces as the Astros took the field. Fifty-five thousand Rockies fans showed up on a Tuesday afternoon in September to show the media and the organization just how excited Denver was about baseball.

It was that enthusiasm for life, for the mountains and everything you could do in them, that had thrilled me when I'd lived in Colorado before graduate school. Two days after that doubleheader, I rolled into Creede. By the weekend I'd made my offer on the ranch.

Did I ask myself whether putting 5 percent down on a 120-acre ranch I had no idea how to take care of and no foreseeable way to pay for might have been taking the idea of *retethering to the earth* to a radical extreme? I did not. Did I ask myself whether my whirlwind year and a half on the road surrounded by people who were rabidly (and unfoundedly) thrilled to make my acquaintance had me so freaked out I bought 120 acres of protection in a town even most Denverites had never heard of? I did not. If buying the ranch was a gross overreaction to either my mother's death or my book's unexpected run, it was a secret I kept from myself.

What I *was* becoming aware of in those days was that something I thought of as the *greater physical world* had always had an uncanny way of looking after me. My parents had been drunk so often—crazy raging drunk, absolutely no-business-getting-behind-the-wheel drunk—and yet they were always getting behind the wheel. As a result, I was in sixteen totaled automobiles before my sixteenth birthday. My parents and I collided with trees, guardrails, other cars and mailboxes; we were catapulted through cornfields and onto median strips and underneath one tractor-trailer.

One Sunday morning in April, my mother sent me in to the local 7-Eleven to buy a copy of *The New York Times* after church because she had drunk so much of the blessed but unused communion wine (a fringe benefit of being a member of the altar guild) she couldn't get her legs underneath her. Just before getting back in the car, I dropped the paper under her MG Midget and was bent over gathering sections together when the wheels began to spin and spit gravel. Leaning over to see what was taking me so long, my mother had jammed her foot onto the accelerator rather than the brake. The car leapt the significant curb, knocking me backward and picking up with its bumper one of those big plastic horses you put a dime in to make rock. My mother's car pushed that horse all the way to the stand-up coolers in the back of the store, where the glass exploded spectacularly, sending cans of soda careening all the way out into the parking lot.

One Christmas Eve, my father and I rolled a Cadillac convertible seven times, into the median, across two lanes of opposing traffic, and down into a creek bottom, shattering every piece of glass, shredding every tire, caving in every piece of steel except the portion of the roof above the front seat where the highway patrol had to cut us out with chain saws.

Not just sixteen car crashes before I was old enough to get my learner's permit, sixteen *totaled* vehicles. And I never, as a result of any of those crashes, spent one night in the hospital.

After high school, having gotten out of my parents' house alive, I predictably replaced the dangers inherent there with risks of my own choosing. I ran class V rapids at flood stage, sat up all night with fresh Dall sheep carcasses in grizzly country, and skied out-of-bounds avalanche chutes and couloirs with the toughest of the boys.

When an avalanche on a moonlight telemark ski on Berthoud Pass failed to pull my skis under the snow and me with them; when the water cooler popped up beside me after I flipped my raft in Big Drop 2 in Cataract Canyon (the highest runnable falls in North America), providing me more than enough flotation to survive Big Drop 3; when I guided a 52-foot sailboat out of the peak winds of Hurricane Gordon through a narrow break in a coral reef and into an unlit harbor on Bimini (the hurricane had knocked the light out) by listening hard to the way the waves were talking to me; it was hard not to believe the earth was somehow keeping my best interests in mind.

It's not so much of a stretch, then, for me to believe the ranch somehow urged me toward it; that it spoke to some ancient part of my brain, which despite all evidence to the contrary, still felt an urge toward home.

I have always taken the greatest comfort in being surrounded by wild things. From the time I was eight months old and my babysitter Martha Washington would take me out in the stroller every afternoon and I would grab the scruff of two neighborhood German Shepherds, Salt and Pepper, one with each hand, and they would flank my stroller like some kind of suburban secret service. Or in my grade school years, when my mother would say "I don't even want to see you until dinner!" and I would disappear for hours with the neighbor girls into the little remnant woods on the other side of Stoke Park Road, where we would hit our own hips with imaginary crops and gallop over fences made from fallen trees. On those first camping trips with Colonel Bob Miller, who would load fifteen neighborhood kids into the back of his station wagon and make us ride under wool blankets, telling us we were headed "out west," which was really just an overgrown portion of Bethlehem's Monocacy Park. He'd teach us how to use a compass and how to keep from walking in circles without one, and how to move through a dark forest without fear. During all the trips to the ocean with my parents, where, on the last day, I would stand at the edge of the sea for hours saying goodbye to every wave. In high school, where I would walk the train tracks alone through miles and miles of deciduous forest, making friends with all the animals, memorizing birdcalls, leaf patterns, every bend in Monocacy Creek. In college, when my roommate Mary and I would head down to Hocking Hills in southeastern Ohio for camping, hiking and cross-country skiing, or farther into the Allegheny Mountains of West Virginia near towns with names like Thomas, Douglas and Job. During the years between college and graduate school when I worked seasonally in ski towns, and lived in the off-season all over Utah's red rock country in my VE 24, eating freeze-dried food, going weeks sometimes without a proper shower. For the decade I spent guiding river trips and hunters. I am never more content than when I am cooking, eating, sleeping, waking and walking in the wilderness.

Even now, in my grown-up professional life, too much of which I spend on airplanes, I am likely to grab the sleeve of an unsuspecting stranger and say, *Look! There! That's Upheaval Dome, or the Mogollon Rim, or the Blue Ridge Escarpment*—as we sail 39,000 feet above the places I've walked in my life, carrying everything I needed on my back. It still makes me so happy just to say their names.

It is no wonder, then, the ranch opened my heart like a tin can. A place with so little light pollution the Milky Way is truly milky. The big mountains—Bristol Head, Red Mountain, Copper Ridge, and Baldy—hold me in place, the gamma grass dancing in great undulating swathes, the aspens quaking their comfort, the creek and the coyotes combining for a lullaby, the big sky, whether full of stars, sunshine or snowflakes is *always* watching over me.

The initial mortgage Dona carried for me was a fifteen-year note, with a monthly payment that verged on $4,000. (In 2003, she would refinance me, extending the mortgage by five years.) Along with the magazine work, I started a bootleg river business where I applied for private permits and then advertised, "Write and Run the River with Pam Houston." I told myself I was more or less within the parameters of the law because I wasn't charging folks for the river trip itself, only the writing instruction that came with it. We all split the cost of the river expenses just as we would have on a private trip, though I'm pretty sure the BLM/Forest Service wouldn't have gone for that explanation if push had ever come to shove. I also accepted offers to read or teach wherever and whenever they occurred.

At one of those college visits, I met a young woman—I'll call her Dani—who was eager to help me with my river business. She had recently received a great deal of money in a trust fund, she said, so I wouldn't need to pay her for her work. I could teach her to row and to crew, and she would work in exchange for the knowledge. I accepted, since that sort of trade was exactly how I had learned to run rivers myself.

Dani and I led several trips together, and to say she was helpful would be a grotesque understatement. She was Radar O'Reilly to my Henry Blake. I would turn my head fifteen degrees to scan the shoreline for a suitable lunch spot, and there she would be, readying the bowline. I would only have to glance at the bottom of the boat and think "bail bucket," and she was already putting it in my hand. I had run river trips over the years with a couple of different boyfriends, but I had never teamed up with someone who was willing to help me *and* let me be the trip leader.

Perhaps that's why, at the end of river season, when Dani offered to buy a third of the ranch from me to alleviate the financial pressure she knew was driving me to distraction, I accepted. In September 1995 I sold her one-third of my acreage and none of the buildings for $120,000. I started a job teaching as a one-semester visitor at St. Mary's College in Moraga, California, and Dani went to Creede to take care of the ranch.

The letter came to my rented cottage in California via FedEx during the first week in October. I was shocked to see it, because at the time I could not imagine FedEx was a thing Creede had. I no longer have the letter, so I'm relying on memory here, but it said something along the lines of "I don't want to own the ranch with you anymore, and I know you don't have the money to buy me out, so I am going to buy you out. Please contact me so we can make arrangements ASAP."

A colleague at work assured me she wasn't serious. "She's just saying 'love me, love me, love me,'" he said. "She thought when she bought the ranch with you, the two of you were going to be roomies. Fly home this weekend, make her vegetarian lasagna, let her read you her poems, and everything will be all right."

I flew home on the weekend. I made her vegetarian lasagna. She read me her poems at length. When I finally got the nerve to ask her if she wanted to talk about her letter she said, "There's nothing to talk about. I'm firm on it. Either you pay me back the $120,000 immediately or I am buying you out."

This was not the same Dani I had known on the river. When I pressed to know what had come over her, she admitted her grandfather had put her up to acquiring the ranch. He was the one, of course, who had set up her trust fund, and he owned property all over the American West.

It is also possible Dani was a little bit in love with me. *Cowboys* made lots of people fall a little bit in love with me, and two things I can say for certain are, it wasn't really *me* and it wasn't really *love*. But Dani was twenty-two, and on the river I had taken her seriously in a way maybe no one in her life ever had. I could imagine her complaining about my absence to her grandfather, and her grandfather seeing an opening, seeing a way to acquire one more piece of beautiful land. This all happened more than twenty years ago, but one thing I remember with perfect clarity is how much Dani feared her grandfather, how terrified she was of disappointing him.

I drove to town to clear my head and so I wouldn't say anything I might regret later. Maybe, I thought, buying the ranch had been a giant mistake after all, and maybe this was a clean way out. For two years I had been running ragged trying to make the payments. I had given the $120,000 Dani gave me straight to Dona Blair, which had lowered my monthly payments from $4,000 to $2,500, putting them into the realm of just barely makeable if I took every single job that came along. My work was all contract work—a freelance article here, a ten-week teaching gig there. No bank in the world was going to give me $120,000 to pay Dani back.

I parked my car in front of the post office and ran immediately into Ann, Dale Pizel's wife.

"Pam!" she said. "I didn't know you were in town. Dale was just asking me about you. He needs you to sign some papers about water rights."

I got the mail and walked down the street to Dale's office. "How's the world traveler?" he said. Dale is a cowboy from his ten-gallon hat to his shiny silver buckle to the steel toes of his leather boots. The walls of his office are covered with rodeo photos and fancy saddles—his affect is more horse trainer than real estate man.

"Grounded in California for the semester I'm afraid," I told him. "Trying to earn a little money."

"I've finally got these water rights papers from the original sale," he said. "They basically say you know you don't own the water in Lime Creek and you won't dam it up for your own purposes. But you can take them home and look them over if you want. How long are you here?"

The question tugged at my heart. "Two more days," I said, which was the immediate answer. But what if that was the answer for all time?

"Just take those home and read them, and I'll be here Monday morning if you have questions. Or you can just drop them in the mail before you leave town."

I picked up the document, thanked Dale, and made to leave. "Oh, and Pam," Dale said.

I turned to face him.

"I also have these other papers, the ones I drew up to put those forty acres into Dani's name. I haven't filed them with the county yet. So since you're here in person, you might look them over too."

My heart started pounding in my ears. "You mean . . . ," I began, but everything I could think of to say next seemed unequivocally self-convicting.

"The sale isn't official until we file the papers with the county," Dale said. "Since we did it all over the phone, I thought you might want to lay eyes on them before it's—you know—permanent."

Now my heart was beating so hard in my chest I was sure Dale could hear it. "I'll do that," I said. "Thanks, again." I gathered up the rest of the papers from his desk and walked out his door. Once outside I sank onto the bench in the town park. It had been at least ten days since I had deposited Dani's check in my account, since I had written a check for the same amount to Dona Blair. And now, I was pretty sure the only papers in existence saying Dani owned part of the ranch were in my hands.

I drove back to the ranch feeling significantly more empowered.

I walked into the house and sat down on a kitchen chair facing her. "You may have inherited more money than I will earn in my lifetime," I said to Dani, "but I spent six months of my life looking for this place and it is psychically mine. I don't know right now how I am going to pay you back, but I will, and with interest. Now I need you to gather up your things and get off my property. Tell your grandfather to go find some other beautiful piece of land."

I wasn't surprised when Dani's face flooded with relief. She *had* done this to please her grandfather. Maybe somewhere in there she wanted my love. But what she really didn't want was to live by herself on a 120-acre ranch in Creede, Colorado, and now she didn't have to.

On Monday I went back to Dale's office and told him the whole story.

"We can loan you that money, Pam, at an interest rate that won't kill you." I had forgotten Dale was also the president of the local bank.

"We'll get Dani her money, and I'll write to her on your behalf and ask for a quitclaim deed. She doesn't need to know she was never quite the owner of that land."

The First National Bank of Creede loaned me $120,000, to go with the $250,000 I already owed Dona Blair. Miraculously, that winter, I was hired by Michael Shamberg at Jersey Films to write a screenplay (never made), which knocked the Bank of Creede loan down to almost nothing. Just like that, I was back in the realm of barely manageable.

In the months after Dani's departure, several people in town told me stories. That Dani had been rude on multiple occasions to Conoco Connie at the gas station and Bertie the postmistress, who is possibly the sweetest woman on the face of the earth. That she refused to make eye contact when she ordered her morning coffee at Cafe Ole. That she had called both the Soward Ranch and the county offices to complain about the dust the trucks were making going in and out of the Soward gravel pit. And while it is true those trucks make a lot of dust, everyone in town knew that gravel pit was the only thing allowing seventy-five-year-old Margaret Lamb to pay her county taxes.

I would never have had the ranch in the first place had Dale Pizel not talked Dona Blair into the idea of me, and I wouldn't have kept it without Dale's decision to lend my overextended self another $120,000. In transactions with Dani, he was my realtor, my banker and my lawyer all rolled into one.

I knew better than to ask Dale if he had heard stories about Dani, and if that's the reason those papers sat for ten days on his desk. I knew better than to read too much into it when he would say things to me in the months to come about Creede magic, about how the valley spits some people right out like a pit, and welcomes others, gets under their skin and never lets them go. He probably has no idea how often I think of him, or how grateful I am to him every single day.

I don't see Dale around town very often. He rides in the Fourth of July parade, and I see him at the Elks Lodge dance on New Year's. We wave and smile, but we've barely had a real conversation in years. I did bump into him going into the post office the day I wrote this book's proposal, the day I first put down on paper his role in changing my life forever.

"Hey, Pam," he said, opening the door and smiling broadly. "It's such a funny thing to find you here, because for some reason I've been thinking about you all day."

Ranch Almanac: Donkey Chasing

When the mini-donkeys first arrived at the ranch, there was some—I would have to call it good-natured—chasing. And to be fair, the wolfhounds were used to my returning from work trips with a squeaky toy for each of them. When I brought home the mini-donks, they probably just thought I'd outdone myself.

I hadn't considered, when I agreed to rescue the bonded pair, that my pasture was fenced to keep horses and cattle, but nothing much shorter or skinnier than that. My corral, especially, was not mini-donkey-proof, and neither were a few of the pasture corners that had been left with a small space open so people could slip through. Also, the donkeys really liked people. They would follow me around the yard while I did my chores. They'd pick something up in their mouths—a hose, a rope, a stuffed-lobster dog toy— and play tug-of-war with it, mostly, it seemed, for my amusement. They had no problem negotiating with their little high-heeled hooves the three steps that led up to the dog porch, where they would spend several minutes sniffing the bowls and beds as if solving a great mystery. If I had let them, I believe they would have followed me right through the front door into the living room, and curled up with me on the couch.

The wolfhounds at first were curious about the donkeys and then affronted at their hubris. Fenton, especially, had a strong belief system around animals staying in their place. He felt Mr. Kitty belonged outside, in the mudroom or in the basement. The sheep and the chickens belonged in their indoor/outdoor enclosure. Horses belonged in the corral, the barn and the pasture. Who were these newcomers, who'd been given the run of the place?

Fenton would watch them nervously for hours until his outrage got the better of him, and then with no particular provocation, he would leap up and chase the donkeys around the yard. And because William did everything Fenton did exactly one half-second later, the donkeys found themselves on the run a couple of times each day.

The wolfhounds are just about a head taller than the donkeys, and the donkeys were younger and maybe even a little smaller back then. I don't believe the dogs had any intention of hurting the donkeys, but wolfhounds are bred to chase fast-moving objects, and those little donkeys can turn it on, in spite of their super-short legs.

Sometimes Isaac, the bigger, brassier, donkey, would manage to turn the tables, would reach out his big square teeth and take a nip at a wolfhound haunch, and then the chase, for a little while, would go the other way. This strategy backfired of course, because the dogs thought that game was even more fun than the original, and so did everything possible to encourage it. On the one hand, everyone was getting lots of exercise, but on the other, said my nascent rancher voice, someone was eventually going to get hurt.

I could fix the spaces in the fence given a little time, but I would need poles, and a bag of cement and a few days when I didn't have writing deadlines, so I decided to give communal living a try. I rewarded peace when it occurred, and was vigilant about calling off the dogs, bringing them inside with me so the donkeys could enjoy some quality yard time alone.

After a couple of weeks, I needed groceries, sheep feed, a mineral lick and about a million other things I would think of once I got to the Monte Vista Coop, a little over an hour's drive away. I locked the dogs in the house and left all the gates but the front one open, so the equines could graze in the yard together where the grass was greenest and sweet.

Five hours later, the truck loaded down with a month's worth of barnyard supplies and groceries, I got out to open the gate at the end of the drive. I heard Deseo whinnying and whinnying as he trotted nervously up and down the fence line. Deseo is a worrywart, the fussiest of all the animals on the ranch—a little like someone's urbane great-uncle set loose against his wishes on the farm—but he's also a very good alarm clock. When anyone or anything is threatened, Deseo makes sure to let me know.

I wrenched the gate open and went flying up the driveway to see who was injured or dead. I took a quick head count. Six chickens, five sheep, two horses, two donkeys and, pressed up against the kitchen window, the noses of two interested dogs. I caught Deseo with a lead rope, looked him over and petted his neck. He was all frothed up but seemed unhurt. Everyone else was strictly business as usual, Roany ingesting as much tender yard grass as he could before I turned him back to his 120 acres of pasture, Simon and Isaac on either end of a knotted rope dog toy, pulling each other across the driveway.

I let Deseo go and turned back to the truck to unload the groceries. When I carried the first bags up the walkway to the dog porch, I didn't at first comprehend what I was seeing. And when I tell you the dog porch was covered in donkey shit, I want to make sure you don't picture two or four or even ten piles of steaming *donkey pucks placed here and there on the wooden decking. The dog porch is roughly eight by eight, and every square inch of its surface was covered in donkey poop. I mean to say those donkeys shit and shit again and spread it around with their little hooves, and then they shit some more and spread that around, and then they shit again. They shit on all four dog beds, and in the case where there was more than one bed piled on top of another, they had pulled or kicked the beds apart so they could shit on the ones underneath. One of them shit into an open rectangular cooler I had washed and put on the dog porch to dry. They had upended the trash can that lives on the porch and kicked the shit and the trash together. They had even somehow smeared shit on the porch railings.*

It had to have been a premeditated attack and it seemed utterly impossible it had been committed by only the two of them. Had they somehow saved up for days? And if so, how had they known I would pick that day to go to the valley? The transgression had the scope and feel of a well-executed fraternity prank, though there wasn't a college within three counties.

I had always heard donkeys were smarter than horses, and I imagined how much satisfaction they must have taken, shitting away, kicking stuff around, while the dogs' noses were pressed tight to the kitchen window. I believe Isaac wanted me to understand there was no insult directed at me personally, because nothing that was not on the dog porch had been tampered with.

This was what Deseo had been trying to tell me as he trotted up and down the fence line while I fumbled with the gate. "Ohhhhhhh. . . . she's gonna see the do-o-o-o-o-g p-o-o-o-orch," he whinnied, at the first sight of my car coming down Middle Creek Road. Closing up those spaces in the pasture fence moved to the top of the chore list. It was a brief but effective revolution, and the donkeys maintain their sovereignty to this day.

PART TWO

Digging In

The Season of Hunkering Down

By the first of October, the aspens are done showing off for the year. First dusting of snow on the peaks, then first dusting of snow on the pasture. The color is almost gone and with it the tourists. My neighbors from the Soward Ranch have moved into town for the winter. For the next seven months, I'll be the last occupied house on my road. The horses hang around the corral, looking a little grim. They know what's coming.

I'm just back from a fourteen-day research trip to the eastern Canadian Arctic on an icebreaker, and three separate weeks teaching—on the island of Ile de Ré off the Atlantic coast of France, on a 140-year old schooner out of Rockport, Maine, and at the Omega Institute in the beautiful Hudson Valley. I have two weeks at the ranch before I have to leave again.

I've all but missed this year's color change in the high country, so even though there's much to be done to prepare for winter, this morning Fenton, William and I take a hike up to Phoenix Park—one of the most wind-protected places in the valley—hoping to find a few groves of aspen still holding their leaves. We climb for an hour in light drizzle and under my boot soles is a carpet of green and gold. We surprise a mule deer buck, a four pointer, at the place where the forest gives way to meadow. When we reach the waterfall at the top of the park, the sun peeks through the clouds just long enough to turn the whole scene Kodachrome: the heavy gunmetal sky, the ghost aspens, with only a fraction of their leaves left glowing like a fluorescent pencil sketch beneath it, the water tumbling down the face of the cliff, beads of it lit up against the dark rock and spinning earthward like fireflies.

In the summertime this trail sees a fair amount of use, from hikers and horsemen, sometimes four-wheelers, and even the occasional 4-x-4 truck, but summer feels long over and we are between hunting seasons, so the dogs and I have the place to ourselves.

Years ago, on an August hike right at the tail end of the monsoon, I got caught in a thunderstorm halfway across the big meadow that leads to Phoenix Park. I was new to the valley and had not yet learned how a bright white micro-puff in one corner of the sky can morph into a cumulonimbic monster in the amount of time it takes to go around a couple of bends in the trail.

If you have never gotten caught in a thunderstorm at high altitude; if you have never felt your long straight hair stand on end as if someone above you has strings attached to it; if you have never smelled sulfur in the air just before a crack you can feel at the center of your ribcage splits the sky in two; if you have never run between lightning bolts that are hitting the ground on every side of you, your brain racing to determine whether you will improve or diminish your odds of surviving if you take five seconds to unbuckle your pack and throw its contents, including your stainless steel water bottle and your waterproof camera to the ground; then you might not understand what a pleasure it is to hike that same trail in October, on a cool dry day where the odds of a thunderstorm, while not impossible, are about 10,000 to 1.

After a snack and a long drink out of that same, time-tested steel water bottle, the dogs and I make our way back down the trail, smelling not sulfur, but the slow rot of dying leaves in a dry climate and the occasional tang of pine pitch. An immature bald eagle rides a thermal down canyon, and it's windless enough that I can hear sun-warmed rocks—newly freed from last night's frost—slip and settle in the big scree field across the creek that rises up toward Wason Park.

In the house I grew up in, fall marked the start of the most dangerous season. My mother dreaded the snow and ice and the perpetually gray skies of a Mid-Atlantic winter. Either she never learned how to buy a serious winter coat, or her vanity wouldn't allow it. She played indoor tennis but the reservations were expensive and in high demand, so she didn't get enough exercise for her to justify the few food calories a day she normally ingested and her perpetual hunger was the loudest thing in our house. The shortening days meant she drank more and started earlier. By the end of September she was headed into a tailspin from which she would not emerge until the crocuses came up in the spring.

By the time my mother died in 1993, the drug Prozac had been taken by more than ten million people. And yet I don't believe the word "depression" had ever been uttered in my childhood home until once, during fall break of my junior year of college, I told my mother I had started taking advantage of Denison's free psychological services.

A boy I had befriended from my geology classes was showing strong self-destructive tendencies—he had just left a severed pig's head in the ice machine in one of the all-female dorms—and I'd made the appointment hoping to get advice on how I might help him. After giving me advice, the therapist, a kind, smart and soft-spoken man by the name of Jeff Pollard, asked simply, "And how are you feeling these days?"

I felt my body go utterly still for the count of one, two, three . . . and then I burst into sobs that lasted upward of ten minutes. I can still feel that office around me as if it were yesterday, the leather books, tall ceilings and high windows, through which I could see all the trees on the quad ablaze in fall color. I can still feel my dawning understanding that therapy was a thing that had been invented to, among other applications, help people who had suffered exactly the sorts of things

I had suffered at the hands of my father. Even then it had taken many sessions for Dr. P to convince me that it was okay to accept that help.

My mother and I were driving back from an unsuccessful trip to the mall. I had arrived at my parents' house wearing a peasant blouse and a long colorful hand-painted skirt I'd bought for more than I could afford at an art fair. She said the skirt made me look fat and we'd go buy something she could stand to look at me in. I had fended off several pencil skirts and dart-heavy blouses, as well as several items designed by Liz Claiborne.

We hadn't exactly stopped speaking to each other, so after ten minutes of car silence I decided to tell her about Dr. P. "He says I suffer from PTSD, which manifests in bouts of depression and low-level anxiety, but the good news is, he doesn't think I'll need drugs. He thinks the talking will work."

My mother kept her eyes on the road, but I saw the corner of her mouth twitch slightly.

"I wasn't sure about it at first," I said, "but now each week I find myself looking forward to the hour I spend in his office." I fiddled with my seat belt. "Dr. P says I'm learning to hear the sound of my own voice."

"Depression, huh?" my mother said, louder than I expected. I'd been hoping she'd ask me what the letters PTSD stood for. "You know what we did for depression when I was your age?"

Drank? I managed not to say.

"Drank!" she said, her eyes shooting to the car clock confirming that we were, in fact, at least thirty minutes past cocktail hour.

Back at the ranch after our hike, I give a couple of hours to one of the larger fall projects: coating the exterior logs with UV protector. At 9,000 feet, at this latitude, the UV eats through everything over the course of a summer: paint, plastic, enamel and, if I don't reprotect them every fall, the logs themselves. The instructions on the giant can warn it takes the coating twenty-four hours to seal correctly and during that twenty-four hours it must not encounter rain, dew or temperatures below 40 degrees. It almost always gets below 40 degrees at the ranch at night, except sometimes in July, during the monsoon. However bad cold is for the sealant, I feel certain half an inch of rain in forty-five minutes would be far worse. If we are not in a drought year, it dews heavily every night until everything freezes solid. Given the impossibility of following the instructions on the can, I slap some coating on the logs in the heat of every afternoon, and hope to get the whole house covered before the snow flies.

The air at the ranch is thin, dry and cold, and the snowstorms get stuck in the dip and swirl of the basin, turning back, and back again on themselves, sometimes dropping as much as four inches an hour. On any given morning from the first of October on out, I might wake to frozen ground and flurries. By dinnertime the split-rail fences may have all gone under, and I might not see the tops of them again until March.

That will be the day that launches four solid months of worry. For my elderly geldings, Deseo and Roany, who get so stiff standing on that frozen moonscape with their achy old-man legs they sometimes won't eat, won't even take the short walk to the water trough. For the mini-donkeys, Simon and Isaac, who are far younger than the horses but no taller than the split-rail fences. In the biggest blizzards they have to power through the pasture like Tonka trucks, leaving their belly marks in the fresh powder. I spend too many hours imagining them high centered in a drift some howling night, their little legs spinning and spinning but gaining no purchase at all.

I worry about my Icelandic sheep, especially Jordan, my best ewe, who has a healthy lamb of her own each year and is always willing to nurse the orphans. She is prone to respiratory illness brought on by sudden cold snaps. I worry about my chickens, who tend to attack (and sometimes kill) one another in extreme weather of any kind.

What edges out the worry, of course, is the wonder. Because what could be better than 48 inches in twenty-four hours (76 inches is the local record), than a couple of Irish wolfhounds leaping though bottomless powder with giant smiles on their faces, than a herd of two hundred elk making their stately way chest-deep in the snowbound pasture toward the river? Best of all, what accompanies each snowstorm is the knowledge that the aquifer is getting replenished, that summer wildfire fear is assuaged, if not abated, that the rivers will be full of trout and the pastures full of flowers come July.

The autumn I was twenty-five, I flew from graduate school in Utah to my parents' house in Bethlehem, Pennsylvania, something I did with relative consistency up until my mother died. Downstairs in the TV room, my father and I were watching the Phillies get beat up by the Mets, when the phone rang and my mother answered it upstairs. A few minutes later we heard her banging around with some fervor. My father leaned toward me, said, "Go see what your mother is up to, will you?"

In her bedroom she was packing a small suitcase.

"What's going on?" I asked her.

"That was Jean," my mother said, without looking at me.

"Jean, as in your sister?" I asked.

In the quarter century I had been on the planet, I had maybe heard my mother say her sister's name five times.

"Yes," she said. "My father is dying in a hospital in Florida, and he says he wants to shake my hand."

I looked at my mother for signs of fracture, but as she gathered her makeup into a little cloth case with red foxes printed on it, she seemed exactly as she had been before. If my mother had mentioned Jean five times in my life, it was five more times than she had talked about her father.

The story I'd been told (who had told me, I wondered in that moment—my father? Martha Washington?) was that on the very same day my mother's mother died in childbirth, her father abandoned the girls.

Aunt Ermie and Uncle Marion, who had never wanted anything to do with children, agreed to raise them. Less than a year after my mother ran away to Broadway, Jean joined her as a way to get out of their sad and angry house. They had a sister act, at first, and eventually went abroad with USO.

Even though Jean was older, my mother had always been the wilder sister. When showbiz got too unruly for Jean, she returned to Spiceland, Indiana, found religion and married her high school sweetheart. My mother had told me, but only once, that Jean never forgave my mother for corrupting her, for luring her to the big city, tarnishing her reputation and ruining her life. The sisters stopped speaking when Jean returned to Indiana, and as far as my father or I knew, this was the first time Jean had made contact in more than forty years.

"So what are you going to do?" I asked, though the suitcase was making the answer apparent.

"I'm going down there," she said. "I've never laid eyes on the man, and this is apparently my last chance."

"Do you want me to go with you? Or drive you to the airport?" I offered, something about her matter-of-fact tone scaring me a little.

"No, no, stay here. Get your father to take you out to dinner. I won't be gone that long."

The next day, at nearly the same hour, the Mets taking it to the Phillies once again, my father and I heard the garage door open. My mother climbed the stairs without glancing in our direction, and my father indicated with his head.

By the time I got to her room she was already unpacking.

"How did it go?" I asked her. "What happened?"

She looked at me as if I were crazy. "What do you think happened?" she said. "I shook his hand."

And with that she turned back to her suitcase.

I went downstairs to watch the ninth inning. A few minutes later we heard her in the kitchen, starting dinner, humming one of her old torch songs, mixing herself a drink.

I finish coating nearly the entire west side of the house with an hour to go before sunset. If I extend my ladder fully, and stand on the second step from the top I can reach all but the four logs closest to the peak, and those logs are protected from the worst of the sun's rays by the roof's eaves anyway. Because I have not successfully taught William to dial 911, I leave it, each year, at that.

Tomorrow I will get on to the roof with a coarse-bristled round brush and the series of screw-in poles that allow me to sweep my chimney. I will force that brush from the top of the chimney all the way down into the basement and scrub for all I am worth for a good twenty minutes. Then I will climb down from the roof with my face and arms blackened by soot, relatively secure in the knowledge that if this turns out to be the winter that ends all winters, at least we have begun it clean and creosote free.

About six months and four cords of wood from now there will be an April night so warm it will seem like overkill to build a fire. The next morning I will open the windows to air out my bedroom and closet. I will hear the hum and whir of the automatic pump in the basement as it gets to work on the water that has inevitably seeped inside as 120 acres of snow turns to liquid and then tries to displace itself. I will trade my snowshoes for my XtraTufs because almost overnight the pasture will have turned from mostly snow to mostly muck. As I zigzag across it, trying to stay out of the deepest mud, I will spot a flash of blue so simultaneously bright and deep it won't quite make sense in this late winter color scheme of bare branches, dusky clouds and dirty ice. The Rocky Mountain bluebirds will have arrived, only the males at first scouting my pasture for a nesting place.

I'll return to the house, and load the sled with the four new bird boxes I ordered from Audubon, an electric drill and some screws. I lose two boxes a year, on average. Sometimes a martin pries the lid off, sometimes a horse uses one for a scratching post, and sometimes the wood turns to dust when the high-altitude sun works on it for a decade, so mounting four boxes a year on trees and fence posts keeps me ahead of the game.

I'll watch the bluebirds flit along the fence line, hear the warble, high and clear, and I'll know the 35 below zero nights are over, that there will be one more big dump of snow so heavy the horses will go on a water strike rather than slog through it to the trough, but it will melt in a matter of days. And before too long, there will be tiny buds on the aspen trees, the ice-choked river will run free again, and a green so subtle I think I might be imagining it will tint first the yard, then the pasture.

The horses' spines will relax all the way to their tails, the chickens will venture out of the coop and even the coyotes' barks will seem lazier, a little less hungry, a little less lonely. The wild iris will push up through the soil, and the roan, whose winter coat is burgundy wine, will shed out to a bright, barely speckled gray. In a matter of weeks, the paint-by-number landscape will have filled in around that first flash of blue: pale green aspen leaf, crimson paintbrush, purple lupine, red-tailed hawk.

A few days after we talked about depression, my mother came into my room while I was sleeping, took the hand-painted skirt out of my closet, washed it in hot water, took the waistband in, and then returned it without a word. When I went to put it on for my return flight all of the beautiful colors were muted and it was a length that had never been and would never be in style. I put my jeans back on and stuck my head in her bedroom with the skirt in my hand.

"Why can't you like me the way I am?" I leaned against the door-jamb, trying to look calm. There were rules against such questions in my household and I knew it.

"Is that the kind of thing they teach you to say in therapy?" she said.

"I guess maybe it is," I said. Her eyes were focused, as usual, on herself in her makeup mirror.

"I gave up everything I loved for you," she said, for maybe the five hundred millionth time.

"I'm sorry," I said, and I was.

There were so many things that made my mother sad: the weather, my wardrobe, the choices she made, most notably, it turned out, having me. I want to write here that I understand, that I know she did her best, that there was no one in her early life to teach her how to love, how to take responsibility, how to be something other than a victim of the circumstances life had dealt her. And as I write the words I can see that they are true. But the other thing I need to say is this:

For all of my childhood and throughout my teens, I prayed to have myself sucked right back up into the aether, because I thought it might give my mother back her hopes and dreams and joy. But the universe wouldn't make that trade with me, and so my mother died, drunk and unhappy, and I found my way to this ranch, this place where I protect and am protected by animals, this place where nature controls how I spend my days and how I spend my life, this place where I can love every season.

When the sun sets tonight, the temperature will drop in thirty minutes from 55 to 38. They are calling for a cold front to move through the valley and if they are right, tonight we'll get our first truly hard frost. I've got a pot of green chili stew on simmer, and the dogs are snoring by the woodstove. There's nothing I would trade this for. Now, let it snow.

Ranch Almanac: Leonids

I read a headline the other day that said 80 percent of Americans live in a place where they can't see the Milky Way, which is why, in mid-November, I set my alarm for 3:00 a.m., pull on fleece pants, upper body layers and my arctic hat and mittens. I grab a thick-walled sleeping bag and go out into a night cold enough to lay a thick layer of ice down on the wooden walkway, lie on the frozen grounds, and look up at the sky.

The first one is on the southern horizon, nowhere near Leo, closer to the place where Scorpio sets, burning itself out in a thin flame over the silhouette of Red Mountain. Next are a couple of fainter travelers, right overhead, ones I will begin to see better as my eyes adjust to the black. Then a big one, running all the way from north of Cassiopeia, across both Dippers, and into the Gemini twins. A real bright burner . . . gold with a hint of red.

This is the annual Leonid meteor shower, a performance the sky puts on for us here in the high country each fall. There is another, less chilly show in mid-August called the Perseids, but sometimes our monsoon clouds us in so much we miss the peak of that one.

Tonight the meteors are beautiful, plentiful (they were predicting four times as many as normal this year) and thrilling. I'm enjoying, just as much, the gorgeous cloudscape of the Milky Way itself, that thick river of light rising up from beyond Bristol Head and flowing right over the ranch before it disappears behind Copper Ridge to the south.

I snuggle down in my sleeping bag and stare into the thickest part of the china plate that is our galaxy and catch meteors out of the corner of my eye. The resident coyotes sense my presence, wonder what I am doing out here at their time of night and start singing to one another about it, which activates the sheep who begin to discuss it too, until everybody gets used to the idea and the quiet returns. I contemplate stardust, try to get my mind around light-years and reach for ways to describe the subtle differences between the colors of the stars. At first light I wake, more heavily frosted than the yard stubble, stand and, without shedding the sleeping bag, walk/hop back into the kitchen to make coffee and avocado eggs.

Mother's Day Storm

In 2014 I lost Fenton Johnson the wolfhound—Mother's Day weekend was his last—which, I know from experience, will make all the Mays from now on a little sadder.

Eleven years is a big number for an Irish wolfhound, and Fenton had made excellent use of every one. I named him after my dear friend the novelist and essayist Fenton Johnson, and as Fenton the dog grew up, he revealed more and more ways the name was apt. Like Fenton the human, he was wise and reticent, the best kind of grandfather even when he was only middle-aged. He wasn't big on asking for affection, wouldn't wiggle up to you like a black Lab or a Bernese mountain dog, wouldn't even very often bump his head up under your resting arm for a pet. He preferred to sit nearby, keeping a loving and watchful and ever so slightly skeptical eye, as if the humans were always potentially on the verge of making a really bad decision, and he would be ready, in that case, to quietly intervene.

When Fenton was a young dog, he would bound through deep snow with an expression of such pure joy on his face it could make even a non-dog person laugh out loud. He'd only drink water out of the very edge of a bowl, and only then with his top teeth pressing firmly against the metal rim. When he wanted something he would come over and scratch on the chair or the couch I was sitting on, as if it were the wrong side of a door. When he was happy—for instance, if I rose from a chair with a leash in my hand—he would wag his tail heartily, but when he was ecstatic, like when I came home after a week of working on the road, his tail would make huge happy circles, the scope of his happiness too big to be contained in a movement that only went from side to side.

To say Fenton was intelligent; to say he had a wider range of emotions than anyone I dated in my twenties and thirties is really to only scratch the surface of what a magnificent creature he was. He was the ranch manager, hypervigilant but not neurotic, keeping his eye on everything—animals, people—making sure no one was out of sorts or out of place. Because of his watchfulness, he had perfected the art of anticipating what would happen next better than any person could have. He knew all of my tastes and my tendencies, and he was always ready to be of service in any undertaking—moving the sheep from one pasture to another, walking the fence line to look for breaks, riding into town to drop off the recycling, cheering me up on a sleepless night by resting his heavy head across one of my ankles, reminding me to get up from the computer after too many hours of writing and go take a walk outside.

This last year, though, the arthritis that first made itself known when he was about eight years old was getting severe. He'd been on Rimadyl—the canine version of Advil—for years. We had had good results from acupuncture, massage and glucosamine chondroitin. Doc Howard had shelved his country vet skepticism to give a laser gun a try and had been surprisingly impressed with the results, using it on many patients for pain relief, as well as on his wife and himself. Once a week I loaded Fenton in the 4Runner and we drove to Doc's, donned our Keith Richards goggles (Fenton got some too) and Doc's granddaughter gave Fenton six shots of laser light in his back end. Lately, even the laser gun treatments were reaching the point of diminishing returns.

I'd been away for a few days, in Boston, when I got the call from Kelly, my ranchsitter, that Fenton was down and didn't seem to want to get up anymore. A wolfhound isn't meant not to be able to stand and walk around, however comfortable we might be willing to make him.

Months before, I had written on my calendar the words "This weekend keep free in case Fenton . . . ," and there was the old boy, as obliging as ever, doing everything, even dying, right on time. I flew to Denver immediately, and invited some of Fenton's closest friends to the ranch for the weekend, knowing that in order to come, they would have to brave the predicted Mother's Day blizzard during the five-hour drive from the Front Range to the ranch.

In Boulder I bought dry-aged organic beefsteaks for everyone I thought might make it, plus a mountain of other groceries. I figured if we were going to be sad—and we were going to be sad—at least we were going to have good food to eat. When I selected the steaks, the butcher, whose name is Jerry (and whose dog's name, I would learn later, is Gristle) took a lot of time and great pleasure describing the dry-aging process, and when I asked for six T-bones, one for each of the potential guests and another for the old boy himself, Jerry said, "You must be having quite a party." And since he had been so kind and thorough in *his* explanation, I said, "Well, what I am actually doing is having a kind of living wake for one of the best dogs who has ever lived, and I want to buy the very best for him, and for his friends who are making the drive up to my ranch in Creede to be with him." Jerry lifted one of the massive T-bones off the top of the pile sitting on the scale.

"You shoulda said so to begin with," he said. "In that case Fenton's is on me."

My friend Tami Anderson had a wonderful dog named Taylor who she was as deeply connected to, I believe, as I was to Fenton. I have loved all my dogs, of course, but there is the rare dog—I have had two so far in my life—that asked me to transcend my human limitations and be, at least occasionally, a little more evolved, like them. Fenton was such a dog, and so was Taylor. Taylor and Fenton were puppies together, and they loved each other truly all their lives. When

Taylor was coming close to the end, she and Tami would often lie on the bed together and look into one another's eyes. One day, Tami told me, almost in a whisper, they were in such a position, and Tami said, "Maybe next time, I'll be the dog."

But Tami couldn't be there for Fenton's weekend, and neither could Greg, so it turned out to be me and Kelly, and Linda, who had cared for Fenton so often over the last five years of his life he belonged to her nearly as much as he belonged to me. She had flown in from Reno and met me at the Denver airport and we had driven together. The storm had kept everyone else away.

The weekend was everything all at once. It rained and snowed and blew and eventually howled, and I slept out on the dog porch with Fenton anyway, nose to nose with him for his last three nights. The storm seemed to have been ordered especially for the old boy, who loved the cold and snow most of all, who hated the woodstove and preferred it when I kept the house in the 55–60 degree range, who all his life would literally raise a disapproving eyebrow at me the moment he suspected I was going out to chop kindling.

Linda and I gave him sponge baths and rubbed his face and ears until he didn't want us to rub his face and ears anymore, and then we sat quietly beside him. I will admit to even loving cleaning him up, changing his dog beds, washing and drying him, fine-tuning my attention to meet his every need.

When I could stand to tear myself away from him, I cooked— giant pots of soup and pesto and grilled vegetables and salad. I had no appetite but the kitchen was warm and smelled good whenever I walked into it. Fenton ate Jerry's giant dry-aged T-bone in three sittings over two days and enjoyed the bone as much as I've ever seen him enjoy anything in his life, even though he'd mostly lost interest in other food by then. There were times I was sure we were doing exactly the right thing by Fenton, times I thought that if *my* last weekend could be like his, it would be better than pretty much anybody's last weekend I had heard about in the history of the world. Other times, I was in a flat panic. How could I be trusted to make this decision? What on earth gave me the authority or the wisdom to decide when his quality of life had crossed over some determinate line? And all that aside, how would I live in a world without him, without his tender presence beside me, without his increasingly stiff rear end galumphing down the driveway to meet me, without his quiet vigilance as I sat in a chair and did my work?

Fenton was my seventh Irish wolfhound and my tenth dog overall. I was not new to being the decision maker, but no amount of times down this difficult road made it any easier. At one point I got myself so freaked out I thought maybe we would get in the car together—just him and me—and drive and drive and see if we could outrun death.

On Monday morning I saw he was getting the very beginning of tiny sores from sitting still for so long, and I knew Tuesday morning would have to be his last. My friend Kae Penner Howell called from Denver and said she had tried to make it on Sunday, but they had closed Highway 285 because of black ice and so far it had not reopened. She asked me if I was okay, and I told her I was. I have always called Kae the moral center of my large and wonderful group of women friends, in part because she was raised by preachers, in part because she has so much backbone, but mostly because she has a remarkable way of orienting toward true north.

Kae and I have the same exact Prius—year and model—and when she pulled in the driveway ten hours later Fenton got more excited than I had seen him all weekend, even though I was sitting right there beside him. Like there might be two of me, and I might come home all over again and start caring for him as I already was. This was another unexpected gift of the weekend. How many hundreds of times had I seen Fenton at the bottom of the driveway, his tail going in giant crazy circles? But because I was always the one *in* the Prius I had never before witnessed that moment of recognition, the moment he became sure *that* car was my car. Who in your life has ever been that ecstatic over your arrival? Someone, I hope. Some living being.

But of course, it wasn't a second me who got out of the Prius. It was Kae, and when he recognized her, he danced and danced, on his front legs only, because he loves her too, and he knew she had come to see him. As a culture, whenever we want to treat someone or something inhumanely, we declare they don't have emotions, but anyone who thinks dogs don't have emotions should have been on the porch that night in the snow.

Kae had driven ten hours in whiteout conditions, doubling the length of the drive. When I asked her if it was awful, she shrugged. "You never *ever* ask for help, so after we talked, I figured I needed to get here."

"I don't think I asked for help this time."

"Maybe not," she said, "but you were close."

We bedded down on the dog porch in sleeping bags under the swirling snow. She said, "You are doing the right thing, Pam. He's not going to get better."

I said, "It feels like a betrayal no matter what I do."

And she said, "I don't think 'betrayal' is a word that belongs on this porch."

I teach sometimes with the Colorado writer Laura Hendrie, and she gives a craft lecture on something she calls the Jaws-of-Life character, the person who sweeps in and pulls your protagonist from the burning car just when it seems all hope is lost. Kae Penner Howell was my Jaws-of-Life character that weekend. She came just when all my intrinsic strength and broad-minded philosophy about the cycle of life was about to fail me. She drove ten hours in a Prius on black ice to sleep on a hard wooden porch in a poorly rated sleeping bag with Fenton and me on his last night on earth.

I didn't want to go to sleep because the hours were short now and I didn't want to miss a minute. After we had been quiet a while, a coyote barked and another howled back from a greater distance. Before long and for the last time, Fenton joined their song.

A few hours later, when it was barely getting light, I lay nose to nose with him and petted his perfect ears and said, aloud, "You did such a good job, Fenton. You did such a good job taking care of me." He looked right at me, right into me. He wanted me to know he knew what I was saying. "And I think you already know this," I said, "but you don't have to be afraid." I didn't know where those words came from—if it were me getting the shot in the morning, I sure as hell would be afraid—but I knew when I said them they were the most important ones. In the gathering light he looked in my eyes not with fear exactly, but urgency. He said, *Now it's my turn to trust you* and I said, *You can.*

An owl hooted, some geese honked, and Kae stirred in her sleeping bag. One of the lambs started baaing—Queenie probably, the one with the higher voice. I heard Roany nicker softly, heard him walk around on the crunching snow. Somewhere in the distance, the sound of a woodpecker. All the sounds the ranch makes every morning.

Doc Howard came at ten, through the snow, to give Fenton the shot. Doc is getting older and had told me he would be sending his granddaughter in his place, and I didn't protest, though I know he heard the disappointment and fear in my silence, so I was unsurprised and very grateful to see his small gray head behind the wheel. When I saw he did not have the sedative most vets give initially, before they give the drug that stops the heart, he again heard my unasked question. Doc said, "What's in this syringe is the world's biggest sedative. I don't like to mess around with lots of reactive drugs." Fenton was calm—almost smiling—for the very few minutes it took to put him to sleep forever. I believe he knew what was happening. I believe he was ready to put his head down on my lap one last time.

Everybody cried, even sweet Jay, Doc's brand-new vet tech who had only met Fenton a couple of times. When I found my voice again, I told Doc the story about Jerry and the steaks, and he said, "Pam, it turns out there are a lot of really good people in the world."

After we loaded Fenton's body into Doc's truck to be taken to the morgue for cremation, Kae and Linda and I took a pasture walk in his honor. A couple of inches of snow covered the ground, and the bluebirds who had returned recently hoping for better weather were almost too beautiful against the freshly whitened pasture to bear. The sun came out, and we fed all the equines apples and carrots from our hands.

Eight hours later I found myself back in the Denver airport, which was full of opportunities to do the things I hadn't found the time or the wherewithal to do all weekend: drink water, go to the bathroom, eat food. My plane was delayed two hours, and the corn chowder at Elway's bar tasted miraculous. I was riding on something I recognized as "having lived through the thing you thought you might not live through" adrenaline. I marveled at all the people around me who weren't grieving, who had had normal days in board meetings or at home with their kids. I wasn't sleepy exactly. It was more like the insides of my eyes had been scoured with a Brillo pad.

Fenton the human sent me a text saying Fenton the canine loved and was loved all his life, and there is no condition in all our living and dying that could be more satisfying. Months later he would write Fenton a eulogy quoting both Thomas Merton (*What we have to be is what we are*) and Whitman (*Life is the little that is left over from the dying*), and saying, "Fenton the canine, was a teacher . . . he taught through the simple fact of being who he is, who he was. . . . In the losses lie the lessons. . . . [I]f we would only embrace death as another aspect of life—if we would let the animals teach us how to live and how to die— we might just treat each other and our animals better than we do."

As I waited for my plane I found myself thinking back, as I had many times that weekend, to Jerry the butcher pulling that steak off the top of the pile. He might have thought what he did was a small thing—though the price of those dry-aged steaks makes it at least a medium thing, even by the most objective measure—but the relative magnitude of his kindness to me, at that moment, was frankly immeasurable—and I had held on to it all weekend, and would continue to for the weeks of grief to come.

Back in 2000, to help pay for the ranch, I took a teaching job at UC Davis, requiring me to be there for two ten-week quarters each year. I chose spring and fall, because summers are glorious in the high country and miserable in Davis, and because farm animals die most often in winter. Twice yearly I'd trade my down, fleece and XtraTufs for corduroy and linen. Twice yearly, I became a teacher who rode her bright yellow bike to school, who formulated sentences containing phrases like "contemporary fabulism" and "Paul Celan-esque," who had regular meetings with the dean and the provost and who usually brushed her hair for them. I read my colleagues' books on Noir Cinema in a Postcolonial Age and Situatedness and spent a fair amount of time apologizing for my SUV and the percentage of my clothes that bear sports logos.

In Creede, there is no movie theater and no drugstore and no one who would ever use a phrase like "Paul Celan-esque." In Creede I talk to my neighbors about shrinking water tables and bingo at the Elks on Saturday night. When I go to the Monte Vista Co-Op to buy sealant to shoot into the water trough, and mineral licks, and big tubes of Ivermectin horse wormer and Carhartt overalls, I notice how different it is from the Davis Co-Op, where I buy organic turmeric and homeopathic allergy medicine, and where people take their groceries home in environmentally friendly macramé nets. To the people in Creede I am intelligent, suspiciously sophisticated and elitist to the point of being absurd. To the people at UC Davis I am quaint, a little slow on the uptake and far too earnest to even believe.

In Creede, people believe in hard work, the restorative power of nature and, in many cases, God. In the English department at UC Davis, my colleagues believe in irony, analysis and verbal agility. God has been replaced by literary theory, of course, which has rolled all the way over, in the seventeen years I have taught there, from deconstruction to Marxism with brief side trips into feminism and the postcolonial. In Creede there is no need for literary theory of any kind because there is such an overabundance of things that are actual. Cold, for instance, sometimes minus 50 degrees of it, and wind and drought, and wildfires that can chew up ten thousand acres in a day.

When I began teaching at UC Davis, it was still the home of the poet Gary Snyder. It was then, and still is, one of the finest environmental literature departments around. But times change, and over the years the talk has changed from riprap and plate tectonics to cyberspace as environment, Prius commercials as representations of nature, the suburban lawn as (and here I quote) "a poetic figure for a space, or spacing, around or under figurality—The lawn therefore a figure for what is excluded in the idea of figure itself—the very substance and / as dimension in which figurality can emerge in itself."*

My colleagues are brilliant, and so is their research, which proves to us, mostly, our own absurdity—tending our lawns, saving the earth with our Prii—the hollow chuckle often aimed at ourselves. The earth is already lost, they reason, and all that is left is to study the simulacrums, the *Man vs. Wild* video games and *Survivor*. I understand that this *is* the new environmentalism, and I respect it as such.

Last winter, a colleague taught a class in something called "distant reading." Because I have spent my life trying to teach students *close* reading, when the grad students first told me about it, I thought it was a joke. But distant reading, according to *The New York Times*, is "understanding literature not by studying particular texts but by aggregating and analyzing massive amounts of data."

"It's not actually done by people," my student Becca told me. "You take a body of literature, say, all the books set in Paris from 1490 to 1940, plug them into a computer, and the computer can tell you how

* Timothy Morton, "Wordsworth Digs the Lawn," *European Romantic Review* 15, no. 2 (2004):318.

many mentions of the Pont Neuf there were." It was, I understood, an attempt to repurpose literature. As if all beings are best understood only in terms of their aggregate, as if by making things less particular, one made them more powerful or clear.

Last semester, when I asked my class, as I do each quarter, how many of them had ever spent a night sleeping in the wilderness the answer was zero, and I realized for the first time in my teaching life I might be standing in front of a room full of students for whom the words "elk" or "granite" or "bristlecone pine" conjured exactly nothing.

I thought about the books that had shaped my sensibility as a young writer: *Pilgrim at Tinker Creek, Silent Spring, A Sand County Almanac, Refuge, A River Runs Through It, In Patagonia* and *Desert Solitaire*. Now, amid the most sweeping legislative attack on our environment in history, a colleague wondered aloud to me whether it was feasible, or even sane anymore, to teach books that celebrate nature unironically. This planet hadn't even been mapped properly a couple of hundred years ago, and now none of it, above or below ground, remains unsullied by our need for *extraction*. As we hurtle toward the cliff, foot heavy on the throttle, to write a poem about the loveliness of a newly leafed out aspen grove or a hot August wind sweeping across prairie grass or the smell of the air after a three-day rain in the maple forest might be at best so unconscionably naïve, and at worst so much part of the problem, we might as well drive a Hummer and start voting Republican.

Maybe. But then again, maybe not. Maybe this is the best time there has ever been to write unironic odes to nature.

I have spent most of my life outside, but for the last three years, I have been walking five miles a day, minimum, wherever I am, urban or rural, and can attest to the magnitude of the natural beauty that is left. Beauty worth seeing, worth singing, worth saving, whatever that word can mean now. There is beauty in a desert, even one that is expanding. There is beauty in the ocean, even one that is on the rise.

And even if the jig is up, even if it is really game over, what better time to sing about the earth than when it is critically, even fatally wounded at our hands. Aren't we more complex, more interesting, more multifaceted people if we do? What good has the hollow chuckle ever done anyone? Do we really keep ourselves from being hurt when we sneer instead of sob?

If we pretend not to see the tenuous beauty that is still all around us, will it keep our hearts from breaking as we watch another mountain be clear-cut, as we watch North Dakota, as beautiful a state as there ever was, be poisoned for all time by hydraulic fracturing? If we abandon all hope right now, does that in some way protect us from some bigger pain later? If we never go for a walk in the beetle-killed forest, if we don't take a swim in the algae-choked ocean, if we lock grandmother in a room for the last ten years of her life so we can practice and somehow accomplish the survival of her loss in advance, in what ways does it make our lives easier? In what ways does it impoverish us?

We are all dying, and because of us, so is the earth. That's the most terrible, the most painful in my entire repertoire of self-torturing thoughts. But it isn't dead yet and neither are we. Are we going to drop the earth off at the vet, say goodbye at the door, and leave her to die in the hands of strangers? We can decide, even now, not to turn our backs on her in her illness. We can still decide not to let her die alone.

I have always believed that if I pay strict attention while I am out in the physical world—and for me that often means the natural world—the physical world will give me everything I need to tell my stories. As I move through my day, I wait to feel something I call a glimmer, a vibration, a little charge of resonance that says, "Hey writer, look over here." I feel it deep in my chest, this buzzing that lets me know the thing I am seeing/hearing/smelling/tasting on the outside is going to help me unlock some part of a story I have on the inside. I keep an ongoing record of these glimmers, writing down not my interpretation of them, not my imagined connection to them, not an emotional contextualization of them, but just the thing itself. Get in, get it down, get out and move on to the next glimmer. Then, when I have some time to write, I read through the glimmer files in my computer and try to find a handful that seem like they will stick together, that when placed in proximity with one another will create a kind of electricity.

I try to keep my big analytical brain out of this process as much as possible, because I believe my analytical brain at best only knows part of the story and at worst is a big fat liar. I believe—like religion—that the glimmer, the metaphor, if you will, knows a great deal more than I do. And if I stay out of its way, it will reveal itself to me. I will become not so much its keeper as its conduit, and I will pass its wisdom on to the reader, without actually getting in its way.

In addition to being my method, the way I have written every single thing I have written, it is also the primary way I worship, the way I kneel down and kiss the earth.

On Memorial Day weekend 2015, I drove William back to the ranch after ten weeks in California. He's a good sport about our time in Davis but there was no mistaking the smile on his dog face when we crested the top of Donner Pass and got back over to the leash-less side of the Sierras. We stopped every four hours for walks along Forest Service roads or multiuse trails all the way across Nevada and Utah, but nothing ever feels better than the first pasture walk back at the ranch.

On Sunday morning, we did what we call the large pasture loop, out to the back of my 120 acres and then over the stile into the national forest, up Red Mountain Creek and across one edge of my neighbor's 12,000 acres, and then back down alongside the wetland and back over my fence again. It was me, William, and another writer friend, Josh Weil, who would be watching the ranch for the next several weeks while I went off teaching in Vermont, Marin County and France.

We were nearly back to my fence line when we heard a high-pitched cry, which I first thought was a red-tailed hawk, until it cried a few more times and I realized William had found himself a baby elk. We ran up the hill, called off William and watched as the calf took a few sturdy steps and then settled back into the underbrush where she had been hiding. Satisfied she was unhurt, we went another hundred yards down the hill only to find a dead cow elk, the blood in the cavity still wet where the coyotes had pulled her guts out.

I tried to make the hole in the neck look like something other than an entry wound—the tooth of a coyote perhaps or the peck of the little-known round-beaked vulture. I did not want to believe one of my neighbors would shoot a cow, illegally, at the peak of calving season, right here at the edge of my property, where my horses spend summer nights grazing the edges of the wetland. I didn't want to think anyone would shoot an animal for practice, for pleasure, and then leave the meat to spoil.

"That baby doesn't have a chance," Josh said, as we stared down into the cow's pecked-out eye, as we kicked at the wet grass that had been pulled out of her stomach. "It's probably starving already."

We both knew the rule of thumb was to leave abandoned calves alone; we also knew we might be in the presence of an exception. Those unspeakably long legs, those airbrushed spots, the deep brown eyes, and slightly pugged-up nose.

"I wish we hadn't seen the cow," I said, stupidly.

"I do too," Josh said, "but we did."

We were both thinking of the two rejected domestic lambs my spring ranchsitter had been feeding, and the mudroom full of milk replacer. We were both looking at the sky, which had begun serving up one of Colorado's famous May blizzards: the temperature was dropping, the snow was sticking and the wind was starting to howl.

"Let's take William home," I said, "and heat up some milk and bring her a bottle. If she is still here when we get back, if she lets us approach her, maybe you carry her back to the barn."

We took our time getting the bottle. If her mother was still alive we wanted to give her plenty of space to react to the distress cries once we were out of there. We drove the 4Runner around to the closest road access, so Josh would have to carry her three hundred yards instead of three thousand. We found her easily, and she blinked up at us sweetly, apparently unafraid. Maybe she was already too weak from hunger to save, I thought, and yet she had jumped right up to get away from William.

I sat down beside her and offered the bottle. She wasn't too keen at first, but when I gave up and drew it back across my chest she stretched herself across my lap to give it another sniff and chew a little on the nipple. She'd only take a little at a time, but before long we'd gotten about a cup down her. She put her head in my lap and started to go to sleep. Josh said it might be a good time to try to transport her.

She did not love being carried. She wiggled and squeaked like she had when William had found her, and I prayed a giant elk cow would come crashing through the trees to fight us for her, but the woods were quiet and Josh held on tight and once we got to the 4Runner she curled up in the dog bed in the back like she had been doing it all her life. Back home, Josh carried her the short distance to the barn, where we made a bed of straw for her, which she rejected in favor of the dirt floor, and I went inside to heat some more milk. That time she drank almost two cups. She shivered in the cold, and I rubbed her warm with my jacket. It was at that point Josh named her Willa.

The internet said it wasn't uncommon for cow elk to leave their babies for several hours, because the babies could not keep up with the herd at the pace of their daily grazing. It said the calves were scentless, and would not attract predators, and the herd would come back and pick them up around dusk.

"If the dead cow isn't her mother," I said to Josh, "we may have just done a really bad thing." But it was snowing in earnest now, the wind screaming, and mistake or not, Willa was warm and dry in the barn.

I did what I always do in Creede when I don't know what to do and that's call Doc Howard. He said there was a sanctuary near Del Norte that would take her and raise her. He told me to call Brent, the wildlife officer, and that Brent would come get her, take her to the sanctuary and, while he was at it investigate the shooting. He said, "There are several other things you could do, Pam, but not without violating ten different laws."

I knew everybody had gotten freaked out about elk since chronic wasting disease became a thing in Colorado, but I also knew we had never had a case of it in Mineral County and they checked every elk the hunters took out. Still, I didn't really want to raise an elk baby with a bottle. What I wanted was for some yahoo not to have shot her mother. The website said to feed your orphaned elk four cups every four hours, so I left Brent a message and went out with more warm milk. This time she was interested and drank with less coaxing. She followed me around the stall, and when I would sit down in the straw with her, she would touch her nose to my face and hair.

Josh and I spent another hour with her, watching her walk around on her long long legs, greeting her when she wanted to make contact, feeling what it was like to be in her presence—which had a mystical quality to it, a visitation from some otherworldly being. So calm, she was, so delicate and full of light.

"Now, Pam, I'm going to need you to trust me a little bit," Brent said on the phone, and because of the tone in his voice when he said it, I did. "The sanctuary in Del Norte won't take elk anymore because of chronic wasting. There's a place in Westcliffe I might get to take her, but her best chance at the life she is meant to have is if you put her back out there, exactly where you found her. There's a good chance the herd will come pick her back up."

"Even if the dead one is her mother?"

"Even if," he said. "If the herd has another cow nursing, she'll probably be okay. I'll come up at seven in the morning and if she's still there I'll put her in a kennel and take her to Westcliffe."

It's hard to put a week-old elk calf back in the woods at sunset within a hundred yards of a ripped-open elk carcass the coyotes already know about, but by the time we talked ourselves into it, I had gotten two more cups of milk down her, it had stopped snowing, and the last sun of the day was warming things up a bit. Josh carried her back to the 4Runner, we drove her around to the back fence and Josh carried her, kicking, squeaking, back to the exact tree where William had found her. We didn't know what we were going to do if she followed us, but she didn't. She curled back in right where her mother had put her, and waited, we hoped, for the herd to come at dusk.

"What a story she'll have to tell her friends," I tried, as we turned our backs on her.

"Oh, she just thinks this is what happens to everybody," Josh said. "On the seventh day of being an elk you get to ride in the back of a car."

The next morning, I had to leave for the airport at four thirty, and the air was clear and full of stars and 29 degrees on my car thermometer. I said another prayer that the herd had come back for Willa, that her mother hadn't been the shot one, and nobody minded she smelled a little like humans and the back of a 4Runner usually occupied by giant dogs. "We might have messed up," I said, to whoever I thought was listening at that hour—some genderless Druidic earth power, I supposed, perhaps the mountain itself—"but we talked it out every step and tried to make the best decision."

I watched seven come and go as I drove farther away from Creede and closer to the Denver airport. I knew news wouldn't likely come until nine, but every minute after seven was torture. Finding her dead would have been the fastest outcome; loading her into the kennel and sending her off with Brent the next fastest after that. Searching the woods for her would take the longest. It was hard to even know what to hope for.

Finally, when I was sitting at gate B23, Josh called. The cow had been shot; that was certain. They had looked long and hard for Willa and found no sign of her. They had also looked up and down the road for a shell casing to help identify the poacher and had not found one of those. Brent would go up to Spar City and ask around, but he wasn't hopeful he would find out anything more.

I have decent intuitive skills, which have improved with the onset of menopause, so I tried to quiet my mind to get a sense of Willa. For whatever it is worth, she did not feel dead to me. I know how potentially self-deceiving that sounds. But she was, among other things, a magical being. Josh and I gave her up to the mountain, and I believe the mountain took care of her.

It's hard to be ironic about a dying dog. It's hard to be ironic about an elk calf when her nose is touching your face. It's hard to be ironic when the young writer who tends your house and cuddles your dogs and who you know loves the earth with the same passion you do is walking behind you down a dirt trail with thirty-three pounds of baby elk in his arms. It's hard to be ironic when your pasture erupts after an unexpected May blizzard into a blanket of wild iris. It's hard to be ironic when the osprey that returns to your ranch every summer makes his first lazy circle around the peak of your barn.

Last January, I was speaking with an environmental scientist who said he was extremely pessimistic about the future of the earth in the hundred-year frame, but optimistic about it in the five-hundred-year frame. There will be very few people here, he said, earnestly, but the ones who are here will have learned a lot.

There are times when I understand all too well what my colleagues in Davis are trying to protect themselves from. Times when seeing the world's bright beauty is almost more than I can bear, when my mind is running the grim numbers the scientists have given us right alongside. And it is also true, had I never laid eyes on Willa, I would not have spent five sleep-deprived hours weeping—often sobbing—in the car that morning on the way to DIA. If I hadn't slept those three nights on the porch with Fenton, it would have been three fewer nights of my life spent with an actively breaking heart. But a broken heart—God knows, I have found—doesn't actually kill you.

And irony and disinterest are false protections, ones that won't serve us, or the earth, in the end.

For now, I want to sit vigil with the earth the same way I did with Fenton. I want to write unironic odes to her beauty, which is still potent, if not completely intact. The language of the wilderness is the most beautiful language we have and it is our job to sing it, until and even after it is gone, no matter how much it hurts. If we don't, we are left with only a hollow chuckle, and our big brains who made this mess, our big brains that stopped believing a long time ago in beauty, in everything, in anything.

What I want to say to my colleagues is that the earth doesn't know how not to be beautiful. Yes, the destruction, yes, the inevitability, but honestly, Doctor Distant Reader, when was the last time you slept on the ground?

How will we sing when Miami goes underwater, when the raft of garbage in the ocean gets as big as Texas, when the only remaining polar bear draws his last breath, when fracking, when Keystone, when Pruitt? I don't know. And I imagine sometimes, often, we will get it wrong. But I'm not celebrating the earth because I am an optimist— though I am an optimist. I am celebrating because this magnificent rock we live on demands celebration. I am celebrating because how in the face of this earth could I not?

Ranch Almanac: Puppy

Today, Isaac rolled the puppy, with, I believe, the intent to kill her. I have always been told donkeys offer the best coyote protection possible, but I didn't fully understand that statement until I saw the efficient and systematic way Isaac got the twelve-week-old pup up under his feet, his legs creating a kind of cage around her, and then proceeded to pummel her with all four hooves at once.

Olivia—Livie, as we call her—seems to have come through the incident unscathed and is currently chewing on a dinosaur toy bigger than she is, dragging it around the living room by its neck. I spent a few hours watching her closely for signs of internal or external injuries, but everything seems to be working okay. No blood coming out of any orifices.

William gave himself away completely in the moments after it happened, first by trying to get into the corral to kick Isaac's ass, and then by running back and forth between the corral and the house, where Livie had retreated—screaming, shrieking—and then coming back to hurry me along to where she was hiding.

It should have occurred to me that the puppy, in Isaac's eyes, may as well have been a coyote—this long-legged, tail-wagging Janey-come-lately. The donkeys have been at the ranch for two years. The last thing we need around here, Isaac must have been thinking, is another soon-to-be-giant dog.

The idea to get a puppy arose when my friend Steph was over, looking at my table full of framed animal photos, and said, "Which one of these is Fenton?" At the sound of Fenton's name, William swung his head around and looked at me urgently. What in the hell have you people done with Fenton, *his big sensitive eyes seemed to say.*

William was out in California when Fenton died at the ranch. I had assumed that when he returned he would have been able to figure out what happened by the various smells, but now I wasn't sure. I had also assumed William was liking being an only dog—the extra treasured one—but that look he gave at the sound of Fenton's name made me fear he thought Fenton was on an extended vacation and might still one day show up.

William loves all creatures great and small. He tries to make friends with every other dog in the world—and cat and horse and porcupine and skunk, and even each one of his squeaky toys. His great beauty notwithstanding, other animals don't that often dig William. It could be his size, or that he still has his balls, or maybe he's just too eager. The big needy kid at the cool kid's birthday party. A puppy, I knew, would love him, would look up to him, would admire and imitate his every move. He'll love that, I thought, but I was wrong.

To say William was utterly bereft at the sight of Olivia would be a grotesque understatement. For the first two weeks after I brought her home he'd look at me with eyes older than time that said, Why wasn't I enough for you, *and mine said to him,* Quite honestly, you were! But I thought I wasn't enough for you!

Livie was entirely unconcerned her presence had ruined William's life. She'd wind her beautiful little body around his front legs and under his nose while he forced himself not to growl (mostly). If he got up and moved to another spot in an attempt to ignore her, she'd lie down a respectful foot or two away in the exact same position.

It crossed my mind to return the puppy. That I had gotten her for him was not just a story I was telling myself (though I can imagine myself capable of such a thing), and his misery suggested I'd made a mistake. But I did not return the puppy, partly because it would have been painful and embarrassing, but mostly because I knew, more so even than any of my other dogs, William was made of love, and his giant goofy heart would win out over his ego in the end.

I had to admire Livie's chutzpah. She was indefatigable, never more than three steps behind him, mirroring every move he made. You don't like me? she seemed to say. Then teach me how to be a dog you will like better. If she ever felt his deep disdain for her she never let it show.

During those weeks I took a series of photographs of the two of them: William stretched out on the living room floor, Livie three feet behind him, the S curves of their spines identical. William out on the lawn chewing a bone, Livie three feet away with a smaller bone held in her identically crisscrossed paws. The two of them on the floor of the car repair shop wearing their harnesses, front left paws cocked, long tails extended, Livie, a perfect mini-me.

I'm going to make you love me, she seemed to say, every time she sashayed past him, dragging the top of her tail along the underside of his chin, and by the time Isaac rolled her under his feet in the pasture, it was clear: love had done its work.

A Kind of Quiet
Most People Have Forgotten

It's July 2014. I am guest teaching in the Chatham University low-residency M.F.A. program in Pittsburgh, where I have been adopted for these ten days by a couple of smart, talented and beautiful young women named Kyle and Maggie, and their handsome, entirely self-possessed mutt, Apacha. It is always both mystifying and flattering when the cool kids want to hang out with my sturdy, skort-wearing, middle-aged self, and makes for a very satisfying do-over from my teenaged years, during which the Kyle and Maggie equivalents would have rolled their eyes hard if I had taken one step in their direction. Or perhaps there were no Kyle and Maggie equivalents in my teenhood, because along with being the most popular girls in the M.F.A. program, Kyle and Maggie are almost preternaturally kind.

I can see by their eyes, though, they each carry some large and not short-term sadness within them—which is the same thing people say about me when they look into my eyes for the first time, even on the rare days when I feel as though I don't have a care in the world. Maggie, I know, has recently lost her mother, who was very dear to her, and she is swimming in the deep waters of that grief. But Kyle's sadness, about which I have been told nothing, has a different flavor, one as familiar to me as my name, and has something to do—I am nearly certain—with how she is letting herself be treated by a man.

The girls and I have taken Apacha for a walk through the huge, half-wild and fabulous Frick Park, on Pittsburgh's east side, and now we're having a beer—well, they are having a beer—while we decide whether to stay where we are and eat vegetarian, or move on to BRGR for organic bison lettuce wraps. I'm not drinking beer these days, nor any alcoholic beverage, nor soda, nor coffee, nor even green tea. I'm not eating wheat, nor sugar, nor anything packaged, processed, or inorganic, because when I went to the doctor for my yearly checkup in May, I had the first high blood pressure reading of my life, along with a precancer diagnosis in the form of HPV 16. The ecosystem that is me was clearly in trouble, and it was time, I decided, to clean up my act.

As the doctor was writing a prescription for the blood pressure meds, I asked her if I could have six months to right the ship. "No," she said, without looking up, so then I asked her if I could have three. "I'm writing the prescription," she said, "I won't be there to see whether you take the pills or not." Which I realized was true, and which I chose to interpret as permission.

Caffeine has always been my go-to antidepressant, and I've said for years if I ever had to make a choice between giving up coffee and dying I would choose death. But as it turned out, all death had to do was wave at me from the window of a bus at a distant intersection for me to quit all caffeinated beverages cold turkey. To heal, I reasoned, my body needed sleep, and I had not slept properly in decades, if ever. Not if we define sleep as the state that, when you emerge from it, is like coming up from some deep ocean-y paradise of nothingness at the very bottom of the world. Unsurprisingly, I spent my first ten noncaffeinated days wanting to kill myself.

And look just there, how I have used the phrase "wanting to kill myself" as a kind of mildly self-deprecating but good-humored figure of speech.

Surprising, one of my selves says to another. As I was likewise surprised when, a few weeks ago, I was standing behind a podium and in answer to a reader's too personal question I heard myself saying, "There was a period of my life when I would have considered killing myself, but that period is over now."

Is that so? That same self, the cynic, asked.

Yes, another answered—this one has a slightly imperious, almost British accent—*I feel quite confident that's where we are.*

Two mostly wonderful things about life after fifty: I'm never sure what I am going to say until I hear myself saying it, and it's hard to remember, with any real accuracy, feeling any way other than how I feel right now. But if a person's books are any reliable record of her life, and in my case they certainly ought to be, there were periods in both my thirties and forties where—and here I want to be careful with the wording—the possibility of suicide came up a lot.

In my thirties I wrote a book called *Waltzing the Cat* and that book contains a story called "Cataract," about a river trip gone awry, and after the flip where both female characters nearly drown in a series of class V rapids, there is this moment of dialogue:

> "Lucy," Thea said, "if you were to kill yourself ever, what would it be over?"
>
> "A man," I said, though I didn't have a face for him. "It would only be over a man. And you?"
>
> "I don't think so," she said. "Maybe something, not that."
>
> "What then?" I said. But she didn't answer.
>
> "If you are ever about to kill yourself over a man," she said, "get yourself to my house. Knock on my door."
>
> "You do the same," I said. "For any reason."
>
> "We'll talk about what it was like being under the water," she said, "what it was like when we popped out free."

The only decade of my life in which I don't remember having suicidal thoughts—until this one—was my twenties, possibly because I seemed to be trying so hard to kill myself in more socially acceptable outdoorsy ways. In addition to high water, hurricanes and out-of-bounds skiing, I also dabbled in tornados and mudslides, and found myself flat on my back looking up at the underside of any number of bucking, green-broke horses.

Back in Park City, in grad school, I looked after a horse named Whoosie, a beautiful young Thoroughbred just off the track who, kicking up for joy one day while I had him on the lunge line, came into contact with my left arm, his hoof breaking my radius like a breadstick and pulverizing a significant portion of my ulna.

I'd been alone at the barn when it happened, and when I came to, there on the floor of the indoor arena, Whoosie's nose inches from my face in concern, I saw my hand was flipped over backward in relation to my elbow. Glorious shock kicked in, allowing me to sit up, turn my hand the right way round and tie it tight to my body with my scarf, one handed, before stalling the horse, bolting the barn doors and walking nearly a mile to the nearest residence. The temperature that January night was 10 below zero.

Several times along the way I nearly fainted, and when that happened I would sit myself down, take big breaths and nearly nod off or pass out—it's hard to say which in that condition—but then I would hear a train whistle, clear and loud, and I would get myself together and go a little farther.

I told my story many times that evening: to the nice people in the house closest to the barn, who called the ambulance; to the EMTs, who cut all three of my layered coats off of me in strips; to the receiving nurse in the ER; to my grad school friends, who rushed to the hospital and to the intern while we waited for the surgeon—I had somehow, on graduate student health insurance, scored the orthopedic surgeon for the Utah Jazz—to arrive.

It was close to midnight when he did, and as I heard myself describe that train whistle for the tenth time, I stopped midsentence. There were no trains in Park City. "Now wait," I said. "I would swear. . . ."

"Oh," my surgeon said, smiling kindly, "lots of people hear the train." He patted my good arm and told me he would see me first thing in the morning.

Before they wheeled me into surgery, my surgeon told me I ought to prepare myself to wake up to my arm amputated at the elbow. "I'm going to do everything I can to save it," he said solemnly, "but it's a hell of a mess in there."

I'd been too afraid of freaking out my mother to call and tell her about the accident, and now I was glad I hadn't. If I did wake up without my arm, I would need a few days to grieve it before it became something *she* had lost.

The team operated for four solid hours, removing eighty-five bone chips, reconnecting tendons, transplanting a hunk of cadaver bone from the bone bank, and securing their work with two metal plates and eighteen screws. They wheeled me out of surgery and my doctor ordered X-rays. He decided he didn't like the way everything looked, so the team spent four more hours doing most of it all over again.

Waking up with my arm still attached gave me the courage to call my mother, though my surgeon warned me it would be six to twelve months before we knew for certain whether the bone transplant would take.

"No really," I told her. "It's a miracle. I got the best doctor in Utah, and my arm is still here!"

"May-be," she said, in two distinct syllables, and I heard ice rattle in the glass in her hand. "But you're still going to have those big ugly scars. . . ."

The surgeon who spent those nine hours replacing my pulverized ulna with cadaver bone sent me home with a bag full of Darvocet which, within forty-eight hours, created some kind of chemical reaction in my brain that sent me so low I called, for the first and only time in my life, a suicide hotline.

When the guy picked up the phone, I immediately apologized for taking his time. "I know I ought to be happy," I said. "My arm is still here, hurting like a son of a bitch, but more or less intact."

"Are you taking anything?" he asked, and when I told him about the Darvocet he said, "Well for chrissake, stop! Haven't you ever heard of Advil?" Which turned out to be some of the best advice I've gotten in my life.

I spent most of my forties writing a book called *Contents May Have Shifted*, and its working title, for all the years it lived in my laptop was, *Suicide Note, or 144 Reasons Not to Kill Yourself*.

Really? The cynic pipes up again. *Really? If you* were *ever actually suicidal, you must not have been very good at it.* And it's hard to argue with her now, over our daily lunch of hibiscus tea and kale superfood salad. *It's bad business to deny your past,* the earnest self, the one who pays attention in therapy, tells her, and for now they—we—leave it at that.

Much was made of my working title in interviews I gave when *Contents* came out because it was mentioned in the jacket copy, but I had never intended to call the published book *Suicide Note*. Too maudlin, too melodramatic, the contradiction within the longer version of the title dishonest, almost coy. The working title was simply a daily way to describe to myself what I was doing: prophylactically collecting and transliterating suicide prevention nuggets, gathering up all the things about this planet that made me want to stay on it, against some unknown future moment when I might feel it would be better not to. And, because I find myself here on the other side of fifty, trying with all my might to stay alive, it seems reasonable to conclude that at least to some extent, my strategy worked.

The waitress brings Kyle and Maggie their beers and me my Pellegrino with lime, and we are talking about favorite dogs or favorite bands, but Kyle is looking at me so intently with those sad, soulful eyes the next thing I know I'm saying, "You know, there was a period of my life when I thought I might kill myself because a man I thought I loved didn't love me back. It embarrasses me a little to say so, but there it is."

Kyle's face is some mixture of stunned and relieved, which I take as a sign to continue. "I've always measured my sense of well-being on airplanes, when we hit turbulence. You know, how much—or how little—do I care if this plane goes down?" They nod. They both *do* know.

"I can remember actually willing the plane to tumble from the sky a few times, because some Joe I probably could not pick out of a lineup, were he here tonight, didn't call, or went out with one of his four other girlfriends, or lied about where he was last Saturday."

The girls are quiet—even Apacha has stopped licking his balls. It flashes through my mind I might be grossing them out, like in the way you don't want your parents to mention the great sex they had over breakfast.

"You didn't ask me to dinner, I know, so I would sit here and rattle on with my old lady advice," I continue. "But I have been thinking a lot lately about how much power I used to give the men in my life to make me feel okay, or not okay. There are reasons for that—ugly childhood reasons—so I try to give myself a break. I'm not a regretter, exactly—I think writers all need something to push against and that was my thing for a long time—and yet at fifty-two it seems absolutely mystifying to me I would give men so much power. It's power I don't think most of them even really want."

Now Kyle is looking at me like I have crawled inside her brain. We are all silent for a while. "Maggie's got a good man" is what she finally manages to say.

I nod. I don't doubt it. Maggie's grief for her mom is palpable, piercing, but it is not full of the shadows and confusion that come when a little girl is treated badly in a hundred different ways by fathers or father figures, that insidious, everlasting training.

"I don't know anything about your past," I say to Kyle, "and I'm not trying to tell you how to live. Somebody could have said all this to me when I was your age—I'm sure someone did—and it would have probably just made me double down. I had to do it as long as I had to do it, chase those nasty cowboys." I smile and Kyle smiles, but her eyes never do. "I'm just saying, I guess, there's another version, after this version, to look forward to. Because of wisdom or hormones or just enough years going by. If you live long enough you quit chasing things that hurt you; you eventually learn to hear the sound of your own voice."

Apacha groans, maybe signaling the end of the conversation, so I drain my Pellegrino and reach for the check, but Kyle stills my hand.

"What made it change," she asks, "for you?"

There are so many possible answers, including thirty thousand dollars worth of therapy; several New Age healing ceremonies—one involving a man who set his chest on fire and another involving a dust buster; five published books and a precancer diagnosis, but I say the thing that feels first, truest, and most long-term: "I realized I could make my own life," I say. "I could have my own ranch. I finally realized *I* could be the cowboy."

But now it is a gray, late November morning, and I'm here, a cowboy on her very own ranch—120 acres of hard dirt and ponderosa, of 60 mph winds and blizzards that drop five feet of snow in twenty-four hours; of floods and drought and fire; of blue columbine and quaking aspen and 12,000-foot peaks all around; of unspeakable beauty and a kind of quiet, on a winter morning, most people on the planet have forgotten exists. I am here, in the middle of all that, and I am pretty damn sad anyhow.

The days seem impossibly short already and yet we'll lose daylight for another month before this planetary ship turns itself around. I'm worried about old Roany's chances of making the winter, and I can't decide whether it is more humane to move him to a warmer place where everything would be unfamiliar, or try to heat the barn a few degrees with chicken lamps so he can live—or die—in the place he knows. I had to rush little Ingrid, this year's lamb, out of Jordan, to Doc's yesterday with bloat, and he saved her life, but once an animal is prone to bloat it tends to return. Facebook has already made me cry four times this morning. First it was Ursula Le Guin reminding me we don't write for profit, we write for freedom; next it was a video of the Unist'ot'en indigenous camp resistance trying to stop the Keystone pipeline; and then it was the state of Nevada electing a man to their house of representatives who said "simple minded darkies" show "lack of gratitude" to whites. Honestly, who wouldn't be sad waking up in this world? And then I clicked on the Prairie Fire Lady Choir singing a song my friend Annette wrote called "Not a Good Man"—a kind of Irving Berlin meets Laurie Anderson number with all the women wearing lollipop-colored dresses and big hair, and when *that* teared me up I knew I might be in serious trouble.

Cry me a river, says the cynic. *How about we make a short list of all things that could be wrong and are not.* So I do. At this moment, none of my close friends are dying (except inasmuch as we are all dying). I have a job—I have several jobs—and at only one of them am I not respected. I am not underwater on my mortgage. I have a barn full of hay and four cords of wood on the porch and a cabinet full of dark-chocolate-covered figs and almonds. My upstream neighbor has not gotten into bed with the frackers and the condo village at the top of Wolf Creek Pass got defeated yet again. My presence on this ranch means these 120 acres will not be subdivided, will not be paved over, will not be turned into dream homes for people who come here one week a year.

And still, this morning, that dark undertow, the feeling of looking up from the bottom of a dank, wet well . . .

Time to move. On this point, all selves are in agreement. *Put the smart wool on, lace your boots, don your barn coat. Cut the apples, cut the carrots, feed the equines from your hands. Cut the string that holds the bale of hay together, two flakes for the mini-donkeys, six for the horses, everything that's left for the sheep. Top off the horse water, top off the sheep water, double-check the heaters in the troughs. Listen to the reassuring thump of cold boot soles on frozen ground, the contented burps and purrs of the chickens as they peck around after their organic scratch grains, the otherworldly whoosh of wing beats overhead—the bald eagle who winters upriver, back after his one-year hiatus. This is how the ranch heals me with its dailiness, its necessary rituals not one iota different than prayer.*

The forecast is calling for wind and possibly snow tonight but right now it is perfectly still and almost 20 degrees, too warm for my heavy barn coat. The creek at this time of year, with all the freezing and unfreezing, is an ice sculpture, the willows lining it pencil drawings, the mountaintop beyond it already feet deep in snow.

Olivia, still a pup, is charging and leaping to see above what's left of the tall grass while William patrols the perimeter. From here I can see Middle Creek Road, Lime Creek Road, as well as the state highway across the river, and though this represents some fairly large percentage of all the roads in Mineral County, for the hour we'll be walking, not one car will go by.

Out here, on this acreage, I've learned not only to hear my own voice, but to recognize what makes my heart leap up and then go toward it: the snowshoe hare—halfway through his biannual color change—William scares up along the back fence, his big white feet flashing as his still tawny body gains distance. A coyote, sitting, dignified and still as a church, two hundred yards across the pasture, watching us make our way to the wetland, and then the flash, when William sees him, and he sees William see him, his total evaporation into thin air, like a ghost dog come from some other plane of being.

These are the things that have always healed me; it just took me half a lifetime to really trust them, to understand how infallible they are. Moving through space, preferably outdoor space, preferably outdoor space that maintains some semblance of nature, if not *this* nature, some other nature. When I'm happy it's a carnival out here and when I am sad it is almost too beautiful to bear—but not quite. It is definitely too beautiful to contemplate leaving. I climb the hill where John Robert Pinckley—the first man to build a cabin on this land—and his children, Bob and Ada, are buried, and I know well that when I claimed these 120 acres they also claimed me. We are each other's mutual saviors.

Sitting at the Pinckleys' gravesite, William pressed up against one thigh and Olivia on the other, looking across the river at Bristol Head all aglow in the low winter light, I am certain the world is not out to hurt me but to heal me, and I'll hold on to it with both hands for as long as I am able.

This is what I try to explain to Kyle and Maggie over a second round of beers and Pellegrino in Pittsburgh. We decide bison burgers sound better than falafel, so Maggie drives me to BRGR while Kyle runs home to drop off Apacha. Maggie and I talk about the eleven-month trip she and her boyfriend took four months after her mother's death. "I was afraid I wouldn't survive her absence if I stayed still," she said, and I said, "Maybe you were collecting new things to love about the world."

We wait for Kyle for thirty minutes and then an hour. Finally she calls to say she is on her way so we order for her, but by the time she actually gets there her food is stone cold and she barely eats a bite.

She'll send me an email a few weeks later thanking me for the things I said to her, admitting she had been driving around all that time we were waiting, crying, trying to pull herself together enough to join us, but that I wasn't to worry too much about her because since that night she had been working on her writing and spending quality time with Maggie and Apacha and feeling a whole lot better. I wrote back and told her though I thought of her often, I hadn't, exactly, been worried. She sounded so solid, so grounded in her email I decided I didn't need to say the other thing I was pretty sure of: that she had cried that night, not so much for the disappointing past, as for the dawning possibility of an unspeakably beautiful future. I was pretty sure she already knew.

Ranch Almanac: Log Chain

Right before sunset (4:08, during these, the darkest days of December) the dogs and I stop whatever we are doing and take a walk down to the river. William especially likes this time of night because lots of animals are moving around. The river is still open, still has a stripe down the middle of silvery glorious movement between giant white sheets of ice. We've gotten eight inches of snow over the last several weeks, and Livie's got snowballs in her feet, so I sit down on the riverbank and pull her on to my lap to warm her feet and legs. She likes to sit in my lap, which she will be able to do for approximately two more weeks. After that it will be like having a little horse on me.

In spite of the encroaching darkness, there's nothing out here to be afraid of. Coyotes, even a whole pack of them, aren't brave enough to attack a full-grown woman and a 150-pound dog. Mountain lions hunt at dusk and dawn, but in this county, there's never been an attack on a human. A black bear won't be hanging out on the riverbank, but even if he were, he'd hear us before we'd hear him and hightail it back into the forest.

It gets darker as we walk, and we ought to turn around, but the river is glowing so beautifully in the twilight and smelling just how a river smells when it's early winter and there isn't much snow yet but the ground has already been frozen for weeks. Across the river, Bristol Head rises more than thirty-five hundred feet off the valley floor, a massive wall of sheared-off compressed volcanic ash, resembling, especially in this light, Yosemite's iconic Half Dome. There's more than half a moon, which is enough to get us back as long as we stay on the elk trail, and in the worst case, we can go up to the road and return to the ranch that way.

Out here, it never occurs to me to worry about running into a human being with ill intent, not because the humans around here are necessarily harmless (though most of them are) but because there just aren't very many of them. According to the latest census, Mineral County Colorado is made up of 921 square miles, and has 704 residents—fewer than one person per square mile.

For the better part of two years, a man who went by the name of Log Chain—a person of great interest to the law enforcement officials in a Midwestern state—camped out in a sheepherder's trailer just over my back fence. I got used to him being out there, and thought he might be there forever, until one day he vanished, as silently as he had arrived.

Log Chain wore clothes he made from skins he tanned from animals he shot himself. I'd see him out there looking like Davy Crockett, crawling on all fours along my back fence with a .22 or a .270 in his hands, hoping to scare up a fox or a coyote. When I asked my neighbor Scotty Lamb what he'd been in prison for, Scotty said, "I'm pretty sure he killed a man, Pam," but then followed that story with another one about seeing Log Chain in Creede one day, and seeing another guy, a tourist, try to get in a fight with him, and watching Log Chain walk away, gentle as a lamb.

Log Chain earned his living making steel knives with long blades and beautifully carved handles. He built me a hanging pot rack by melting down and refashioning junkyard truck springs. I promised to pay him $200 cash for it, and when he brought it over, I realized I'd need to go to the bank. He asked what time he should come back, flipping one of the many layers of tanned skins in his tunic over to consult a dime-store digital clock he'd sewn in there.

Log Chain helped me dig out my 4Runner one time when I got high-centered in a drift in my driveway I shouldn't have tried. I was grateful to him even though he talked about thalidomide babies and the end of days the whole time. Now there is no telling where Log Chain is, but I stand by the consensus that in his Colorado incarnation he was not only harmless, but helpful.

The Sound of Horse Teeth on Hay

This morning the wind woke me at first light, howling against the storm window and threatening to tear a loose piece of flashing off the kitchen gutter. I'd been awake writing until two, and hoped to sleep until eight, but William was worried, emitting a micro-squeak the way he does every thirty seconds—just long enough for me to have nearly dropped back off to sleep—so I was worried too, not about the house, but the horses.

We've made it to February 1, which means, hopefully, there won't be too many more nights of 35 (or worse) below zero. We've had a lot of those nights this year, in December and January, too many for the comfort level of my old horses who manage to endure, year after year. A storm like this will elevate the temperature to zero or above. Still, a 40 mph wind can turn 20 above into 20 below, and I am starting to suspect that Isaac, the mini-donk, who has a bit of a Napoleon complex, has begun bullying the horses, keeping them out of the giant stall I leave open for them. If he's successful, it means two tiny donkeys are (relatively) warm and dry right now, while the horses are doing their best to use the angles of the barn to stay out of the wind.

I roll out of bed and cautiously open the door to the wood porch (I've lost doors to big wind twice in the past), but this wind seems to be from the south, and though the snow is swirling around the porch like some kind of ghostly special effect, the door opens normally. I tump the snow off of a couple of logs and bring them inside, knock the coals around in the woodstove and add the new logs to the fire.

If there is any doubt about how cold this winter has been, my wood and hay supply attest to it. I am going to run out of both, probably by mid-March, and since the pasture doesn't come in until late May and since it can snow anytime until the Fourth of July, I am going to have to buy another two cords and another hundred bales.

It's not the buying that's punishing; hay and wood are reasonably priced around here. It's moving the hay from the plowed part of the driveway to the barn, and moving the wood from that same spot, across the front yard and around the house to the covered porch—all of this with four feet of snow still on the ground. It will involve packing a trail with snowshoes, and then sledding the rounds of wood and bales of hay, one or two at a time to their destinations. And then there is the stacking them once I get there.

Rick Davie will help me move and stack the hay—he's too much of a gentleman not to, but I'll move and stack the wood alone.

It's easy to lose track of the days out here, but I know this is Sunday because the blizzard was supposed to arrive Thursday, but only amounted to flurries until yesterday (Saturday) morning, when it started to come down in earnest. The forecast kept edging the winter storm warning forward—increasing its duration by two or four hours at a time, as if they didn't want us to notice—but now they've gone ahead and said we are in for it pretty much continuously until Tuesday night. There is so much wind it's hard to say from the kitchen window whether we've gotten two feet or four, but I know the drifts will have made the driveway out of the question, even in the old reliable Toyota truck with the manually locking hubs.

I'm mostly here by myself during the winter, or I guess, more correctly, I am the only human on the ranch, which feels the opposite of being alone to me. I am in the good company of two wolfhounds, two horses, my bonded pair of miniature donkey jacks, three Icelandic ewes and a ram, and one aging mouser named Mr. Kitty. I have well-stocked cabinets and there's always something in the freezer to make soup out of. Randy Woods, who plows my driveway, usually gets to me within twenty-four hours, unless it's a three-day storm and then he gets to me twenty-four hours after it stops.

I make some cinnamon tea—double warmth—and dress in layers of wool, fleece, down and whatever it is snow pants are made of these days, and step out onto the dog porch into the blow. I squint to see the horses in the corral, their manes, backs and tails frosted with snow. No sign of the donkeys nor the sheep, who have wisely decided to stay inside their enclosures.

I have always preferred the company of animals to the company of people. I've been told this means I am emotionally stunted in some way, and perhaps I am. But when I compare myself with the people I've known who can't handle being without the company of another human being for even five minutes, I think I might be less emotionally stunted than they are.

My childhood home did not have any safe places. When my parents were drinking, when my father stomped through each room of the house looking for a target, I often hid in the basement, in the clothes dryer with the round Plexiglas door cracked just enough for air. Yet, beginning with Martha Washington, who entered my life when I was two days old, I have felt safe in the presence of more than enough human beings to offset, at least cognitively, all the ways I was conditioned to distrust them. There were so many teachers—Mr. Kashner in grade school, Mr. Miller in high school, Dr. Kraus, Dr. Burkett, Dr. Bennett, Dr. Consolo and Dr. Gamble in college—who took a special interest in me, who made me feel loved and safe and smart and valued. I have had men in my life, off and on, who have loved me (and a few who did not), and if I never learned to trust them, exactly, at least I learned to reach for trust. I have good and loving friends spread from coast to coast and elsewhere whom I visit, and who come to the ranch, people who have had my back in every situation and enriched my life in more ways than I can enumerate. And if I say, even so, that it has been only the rare human who has given me an animal's worth of love back, it's not because I underestimate the power of human love. It's because I have been lucky enough to live in the unconditional, unwavering, uncommon, gale force of love directed at me from my animals.

The wind stills for a moment and the whole world is silent as a prayer. In the aftermath of a blizzard, the snow looks more like a painting of snow than snow itself. Everything sculpted and softened by all that power pushing it for hours in one direction. The hill that rises behind Bob Pinckley's old cabin looks less like landscape and more like contemporary art. White on white, a tiny row of fence poles the only distinguishing factor. And then the wind starts howling again.

I go back inside and call Randy Woods and get on his schedule for Wednesday morning. I slice two apples and break eight carrots into pieces while William sits patiently beside me. I don the hat I bought right out of an Inuit lady's kitchen in Arctic Bay, Nunavut, Canada (the warmest hat I have ever owned), my neck gaiter, my winter work gloves, and my Carhartt barn jacket. No need to call William, who is already standing at attention in the mudroom. It is just as well that Livie, who is snoring soft puppy snores by the woodstove, sits this one out. I open the door and off we go.

From what I can see, and I can't see all that much in this gale even though it is full daylight now, we've gotten about two and a half feet of new snow since midday yesterday. But the drifts between me and the barn run anywhere from one to three feet higher than that. My beautifully engineered two-weeks-in-the-making snowshoe-packed trail to the barn is nothing but a distant memory, but it still behooves me to try to stay on top of its old footprint, because when I fall off of it, I sink yet another foot and a half down into the last storm's uncompacted snow. I get about thirty steps into my trek when a wind blast stops me cold and I realize I've left the porch without the snow shovel, so back I go, using the boot-sized post holes I have just created to retrieve it. William doesn't really love snow this deep. It gets up in his paws and makes ice balls which eventually bleed, but he's nothing if not loyal, so he returns to the porch with me.

Today, I don't need to shovel my way to the barn (though one year we got five feet in one storm and then I *did* have to shovel my way there). In this wind, any progress I'd make trying to use the shovel to remake my old trail would be erased in minutes. I'll need the shovel once I get there, to shovel out the orange gate, which lets me into the corral, and then to shovel out the barn door, which lets me get to the hay.

But first things first. The remaining hundred or so steps to the barn. It seems impossible, but it is snowing even harder than it was five minutes ago. A giant gust of wind lifts more snow into the air, and the barn, which is only about a hundred yards from the house, disappears entirely. This is the kind of day that makes a person believe those stories where the farmer gets lost between the house and the barn and freezes to death in a snowdrift while his wife cooks his dinner. If I get lost in a snowdrift today, no one will know I'm there until the spring thaw.

One time, after a big storm, I fell off the side of the ghost of my old trail into a very deep drift. My legs were trapped under me in a strange position, and being more or less armpit deep in snow, there was a moment when I wasn't sure I *could* get myself out. I gave it another try, and got one leg around to the front of me, and then another, until I was in a half-buried sitting position. I tried to use my arms to roll myself over, to get on my hands and knees, but everything beneath me still felt bottomless. I wasn't exactly scared, I hadn't yet had *time* to get scared, and though it was well below zero with a moderate wind, the sun was shining.

I decided to rest for a minute before the next try, and lay back in the little cave I had inadvertently fashioned to look at the sky. No sooner had I gotten into that position and let out a long slow exhale than William was right by my side—the windward side—the whole length of him tight against the whole length of me, body to body. His first instinct to block the wind, to keep me warm until I got out or until help came.

Today we make it—without falling—to the corral where the horses are waiting, and I distribute apples and carrots through the rails. In spite of the wind, the horses seem calm, a function of the temperature. Ten above beats 35 below in their book, no matter what the Weather Channel tells us the wind chill "feels like." When it is coming down like this it simply can't be 35 below—those conditions are mutually exclusive, and I believe the horses, at this stage in their lives, would choose the snow over the deep freeze on every occasion.

When it *is* 35 below, the sky is clear, the wind is still and it is as quiet outside as the beginning of time. Ice crystals form on the aspen tree outside the kitchen window, on the lead ropes that hang from the barn door, on the horses' coats and eyelashes and whiskers. When the light is right, and you train your eyes just a few degrees off the direction of the sun, you can even see tiny crystals suspended in the frigid air. When I come out to check the animals right before bed, ice crystals swirl in the light of my headlamp. When it is 35 below, I take one step outside and the inside of my nose freezes; the crunch of my boots on the packed powder path is the definition of the word "dry" on my tongue. On those mornings, the equines eat the apples and carrots out of my hands quickly, before they turn into carrot- and apple-flavored popsicles, and I must do everything with great care because a few minutes with exposed skin is enough to cause frostbite.

But today there is time to pet under a forelock, to reach down into the snow to pick up a dropped apple or carrot bit. The mini-donks, Simon and Isaac, crowd in for their share. Simon won't eat carrots, only apples. In between bites he occasionally likes to take a benign flat-toothed love nip out of my hip or thigh. Isaac thinks he's the boss around here even though he is shorter than the wolfhounds. He puts his little hooves up on Roany's neck sometimes just to push him around. Roany, a big Roman-nosed quarter horse, seventeen hands at the shoulder, has been on the planet for more than thirty years, getting along with pretty much everybody, and so lets him.

At one time, Roany was the most powerful beast on the ranch by far. He could have kicked Fenton the wolfhound over the fence with one back hoof if he wanted to stop his barking once and for all, stop all his showing off. But even when Fenton would chase Roany from the middle of the pasture all the way back to the barn, the big gelding would take care where he put his feet, would turn and pin his ears in warning, but never do anything more.

Roany was thin this September and thinner in December. He's staying closer to the barn than he ever has and I fear he might be losing his sight. I've been sneaking him a coffee can of senior sweet feed most afternoons when the others aren't looking. In December I worried he might not make the winter, but here we are in February, and he rubs his ice-crusted eyelashes against me and reaches his giant lips toward my pockets to get another carrot. Maybe the old roan will get to see another summer on the ranch.

When I arranged my UC Davis schedule in order to spend the coldest part of every winter here, I worried a ten-week solo stint at the ranch might make me antsy or lonely, or just plain weird from only talking to animals. It has not.

When I teach the intensive writing workshops that make up a considerable part of my income, I am around people 24/7 for weeks at a time, and I like that version of my life too. But I've recently realized what I've never had enough of since I was a kid is alone time. That kid who hid in the clothes dryer had almost unlimited alone time and she quickly came to realize it meant both safety and the possibility of unrestricted adventure.

At eight, on a vacation to London with my parents, I memorized the entire map of the Underground, got myself to the Tower of London, and took the terrifying beheadings tour at sunset before my parents—who were quite happy in our hotel bar—ever realized I was gone. At five, in the Bahamas, I befriended a giant dappled gray horse and his Bahamian rider, who scooped me into the saddle, galloped me all the way down the beach and chest high into the waves before my mother looked up from her beach towel. (From that moment on, I was horse crazy.) From the time I was ten until I turned sixteen, I rode my bike through the cornfields of Bethlehem, Pennsylvania, to the truck stop on Schoenersville Road, where I racked up ten games on each of the pinball machines and sold them at half price to the truckers.

Here at the ranch, the dogs and I can ski as far as we want for as long as we want. We can drive down those dirt roads we never had time for, just to see where we end up. I can clean the pantry at three in the morning, or do a thousand-piece jigsaw puzzle on the kitchen table or eat a whole bag of frozen peas for dinner with one pat of butter and a liberal dosing of Crystal hot sauce. I can take a bath in the middle of the day and I can stay in there until I shrivel. I can sleep anywhere I want to: out on the couch by the fire, in my bed with William or in his dog bed with him. I can take the bathroom door off of its hinges, bring a four-foot stainless steel water trough in there and raise six Plymouth Barred Rock chickens from pullets.

Every time an alone spell comes to an end, when I'm excited to welcome a friend to the ranch, or I'm off to a city to teach or speak or be public, there is always a sliver of regret as I watch the hours wind down. I always find myself wishing for just one more ranch day.

Today, though, any potential visitor would have to be dropped in by helicopter. On a Sunday, midstorm and this late in the season, I doubt I'll even see the plow out on Middle Creek Road. Margaret closed up the Soward Ranch in early December. And my closest neighbors back toward town, the Albrights, are about two and a half miles walking, when it is walkable, which today it is not.

The big orange gate swings out from the corral. It is the main access to the barn as well as to the large pasture, the gate through which Rick so expertly backs his truck. In winter, the gate does not need to open big enough for a truck, but it's important to shovel it out wide enough that if a horse had to be taken out in an emergency, the horse would not be afraid to walk through. The gate is about twenty feet wide, so, with a couple feet of snow drifted against it, it takes about twenty minutes of bust-ass shoveling to get it to open double horse-width. Then there is the barn door, which is smaller, but has the added challenge of the frozen solid horse briquettes that seem to collect there, and must be pried up along with the snow. By the time I finish both tasks I can feel a new set of blisters rising on top of my calluses.

In this much wind, I would normally put the hay in the three-sided windbreak on the barn's south side. But this is an unusual wind, from the south, which accounts for its unseasonably warm bearing, so I drop the bale in the corner of the corral, on the north side of the barn, hoping the sheep pen will block most of the wind when it starts to clock around to the west, as it is predicted to do in a few hours.

I cut the orange twine with the hay hooks, making sure to pick it up and zip it in my pocket (hay twine wreaks havoc with a horse's digestive system), and close up the barn. If it were grain day, I would give the horses their mix of beet pulp and senior mix for horses with metabolic conditions, joint formula, multivitamins, SureGut, and a scoop of Horseshoer's Secret. (We are *all* big believers in supplements in this house.) Deseo's metabolic condition means he can't handle grain too often, so we stick tight to our every-fourth-day plan. Today is day two, which is going to work out great, because Tuesday, when the storm moves out and it really gets cold, they will be even happier for the grain to warm them up than they would be this morning.

The wind has calmed for a moment so I stand and listen to the altogether satisfying sound of four equines chomping good grass hay on a snowy morning, and think about all the mornings, over the last twenty-five years, I have spent standing right here in the snow.

The coldest January was in 2009. I went though six cords of wood that winter even with propane back up. For the first time ever the dogs had to be encouraged to go on walks, and Mr. Kitty wouldn't even go out to the barn to hunt. He stayed in the basement for days at a time, cozied up to the big gas heater.

There were five feet of snow standing and no warm days to melt any of it. The white ground reflected back all the sun's rays and couldn't soak up enough heat during the short days to raise the temperature even to 10 below. The three-foot split-rail fence surrounding the house went completely under in early December and I walked daily on a white moonscape between the house and the barn. The roof slid so many times eventually there was nowhere for the snow to go and it formed an igloo around the house that actually kept the wind off and raised the temperature in the back bedroom by several degrees compared with a lighter winter. The house threw off enough heat to cauterize the insides of the igloo—like what a candle does on the inside of a jack-o'-lantern. It was beautiful, for the month it lasted, living inside a big old jack-o'-lantern of snow.

But now it is edging toward 15 above, and the horses are feeling it. The wind picks up again and Isaac lets out a big donkey bray that means he is either mad at the wind or happy about the hay or about to climb up on somebody's neck, so I exit the orange gate and start the hundred-yard trek to the water trough.

On a normal day, even on a normal winter day, this walk is easy, but today I have the challenge of memory again, trying to stay above my old trail. Sometimes if I hold my head just right, I can see the faintest ghost of the path on top of all the brand-new snow. It's like one of those magic eye drawings, the way I have to look not directly at it and soften my eyes to see. Only then can I see the slightest change in the snow surface that, princess-and-pea-like, indicates a change in the surface several feet down.

I know the trough will barely need topping off—snow has been falling into it for twenty-four hours and this kind of weather does not engender big thirst in the horses. But I have learned, over the years, that the best way to care for animals, especially barnyard animals, is to repeat the exact same tasks, in the exact same order, every day, forever and ever. A change in the barnyard means trouble, and if I do the same things the same way each day, I am more likely to notice a change. Also, any local will tell you that Murphy lives on a high-altitude ranch in a snowstorm. Were I to decide the trough did not need topping off today, this would be the day the trough heater failed, or the bottom seal wore out, or the pump froze, or a rat with hantavirus drowned himself in there and Isaac would be just churlish enough to eat it.

I am not a good farmer. I am not even a real farmer. Rick Davie is a real farmer and I am only pretend. But the hypervigilance I learned in childhood serves me well on the ranch in general and in big weather in particular. My mind runs a series of potential calamities, and my actions, insomuch as they can, guard against them.

The trough is less than an inch down, but I top it off anyway. All systems go. Then it is back along the trail, easier the second time through, to the sheep pen, and another door that needs to be dug out.

I decide to feed the sheep inside their enclosure, something I don't do often because it radically increases the amount of inside poop. But even with ten pounds each of the warmest wool money can buy on their backs, the sheep don't want to be outside today. I give them their four flakes of hay, and drag my feet around in the snow in the outside portion of their pen until I find the three black rubber feeders that went under hours ago. I dig them out and split a coffee can of grain among all three so they don't ram one another fighting for it.

Outside the fence, William is watching Sheep TV. The whole time I am in the pen he sits perfectly still in the same exact place he sits every day, staring hard, his face so intent, so utterly concentrated, waiting for one of those sheep to make a wrong move so he can tear the chicken wire open with his teeth and rush in to rescue me from them.

I leave the sheep pen and head back on my water trail to the frost-free pump and fill a bucket to carry back to the pen. Last winter, because my back was ailing, I discovered if I carefully plucked all the icicles that hung on the back of the barn—there were hundreds hanging at half-inch intervals in accordance with the corrugated tin of the roof—and added those to the sheep's water, I could save myself a good many bucket carries. The icicles are beautiful; they renew themselves every day until it warms up enough for the roof to slide, and they feel delicious when you hold them in your hand.

Every time I walk one of these little connector trails I improve the conditions. But when William and I turn back toward the house, the trail we made an hour ago has been utterly obliterated. I decide to wait at least until it stops howling to shovel the walkway to the house, or—a much bigger job—remake the path to the propane tank.

Last month, in a long spate of 30 below zero nights, the propane company called to say their man couldn't deliver propane because I did not have an "appropriate path dug from the driveway to my tank." In twenty-five years I had never been asked to dig a path to my propane tank—appropriate or otherwise. I'd always figured any propane man worth his salt owned a pair of snow pants. But perhaps the propane company had hired a new delivery guy who had recently moved here from Florida.

The day I got the call I channeled my outrage into action, went outside immediately and spent three hours digging a walkway to the propane tank so beautiful you could have rolled a red carpet out on it and used it for the Oscars. When I got to the tank and checked the gauge it turned out the lady on the phone had been wrong, the guy *had* crawled through the deep snow and filled it after all, which made me feel better about him generally, and happy to have spent my afternoon making him such a nice path.

Today has eliminated that path, along with the driveway, which is just a suggestion of itself between the ridges Randy Woods made the last time through with his plow.

Back inside, we shake off snowballs in the mudroom. I put some oatmeal on for breakfast, the steel-cut kind that takes thirty-five minutes because why not? It's as good a day for writing as there has ever been so I join William on the couch, open my laptop and get to it.

Monday and Tuesday are much of the same but Wednesday morning dawns clear, as predicted, and 30 degrees colder. I open the back door to utter stillness and ice crystals in the air. Every living being in the county, it seems, is either resting this morning or frozen in place. When I start across the path toward the corral with my apples and carrots I can hear a car crossing the cattle guard three miles and two deep bends of river canyon away.

In a few hours, Randy Woods will be here with his giant blade to reconnect me with the rest of the world, and after I finish shoveling the walkway and the path to the propane tank, William and Livie and I will drive to town, pick up the mail, drop off the recycling, get a few fresh vegetables and a pint of sea salt caramel ice cream.

It will be nice, after all these days, to speak to a member of my own species, someone who can speak back in the same language. But there is another part of me, some eight-year-old part, who wants Randy's plow never to come. It's not only that the eight-year-old feels safer at the snowed-in ranch than anywhere, it's that the snowed-in ranch was a story she used to tell herself—she is certain of it—when she needed a place for her mind to go, when she needed a reason to make it to nine, and then ten and eventually seventeen, and freedom.

Ranch Almanac: Born in a Barn

*In the winter of 2011 I had only two chickens—Sheryl Crow,
who thought she was a rooster, and Martina. Two is not enough
chickens—everybody knows that—but that is how many I was left
with after the summer of ranch fatalities, so I put their henhouse in
the back of the pen with the sheep and hoped for the best.*

*Martina and Sheryl Crow had made it through the fall
okay, but deep winter around here tests everybody. I've been told
Plymouth Barred Rocks put out 33 BTUs per bird, and if that's
true they were probably the warmest animals in the barnyard. But
I had grown attached to Martina—her checkerboard feathers,
the way she laid the most delicious egg you ever tasted each
morning, like clockwork at a quarter to nine. So all that winter I
would wake up in the middle of the windiest nights, the stormiest
nights, the most frigid nights, and worry about everybody in the
barnyard, especially her.*

The thermometer on the front porch was influenced by heat

coming off the house and was therefore unreliable. But a mile down the road, there's a Weather Channel–sanctioned station that reports temperature and precipitation in real-time updates. It was usually around 10 below zero by the time I went to bed, and a couple of hours later, I'd wake up worried, turn my computer on and watch the numbers tumble. 20, 25, 28, 32 below. It's always darkest just before the dawn, goes the saying, and it is always the coldest then too.

During the most frigid weeks of winter—the Arctic blast, as the Weather Channel calls it—my worry gets the best of me, so I get up around five, dress in my snow pants and my big down coat, and head out to the sheep pen with a headlamp and a space heater. I already have two heat lamps going out there on thermostatic plugs, a gesture of compassion that raises my electric bill from $90 a month to $140 in December, January and February. Though the eggs are very tasty, it's not responsible energy use or cost-efficient ranching (what would Rick Davie say?), especially since Martina is the only one who lays. Sheryl crows like a rooster and beats Martina up from time to time, which, I believe, leads Martina to sometimes lay two eggs a day, just to spite her.

I plug the space heater into the one remaining plug in that part of the barn and set it on my lap facing outward. Martina and Sheryl Crow come and tuck themselves in, one under each armpit. The Icelandics too are happy to see me these mornings. Jordan and her twins, Queenie and Natasha, come inside the inner part of the enclosure, an area they usually leave to the chickens, and hunker down into the wood shavings with me. With the glow of the heat lamps and the warmth of the heater, the animals all clustered around and breathing contentedly, it is hard not to think of Mary, all those years ago, and the manger, though I was raised Episcopalian and have since become something I loosely refer to as Buddhist-Druidic, and therefore it's rare I think of Mary for any reason at all.

One morning, when I had lost all feeling in my fingers and toes and went back inside where Greg—home for Christmas break—was making me one of his delicious lattes, I said, "I can kinda see now why Mary wanted to give birth in a barn."

"She didn't want to give birth in a barn, Pam," he said. "There was no room in the inn."

"I know that's how the story goes," I said. "But I bet she was secretly glad."

Ranch Archive

On the top of the hill in the middle of my pasture there is a chain-link fence surrounding the graves of John Robert, Bob and Ada Pinckley. When I bought the ranch I signed a piece of paper saying their relatives were allowed access to the little cemetery into perpetuity, but in the twenty-five years I have lived here, no one has ever come by. I make it a point to come up here at least once a month myself, to bring a fistful of wildflowers, to sit still for ten minutes, to say a whispered thank-you to the man who saw this meadow and thought, This is a place a person could make a life.

I am not a researcher at heart. I don't have anything against librar-ies, except that they are indoors, but my writing rises more often from tactile experience than it does from anything I've read in books. But there are a lot of ways to know a piece of ground and one is to learn what happened here long before I set eyes on the place. So I put my rudimentary researching skills to work to see what I can find.

For my twentieth anniversary at the ranch, Dona Blair sends me a small box labeled "ranch stuff." The largest item in the box is the ranch's Abstract of Title—the original one from 1916. It rolls into a scroll and has a sky blue linen cover. The heavily serifed black lettering on the blue linen proclaims the document as:

Abstract of Title [the capitalization is theirs]: SOUTH HALF of the SOUTHWEST QUARTER of Section EIGHT; The NORTHEAST QUARTER of the NORTH-WEST QUARTER; the EAST HALF of the SOUTH-EAST QUARTER of the NORTHWEST QUARTER; and the EAST HALF of the NORTHEAST QUARTER of the SOUTHWEST QUARTER of Section SEVENTEEN, ALL in Township FORTY North, Range ONE West, New Mexico Principal Meridian.

It is sealed with an embossed gold eagle.

When I open to the first page of the scroll I find out that at 1:20 p.m. on February 11, 1916, the United States of America, by the power of President Woodrow Wilson, conveyed to the Heirs of John R. Pinckley this land (and here it lists all of those halves and quarters again), with patent number 494,126. Just below the release of patent is a notification that on February 8, 1915, at 4:40 p.m., the United States Land Office, received, from the Heirs of John Robert Pinckley, payment in full for those acres. There is no mention of what the payment was.

Below those two notifications, under an embossed number 3, is a record of one George Gerard mortgaging these same acres to Rolf H. Locklin back on November 24, 1905, at 1:45 p.m. The note was for $200 and was due in ninety days; interest at 12 percent. Below that there is a release of the same mortgage, on September 7, 1907, at 2:20 p.m.

Twenty-nine years later, the scroll tells me, in 1944, Robert Pinckley (son of John Robert) sells one-quarter interest in the ranch to Don C. LaFont for $400. This is how the ranch shrunk from the original 160-acre homestead to the 120 acres it is now.

The next page tells me that in 1946, the District Court of the United States:

HEREBY ORDERED ADJUDGED AND DECREED
that all rights in and to a proposed reservoir on public lands
of the United States in Mineral County embracing a total
area of 4,493 acres, more or less, be and hereby are forfeited
for nought, and that all right, title and interest of the defendants herein be and hereby are vacated, cancelled and held
for nought. That the title to the land described in said map
to be used for said reservoir be and hereby is forever quieted
and confirmed in plaintiff as against any claim of right, title or
interest in or to said reservoir rights. That the defendants and
all other persons be and hereby are enjoined and restrained
from asserting any right, title, or interest in and to said reservoir rights, and be and hereby are enjoined and restrained
from constructing any reservoir on said lands.

I don't know what proposed reservoir they are referring to here.
The Rio Grande Reservoir, roughly forty miles upriver from me, was
built between 1910 and 1914, thirty years before this decree. It could be
the Goose Lake Reservoir, which is about fifteen miles up Ivy Creek
in the opposite direction. Or perhaps it was a reservoir that was proposed but never built. In any case, the federal government wanted Bob
Pinckley to know he was not entitled to any of that water, even if some
of it ran across his ranch.

The document goes on to record tax payments in some years and
not others, and to reaffirm several times that the owner of the 120 acres
has no water rights at all. In 1960, two years before I was born, the
record notes that Robert Pinckley signed a contract with the San Luis
Valley Rural Electric Cooperative to have electricity brought to the
ranch. In 1966, John LaFont was notified that Robert Pinckley had
not paid his taxes in 1936. The bill was $17.44, plus interest, which John
LaFont paid. Also in 1966, Myrtle LaFont and May Oates (the other
heirs of John R. Pinckley) turned their stake in the ranch over to John

LaFont via a quitclaim deed for which he paid each of them one dollar. John LaFont continued to pay the taxes on the ranch up until 1969, which is when the record appears to run out. The year after that, John LaFont sold the property for $25,000 to Dona Blair and her late husband, Robert Blair, because John had his own place closer to town and couldn't afford the taxes on both properties.

The next item I pull out of the box is a bill from Dr. Wm. O. Whitaker to Robert Pinckley for $14 dated March 11, 1940. The bill is handwritten with a pen. Under a column labeled "Professional services" words are scrawled that appear to be "deduct horns." And then, at the bottom, "This bill has run quite a while so please remit."

There is another letter, addressed to "Mr. Robert Pinckley, Creede, Colorado," containing a request for official right-of-way for the county road that splits the property. It is postmarked March 23, 1958, at 5:30 p.m. I find myself unduly moved by the record of the exact time of day. When I run my hand over the address I can feel the indentations left by the keys of a typewriter. The hand-cancelled stamp on the letter cost three cents.

There is a letter from John LaFont to Robert and Dona Blair dated October 11, 1970, also handwritten in pen.

Dear Folks,

I have been intending to answer your letter for several weeks but since writing letters is not my favorite pastime that should explain the long lapse in the time. I am very grateful that you folks are going to be the owners of the Pinckley property. It is rather sad to see the old place go as it holds a heap of sentimentality for over 50 years. But I trust it is going to be in good hands. I plan on leaving that old mowing machine and several old items in the cabin.

As to the condition of the cabin. Bob Pinckley lived in it winter and summer year around until he died there in June,

1966, so it is not too uncomfortable. However some new glass needs to be put in the south window which was broken out by trespassers a couple of years ago. I believe that posting the property (within reason) would be a good idea. I will check on the place for you occasionally. As it is a little way off, my visits will probably be infrequent. But at least people will realize that it is being looked after to a degree. The probabilities are that we could find you a place to store some tools and other articles around here somewhere.

Now to clarify the ranch situation—especially Grandmother Pinckley. Grandmother Pinckley (my mom's mother) died from complications following childbirth (twins) in November 1906 in Creede. Her remains were shipped to Longmont, Colorado for burial. Three or four years after her passing Grandpa Pinckley filed on the homestead and moved on to it in a tent. My Dad helped him build the two little cabins and the old log barn down by the mowing machine. There were Bob, Hazel, and Ada at home at that time. The little twin girls were adopted out while they were infants and my mother was already married and in a home of her own. Anyway, Grandpa Pinckley died in June 1913 before he got the ranch proved up on so my mother (Myrtle) moved up on the place and proved up on it and got it patented.

Someday we will have a chance to visit, (I hope) and I can fill you in on different things. It would be a lot easier than trying to write it. The three graves are Grandpa (John R. Pinckley) Ada, the next to the youngest daughter, and Uncle J Robert Pinckley (Bob, my uncle).

My wife joins me in wishing you good luck on the place. She is recuperating pretty well now at home after 15 days in the Del Norte Hospital. She had quite a siege of asthmatic bronchitis, staff infection [sic], and an allergic flare up from penicillin.

Let us hear from you occasionally and I'll try to answer earlier.

> *Sincerely,*
> *John LaFont*

There is nothing else in the box—a few tiny puzzle pieces I try to connect to form a hundred years of ranch history before I came along. I'm glad to have the relationships between the LaFonts and the Pinckleys explicated: Bob's sister Myrtle married Don LaFont and gave birth to John LaFont, who looked after Bob in his old age. It's nice to picture the ranch before electricity, and when the county road was nothing but a dirt trace. But the detail the box revealed that makes me happier than all the others is the one about Myrtle: in spite of the county record giving the credit to her father, it was actually a young woman who proved up on the place, who did the physical work of satisfying the claim and earning the homestead. I picture her out here, with a saw in her hand, a pile of fence poles at her feet and her hair tied up in a gingham kerchief. I vow to name the next female resident of the ranch of any species Myrtle.

A quick internet search reveals that the very same John LaFont who tended Bob Pinckley in his old age, who made it possible for him to live out his years, die and be buried on the ranch, and who claimed to struggle writing a one-page letter to Dona Blair, actually wrote two whole books: *The Homesteaders of the Upper Rio Grande* and *58 Years Around Creede,* both published in 1971. John's father, Don C. LaFont— the one who bought those forty acres behind my back fence from Bob Pinckley—also wrote a book, *Rugged Life in the Rockies,* which had been published twenty years earlier. I find signed first editions (and only signed first editions) of all three books on Alibris and order them, pleased to know I am not the first, nor even the second writer to walk the fence line of the ranch, composing paragraphs.

Rugged Life was published by Prairie Publishing Company in Casper, Wyoming, *Homesteaders* by Oxmoor Press in Birmingham, Alabama, and *58 Years* simply says, "privately printed" in the place where the publishing information usually goes.

"The procedures for homesteading," writes LaFont in *Homesteaders,* "were to take out the boundaries of the tract of land you were desirous of, then locate it in its proper range, township and section number. This way a legal description could be established and the property could be mapped." "Proving up" on the land included everything from constructing a residence of some kind (a homesteader had to live on the claim for at least six months each year) to plowing a specific amount of ground for cultivation, "grubbing off a specific area of willow or brush, or clearing off a set sized patch of timber." It was possible to be awarded a patent in as few as three years, but you could also string the improvements out for five years without reneging. There was a filing fee of three dollars and a patent fee of ten dollars and if the county was satisfied you had proved up adequately, the land was yours. If you were into "homestead flipping," the going rate on a newly patented 160 acres was $1,000. The first homestead in the Upper Rio Grande Valley was patented in 1880 and the last in 1930.

Of the 203 homesteaders who settled the Upper Rio Grande Valley in the late 1800s and early 1900s—from the Old Riverside Ranch, about thirty-five miles downriver from me, to Pearl Lakes, about thirty-five miles upriver and very near the headwaters—25 were women. As of the publication of *Homesteaders* in 1971, only 5 of those 203 homesteaders were left alive and 3 of *those* were women. The only person who had been alive at the time the claim was filed and *still* lived on the ranch that constituted the original homestead was Bob Pinckley's next-door neighbor (and mine), Emma Soward McCrone. In 1971, when John LaFont told Emma McCrone that she was the only one of the 203 homesteaders left on her ranch, she said she must have been "too damn dumb" to be convinced you couldn't survive on a homestead.

Emma McCrone lived out her days on the 1,200-acre Soward

Ranch (we share a long fence)—and her daughter Margaret McCrone Lamb—born on the ranch in 1919—died in March 2015. Margaret spent four years of college at the University of Denver, and a handful of recent winters in the town of Creede, but all my memories of her are sitting at her kitchen table at the Soward Ranch, telling stories of the old days in Antelope Park.

"Well of course the ranch is my whole life," Margaret said in an interview she did for a book called *Women of the Upper Rio Grande: Beartown to Creede, Memories from 1920 Through 1960*, published in 2011. "You know I'll have people say to me in town like in the spring, are you going to the ranch this summer? Are you nuts? It is just so much a part of me. And I guess you know like when I was in the hospital that two months, the guests and the girls who worked for me told me it's just not the same when you're not there. They are used to me being here as a stable thing you know, and that is nice to know because the ranch is me and I am the ranch."

Margaret's obituary from the weekly *Creede Miner* calls her "a self-described eternal optimist." Her father had been the postmaster of Creede and she took over that position after he died. She was the secretary of the school board for more than twenty years.

Of all the landmarks around here, Margaret loved the cliff called Bristol Head best. "I just sometimes look at it and think, 'You know, what are my problems?' It's been there a million years probably looking up at the sky."

There is a disappointing dearth of information about my ranch in John LaFont's books, considering how much time he spent out here, keeping Bob company, but the book does confirm what my Abstract of Title suggested, that "the old Pinckley place" was first filed on by a man named George William Gerard, who was a dentist in Creede at the time. Gerard failed to prove up on it, so it went back to the government, and John Robert Pinckley filed on it. When John died it was left to all his heirs, but it was young Robert (LaFont's Uncle Bob) who fell in love with it, and lived on it for the next sixty years.

Also in *Homesteaders*, I find out about Lambert Fewell, known as Shorty by all the old-timers, who homesteaded 160 acres where the Antelope warm springs were located. I live right in the center of Antelope Park, and the only warm springs I know about are in Seepage Creek, across the river. It's possible the Antelope warm springs have dried up in the intervening years, or they may just be on private property. In any case, according to LaFont, Shorty Fewell worked for a man named Sylvester who had bought up a lot of bottomland in Antelope Park because he wanted to construct the Vega Sylvester Reservoir (this could be the reservoir the Abstract of Title was worrying about). He managed to buy the whole of the river bottom except for the Soward Ranch, and had even talked Dan Soward (Emma McCrone's dad) into selling the land by bringing him a whole suitcase of gold coins, but Dan's wife, Ellen (Emma's mother), refused to let him take the gold, and in the words of John LaFont, "saved Antelope Park from becoming a dried up mud hole."

The first time I read about the Vega Sylvester Reservoir, my stomach plunges, as if it still might be about to happen.

The three LaFont books teach me a lot about Creede and the Upper Rio Grande Valley, but not so much about the Pinckleys, so my next stop is the Creede Historical Society and the database for *The Creede Candle*, Creede's newspaper from 1892 to 1930. My search yields exactly five entries:

> January 29, 1910
> Vol. XIX
> *Creede*
> Wednesday afternoon at 2 o'clock sharp, the marriage ceremony was performed by Justice of the Peace John F. Lees, at the bride's home at Sunnyside, joining in wedlock Miss Myrtle Agnes Pinckley to Mr. Don C. LaFont. C.P. Eades and Quincy Neal were the signing witnesses.

After the ceremony a fine bridal dinner was served to which the following did full justice to the good things to eat: Mr. and Mrs. Arthur Neal; Quincy Neal; Mr. and Mrs. A.G. Petitt and Miss Leonore Petitt; Messrs. Charles Eades, Frank Carl, John Pinckley, and the Misses Ada and Hazel Pinckley and Master Bob Pinckley

The guests dispersed in the evening, wishing the happy bride and groom the utmost of the good things of life in which wish we desire to join.

April 30, 1910
Vol. XIX
In the County Court

County Judge C.Y. Butler held a regular session of the County Court last Saturday, and heard the divorce case of Maude May Pinckley* vs. John R. Pinckley, wherein the plaintiff asked for an absolute divorce, with custody of the child. The defendant was represented by Attorney J.D. Pilcher, but was not present, for some unknown reason. The case, though tried before a jury, was of such a spicy and racy nature, that the Judge decided to hear it behind closed doors, and we and everyone else, were chased out. After hearing the evidence, the jury gave the plaintiff a divorce and also gave her custody of the child.

Late: John R. Pinckley was found on Monday at Locklin's ranch. When seen by the caretaker there, he was walking near the house, with a gag in his mouth and his hands bound in front of him with baling wire. When the gag was released, he said that he had been held up and robbed by some men who took $25.00, and his chewing tobacco. Pinckley, being an inveterate user of tobacco, it can readily be seen what an awful act was committed by the robbers.

---

* Maude May Pinckley was John Robert's second wife and, briefly, the stepmother of Bob, Myrtle, Ada and Hazel. The child named here is James Pinckley, who would eventually die in a snow slide up Red Mountain Creek.

After robbing him the men then kidnapped him, ran off with him, all same Albanian brigands and Ellen Stone.*

He returned to town the same day and at once bought some more tobacco, but will not open his face about his being kidnapped. There must be a dark and bloody mystery somewhere, and we recommend that Sheriff Duncan at once obtain the services of Old Sleuth, the famous detective, in order to have the whole thing fathomed out.

May 21, 1910
Vol. XIX
The County Court

Before Judge C.Y. Butler sitting in the May term of the County court, counsel for John R. Pinckley filed a motion asking for the setting aside of the verdict of the jury in the divorce suit of Mrs. Pinckley, in which she was granted a decree. The motion was overruled and counsel then took exception to the overruling and made a motion for a new trial. Judge Butler thereupon set the case for trial on Monday June 6th.

June 21, 1913
Vol. XXII
Creede

John R. Pinckley, an old time ranchman of Antelope Park, died at his home on Friday of last week, June 14. Mr. Pinckley was born in Carroll County, Tennessee, and was 52 years of age. He is survived by five children, Mrs.

---

* Ellen Stone was an American missionary who on September 3, 1901, was captured in the Ottoman Balkans by members of a Macedonian revolutionary organization seeking independence from the Ottomans. The Macedonians demanded $110,000 in ransom and the American Board of Commissioners for Foreign Missions refused to pay. In early October, Stone's relatives and a Boston ministry began a public campaign to raise the money, but before they did, C. M. Dickinson, an American diplomat in Bulgaria convinced the bandits to accept a smaller amount and Miss Stone was released.

Don LaFont, Robert Pinckley, Hazel Pinckley and two twin girls, May and Fay, adopted by Mr. A.D. Parsons of Creede.*

The funeral services were conducted by the Rev. J. Bruce Mather, pastor for the Congregational church of Creede, and were held at the home of the deceased. Mr. Pinckley was buried on the home ranch. A large number of neighbors and friends attended the funeral.

May 27, 1916
Vol. XXV
The County Court

Creede Colorado will take notice that on Monday, June 19th, A.D. 1916, the hearing upon the final accounts and settlements of the following named estates respectively will be had and made, viz: No. 114 Estate of John R. Pinckley, deceased: Don C. LaFont, administrator, PO Creede, Colorado. Hearing and final settlement on Monday, June 19th, 1916, at 10 o'clock am. And Further Notice is Hereby Given, that at said time and place the Court will receive and hear pro 9 f's concerning the heirs of said deceased persons pursuant to the verified petitions of Don C. LaFont . . . administrators of said estates and will judicially ascertain and determine the heirs of said decedent, it being alleged in said petition of Don C. LaFont that Mrs. Don C. LaFont, Joseph Robert Pinckley, Hazel H. Pinckley, children are the only heirs at law of said estate.

Now therefore any and all persons who are or who claim to be heirs at law of . . . said decedents are hereby required to . . . appear thereat, or abide the determination of the Court thereon. Given under my hand and the seal of

---

* Two children do not appear on this list: Ada, who has died of congenital heart failure since Myrtle's wedding, and James, Maude's son, who on this date has yet to die in the snow slide that will eventually kill him. Perhaps some of the *spicy and racy* content of the divorce trial concerned James's paternity. We will have to ask Old Sleuth!

said court at City of Creede, Co, in said County this 24th
day of May A.D. 1916

As tempting as it is to spend the rest of my summer reading every
single issue of *The Creede Candle*, I decide to ask a few living people to
tell me what they can about the history of the ranch.

"It was John LaFont who fenced the ranch," Dona Blair tells me
over eggs and coffee at MJ's Café in Creede, "but not until after we
bought it. He made his living doing fences for people—he was the best
fencer in the whole valley at the time."

Dona is a kind of human spark plug, optimistic, intelligent, and
energetic. Just when you think you have her pegged as a nice Texan
lady with a summer house in the mountains, she'll let it drop into the
conversation that she just came back from a six-week stint doing NGO
work in Yemen.

"My husband and I would give each other a quarter mile of fencing ever year for Christmas for a decade," she says. "We would buy the
barbed wire and the posts and John would come out and put it in."

"He did a damned good job," I tell her. "That fence is in good
shape almost fifty years later."

"Pinckley had it fenced too, but not so as it would hold anything,"
she says. "Bob was a tiny little fellow, never in that good of health." She
reaches her hand across the table to touch mine and lowers her voice.
"They took him in World War II, you know, and they never should
have taken him. He didn't have the spirit for it. I don't believe he ever
recovered." She takes her hand back and butters an English muffin.
"Bob walked all bent over, you know, from the waist, almost at a forty-
five-degree angle. When we started staying in the cabin and even I had
to duck to get in there I thought, Oh, this must be why."

When Dona and her then husband, Robert Blair, bought the ranch
it consisted of the small barn down at the end of the driveway, which
was in ruins by the time I bought it, the big barn, Bob Pinckley's cabin
and at least fifteen outhouses.

"Pinckley collected them," Dona says. "As the guest ranches around the valley modernized, they would give him the outhouses. He would put them on a horse wagon and drag them down here; he would whittle kindling all winter and store it in the outhouses. He kept balls of string and stores of tin foil. He was a pack rat."

Dona and Robert kept one outhouse on the place in honor of Bob, and it stands behind the chicken coop to this day.

"Bob didn't care for people all that much," Dona says, "but he sure loved his horses. When you go home, see if you can see their names and the day they died, scratched into the wood on that big window's frame."

Sure enough, they are exactly where she said they would be, faint, but still legible: Daisy: 11.14.41, Maisey: 1.6.55, Star: 10.10.60.

Everyone in Creede knows who Bob Pinckley was, but he was a hermit and died nearly sixty years ago, so it's not easy to find people who actually knew him. I run into Tom Payne leaving the bank one day. Tom was born and raised here, and has lived here all his life. I'd been told Tom's father owned a sawmill up on Ivy Creek, above the ranch, and when Tom went up to help his dad mill, they'd always take a six-pack of beer and a carton of cigarettes to Bob.

Tom agrees to my request to talk about Bob sometime, but Tom is shy, and would rather be in the mountains on his horse than talk to anybody, so it takes a few phone calls and eventually the intervention of his wife, Patti, our county treasurer, to make the meeting actually happen.

The six coonhounds who live in Tom's yard greet me first, and then Tom, himself, dressed all in camouflage. He asks me in and pushes three winter sleeping bags with impressive loft off a black leather sofa so I can sit down. Tom manages to make the task of stuffing those giant bags back into their compression sacks last most of the thirty minutes we are speaking. Ten beautifully tanned coyote hides hang from a coat rack next to an equally beautiful beaver. Photos of elk, moose and bears don the walls.

Tom worked in the silver mines in Creede for years and was the Single Jack Mining World Champion in 1983. This means that, in an allotted amount of time, Tom, wielding a four-pound hammer, was able to drive a chisel-pointed steel into solid rock by striking it with the hammer, rotating the chisel ninety degrees each time before striking it again—better, faster and deeper than anybody else. The single jack is the pièce de résistance of the yearly Hard Rock Mining Competition that takes place in Creede and other mountain mining towns, and the best hand steelers will hit the chisel sixty to seventy times per minute, the speed increasing not only the depth of the hole in the rock, but the probability an ill-placed strike will destroy the driller's hand. Also in 1983, Tom—known in competitions as the Trapper—edged out all twenty-eight state champions to win the coveted Colorado All-Around Miner Trophy.

We make Creede's version of small talk for about ten minutes. How cold did it get at my house last night? (21 degrees.) How many bales of hay did I have in the barn? (220.) How many sheep had I lost last winter? (Only one, a yearling ram named Lance who died of pneumonia right after shearing. I was worried about a ewe named L.C. who must have gotten into a poison weed this week, but she seemed to be recovering slowly.) How many moose had I seen that summer? (A cow and a calf a couple of different times up Shallow Creek, a good-sized bull just below Love Lake and a young bull running straight across my pasture in that gorgeous loose-limbed way they have, heading for the hills the day before the start of moose season.)

I ask Tom about the sawmill days, specifically, what Pinckley and his dad talked about in the cabin over beers.

"Oh, you know," he says, "about how much snow they used to get in the old days, and how many elk there used to be in the old days, and how easy it was to trap bobcat in the old days." He grins. "Of course *those* days are the old days now."

"I heard a story," I say, "about Pinckley shooting a hole in his side and you stuffing the wound with flour."

Tom laughs out loud. "Well, first of all, it was a knife," he says, "and it wasn't me who stuffed the flour." He lifts his eyes from the sleeping bag and grins again. "Would you like to hear the real story?"

I nod.

"It was a big old buck knife Bob wore sticking out of his pants in the back," Tom says. "Most of any given day he'd be sitting out there in the cabin, looking out the long rectangular window that looks right up to the high park above the road to Spar City. He'd see an elk up there, and if he was out of meat he'd go up there and poach it. He didn't care too much about hunting season. He'd just go up there and get it. Sometimes he had a horse, and sometimes he'd go on foot." We've hit upon something Tom likes to talk about and it is as if the very walls of the room relax. "Well, this day he went up on foot and shot the elk, but it was too cold to butcher it up there so he slung the whole thing around his neck to carry it home. It couldn't have been a very big elk— I mean a big elk could weigh more than a thousand pounds, and he was a little guy, you know? He walked all bent over. Anyhow, he had that elk on his shoulders, trying to carry it home, and he must have stumbled somehow and came down on that big knife."

"Ouch," I offer.

"What was lucky is that John LaFont had gone out to the ranch looking for him that day—John looked after him more and more as he got older—and found him up there just about bled out. It was John who had the wherewithal to pack that wound full of flour—why John had flour on him that day was anybody's guess—but he packed that flour in there to stop the bleeding, and got him back home so he could get patched up."

"Did he go to the doctor?"

"I imagine he did," Tom says, "though it wasn't his favorite thing." He shakes his head and lets go a little chuckle. "You hear the story about the bobcat?"

I have not.

"Well, this other time," Tom says, "Pinckley was riding a green broke horse way up Red Mountain Creek somewhere looking for bobcat. And he'd gotten one, shot it in the nose with a .22 and tried to strangle it."

"He did what, now?"

"Yeah, yeah," Tom says, letting the sleeping bag drop near his feet so he can talk with his hands, "that's what those guys did. They'd whap the thing hard on the nose with a little .22 bullet, or sometimes even a stick just to knock the cat out. And then they'd strangle it. The hide would fetch more money if it didn't have a bullet hole in it. So he hit this cat in the nose with a .22, and then strangled it, and tied it onto his saddle. He's coming down the mountain, talking a little bit to this green horse he's only ridden a handful of times, trying to keep everything nice and calm, you know? And he turns to look behind him and dammed if that cat hasn't come back to life. That cat's just riding along, with his head bobbing, eyes wide open, taking in the view. The cat's front paws are hanging right over the horse's flank, and Bob knows its only a matter of time until it comes wide awake and digs its claws into that young horse. So Bob very very carefully reaches around with his rifle—he has to hold it way out to the side you know, and he shoots that cat in the back of the head. The horse throws Bob, of course, and goes tearing down the mountain with the dead cat still strapped on. Bob had to walk all the way home, and when he got there, there was his horse standing right next to the cabin, that dead cat still strapped onto the saddle."

The look in Tom's eye is half amusement, half unadulterated sorrow that the old days are gone.

"Pinckley'd shoot rabbits out the window of that cabin." Tom says, "We'd be sitting there talking and he'd lay his rifle right across the sill and shoot. One day his hand slipped and he shot a hole right through his own table. I remember we brought him some plastic glue and he fixed it. He was so impressed with that plastic glue." Tom shakes his head and some bigger emotion crosses his face and stalls him out for a minute.

"Other people in town I've talked to have said he was an old grouch, that he didn't like people very much," I say.

"I don't really think that's true," Tom says, "I just don't think he liked to go to town all that much." Tom's eyes go toward the window. "And really, who could blame him?"

I couldn't blame him. I hardly ever go to town.

"He liked to sit right at the window," Tom says again, "looking up to the high meadow and waiting for something to walk across it."

I admit to Tom that especially in wintertime, I like to sit at the window and look up there myself.

There is nothing shy about Carl Vavak, the only other Creede resident I can find left alive who hung out with Bob. I offer to buy him and his long-distance girlfriend, Lynn, green chili cheeseburgers and fried sweet potato spirals at MJ's in exchange for information.

The first thing Carl tells me is that he wound up with Bob Pinckley's still.

"Bob was making whiskey up there?"

"During prohibition just about everybody was. There were at least twenty major stills in this county."

Born and raised between Creede and Pagosa Springs, Carl worked the silver mines until they closed in 1983. He tells me three things about Pinckley no one else has mentioned. That he was quite happy standing up to his neck in horseshit, but if he got the tiniest bit of cow shit on him he would fuss and scrape for an hour. That he never owned a car, but that in February of each year he would get someone to drive him into town. He would check himself into the Creede Hotel and drink and carouse for two weeks straight. Then somebody would drive him back out to the ranch and that was it for another year. And also once a year, he would make a list of clothes he needed and John

LaFont would go down to the JC Penney's in Alamosa and buy every-thing on the list, but when Bob died and the relatives came to clean out the cabin, all of those shirts and pants John had bought were folded neatly in the corner with the tags still on.

"And mourning doves," Carl says. "He could not abide the sound of a mourning dove."

"Maybe they made him sad," Lynn offers.

"Maybe," Carl says, and takes another bite of his cheeseburger.

I ask Carl if he thinks the killing Bob saw in World War II turned him into a hermit, and he considers the question for a moment and says, "What I always heard is he just couldn't take the discipline. He wasn't a guy who had ever taken orders. Those kids grew up wild on the ranch and Bob never had to answer to anybody. They put him on KP duty, cause he wasn't any good as a soldier, and no sooner had they done that he stood up into one of those cast iron pots and knocked himself out—worked himself a medical discharge."

As Pinckley got older, Carl's dad would drive out to the ranch and get him, and bring him to their home on Miners Creek (about halfway to town) for marathon rounds of a card game called sluff.

"It sounds like a lot of people in town looked after him," I say.

"I'd say that's true. John LaFont most of all. He would ice fish for him up in Spar City. Different people would bring him vegetables sometimes. I don't think he ate very well. Might have been diabetic. He had a temper for sure. I was only fourteen when he died, but all us kids knew to be a little careful around him. He was caged dynamite a lot of the time and we didn't want to get a cussin'. He took kind of a liking to me, though. He had a telescope—a good one for the time—and he gave it to me before he died. I don't think he used it to do anything but hunt for animals, but he sparked a love of astronomy in me I've carried all my life."

"That might be the single most positive thing I've heard anybody say about Bob Pinckley," I tell Carl.

"He had a hard life," Carl says. "Everybody talks about the good old days. . . ." He shakes his head. "LaFont told me that one time back in the early days the Pinckley family needed money so bad they hired out Bob to go on up to Wright's ranch"—about twelve miles upriver—"to drive a team. They were plowing, and building some cabins. So Bob went up there and put in a couple of sixteen-hour days, but pretty soon they had to send him home because he was too homesick. How old do you think he was?"

I shake my head.

"Seven," Carl says. "Let that sink in."

Ranch Almanac: First Warm Day

*In February, all of January's icy blue light gives way to a softer
gold. It's been snowing for six days straight, but this morning the
sun rises with something that feels like a little bit of warmth in
it, and even the equines are in a good enough mood to be silly.
Simon and Isaac have been playing grab-ass out in the corral all
morning. Deseo is crashed out in what we call dead horse position
(DHP) in the snow, soaking up the sun through his dark coat. Mr.
Kitty comes up out of the basement, meows at the door and takes
off on what might be his first kitty bender of the year.*

*The first time he did this, many Februaries ago, I thought
we'd lost him. But he showed up at the front door—not his door,
which is in the mudroom, but the front door—after seven days
of subzero overnights, looking half wild and pretty hungover. He
walked right into the living room, as if he owned the place, which
set off Fenton's animal-out-of-place alert and put both dogs into*

a frenzy. They tore around the house like something out of a Tom and Jerry cartoon until Mr. Kitty slipped out the kitchen door to the mudroom and into his rightful digs.

Today is going to be one of those bluebird days Colorado is famous for, perfect for going out to the pasture and remaking the snowshoe trails. Like everything on the ranch, repetition is the key to successful trail making, and if I make them true after the first big snowstorm, it pays dividends all winter long.

If I stand with my back against the northeasternmost corral pole and cut as perfect a diagonal as I can to the corner pole that marks the half section line where my property and the Soward Ranch meet, I give myself the best chance of retracing my steps after each subsequent snowfall. From the corner pole, I head straight across the pasture to the ridge Bob Pinckley cut some year when he thought he might be able to use the tiny creek that comes off Sheep Mountain to irrigate. His irrigation scheme failed, but the long scar of humped-up earth makes for a great snowshoe trail that runs from one extremity of my property to another. The wind blows most of the snow off that little ridge as it moves the moisture-laden front out of our area. And even when it doesn't, the ridgeline is the easiest place in the whole pasture to find the same trail I have packed down before.

It feels good to be out in the sunshine moving, making tracks. The dogs pay no attention to the old trail. They leap and bound and come up with muzzles full of powder, grinning wildly. I kick along for several hundred feet, waiting for my favorite winter sound of all—the muffled whummmp of snow settling under my shoes. And even though my pasture is essentially flat, the mountains rising in a horseshoe around me out beyond the edges of my property, there will always come a time when my pushing the snow down in one key spot—only the length and width of a snowshoe—launches a kind of horizontal avalanche:

a giant settling of snow in ever radiating quilt squares away from me across much of my big pasture. A whummmp, followed by a longer whummmp, followed by a longer whummmp echoing out all the way to the creek bed and the tree line.

And then the pasture goes silent again.

Eating Phoebe

Back in 2011, I went off to teach in Provincetown, Massachusetts, for a week, as I do each summer, and when I left for the Denver airport on a Saturday morning I had five sheep in my barn: Motown, Yvonne, Jordan, Phoebe and Sampson. I returned the next Sunday, the same day twelve students arrived at the ranch for a private workshop along with Greg, his first ranch visit that summer. On Monday morning, when a student named Laura asked Greg how many sheep we had, he said three.

"No, no," I said, "you're forgetting the lambs, Sampson and Phoebe. There are five now."

"I just let them out of their pen to graze," Greg said, "and I can tell you definitively there are three."

My ranchsitters that year—I'll call them Monroe and Daphne—a young couple of Gen Y-ers who had lived at the ranch for six months, and with whom I had a hard time conversing but tried to think the best of anyway, had not mentioned two sheep were missing before they went off on a weeklong camping trip of their own.

Back-to-the-land types from Georgia, Monroe and Daphne had built raised beds in the yard for the six-week (if you are lucky) frost-free growing season, brewed their own beer in the mudroom and filled my basement with compost worms. They also raised chicks that spring, without asking me, or telling me, in my kitchen.

That April, when I was teaching in California and hadn't been home to check on things in more than a month, I was scrolling through my Facebook feed and found the following status update from Monroe: *I sure hope our Great Dane puppy stops shitting and peeing all over the house before half of the Southeast shows up next month to visit.* I had to marvel at Monroe's efficiency at cramming so many alarming details into a one-sentence update. I tried to imagine a more alarming post: *Cooking meth again in the clawfoot tub with ingredients purchased with forged checks from owner's bank account.*

When I called Monroe and said it would have been courteous to *ask* me if they could get a Great Dane puppy, or even *tell* me in advance that was their plan, since they had one dog already; since I bought for the ranch everything they asked me to, including an indoor compost starter kit, a thousand dollars worth of sheep fencing, a miter saw, a pillow top mattress and even, as it turned out, the chickens they didn't tell me they were planning to raise in the kitchen. There was a pretty good chance, I insisted, if they *had* talked to me about the Great Dane puppy I would have said yes.

During the entirety of our conversation, Monroe sounded like he always did, like somebody who had just come back from a seventy-two-hour rave.

But several months had gone by and now we were all used to Sadie, the puppy, and the aroma of chicken shit no longer filled the kitchen. When we all overlapped at the ranch, Monroe and Daphne tended the sheep and the chickens and I took care of the horses and dogs. Now, somehow, we were down two sheep.

To my surprise Monroe answered his cell phone—in this case "camping" turned out to mean they were staying a few days at the house of a friend in town so they could drink all they wanted at the bar without having to drive the twelve miles to the ranch. Monroe didn't know what happened to the sheep, he said, but he thought he might have seen mountain lion tracks, and the coyotes had been especially loud lately, and he'd heard there'd been a bear nosing around Red Mountain Ranch—five miles up Ivy Creek—last week. When I asked why he hadn't thought to mention the missing sheep when I got home, and why he hadn't locked the sheep in their predator-proof pen at night as we always had, he had no answer.

Remembering that a few weeks before Monroe had drunk an entire bottle of wine with dinner, I asked him if he was having any kind of trouble.

No, no trouble, he said, but he *was* sad about the loss of the sheep. "Those sheep were my friends," he said, but he seemed to have already forgotten which two of his friends were missing.

So me, and Greg, and my student writers spent several hours that day combing the surrounding hills, calling for Sampson and Phoebe.

"Something's not right about this," Greg said, though I was usually the conspiracy theorist in the family. "He isn't surprised or worried enough that they're gone."

On the phone Monroe had said he and Daphne would come out and help us look for Sampson and Phoebe, but two more days went by and they didn't show.

On the third day, my friend and farrier Dex Decker showed up to trim the horses, and when I asked him whether he thought sheep in distress would move uphill or downhill, Dex, said, "I don't think you're asking the right question."

"So what's the right question?" I said.

Dex thought for a minute and then said, "Well, shit, I guess it's gonna be me who throws those kids under the bus."

After I heard Dex's version it was time to call Sheriff Fred Hosselkus.

"Pam!" he said, when he picked up the phone. "I was wondering when I was going to hear from you. You missing a couple of sheep?"

I said I was, and he said, "Well, you might check the freezer down at the Far Dog."

The sheriff's version and Dex's version lined up remarkably well, given the way news travels in a small town, and those versions synched up with other versions I heard over the next several days.

It seemed Monroe and two of his friends got wasted the last night I was in Provincetown, and in the throes of what Dex called "a bad idea at the bottom of a bottle," decided to slaughter Phoebe, the yearling lamb. They killed her in the barnyard, in front of all my other animals, including Phoebe's mother, Jordan, the other sheep and the chickens, the horses and the donkeys, and for all I knew, the dogs and Mr. Kitty, using one of my good cooking knives.

One of Monroe's friends held Phoebe up off her front feet and Monroe leaned in to slit her throat. Phoebe struggled hard, causing Monroe to cut not only her throat but also his friend's brachial artery. But the friend was too shitfaced to *know* he had a severed artery, so the drinking party loaded Phoebe's body into the truck and went into town, to a restaurant called the Far Dog, where the other friend worked as a prep cook, and therefore had a key.

In their enthusiasm for whatever Bacchanalian ritual they were enacting, they forgot to lock the other sheep away, and so little Sampson—only a month old—must have been dragged away in the night by coyotes.

One can only imagine the 3:00 a.m. scene at the restaurant. The part-time chef butchering Phoebe, wrapping her in white paper and putting her in the freezer, Monroe chugging a beer, sautéing a little garlic for the tenderloin steaks, the third guy slumped at a four top in the corner, quietly bleeding out. Across the street a well-meaning insomniac notices a light on in the Far Dog, calls the sheriff's office, and suddenly Fred Hosselkus's pager goes off.

If Fred had not shown up at the restaurant when he did, I heard from Deputy Billy Fairchild, the bleeder probably wouldn't have made it.

As it was, he was taken all the way to the Front Range by ambulance—
five hours over passes—and even then doctors weren't sure they'd be able
to save his life. Meanwhile, one imagines, Monroe and the prep cook sat
around in the Far Dog, toasting the manly life, eating Phoebe.

I had gotten those sheep in the first place because the county tax laws had
changed so pleasure horses no longer counted as livestock when determining agricultural status. In Colorado land status designations, there
is no category between agricultural property and vacant land, no "gentleman farm" category for people like me who love to be surrounded by
animals, but who don't make the largest part of their living from them.
The taxation difference between agricultural property and vacant land
is not two or three times, but twenty. If I lost the ranch's agricultural
status—which it has had since homesteading days—not only would I
have to move because of the tax burden, I would be doing a disservice to
the land itself, and to anyone who owned it after me. Eventually it would
fall into the hands of a developer who'd likely pay the taxes for one year,
and then subdivide it into one- to five-acre ranchettes.

Early that spring, Monroe and Daphne and I had talked at length
about what kind of livestock I should purchase. We had decided on
sheep because chickens only counted if you had them in the hundreds,
and I'd heard too many stories of goats eating sideview mirrors off cars.
We could've raised a calf or a pig every summer, but that would mean
sending it to slaughter at the end of the season. We agreed none of us
wanted to get attached to an animal with a death date stamped on its ear.
With sheep, we reasoned, we could shear them and sell the wool, and
sell a yearling ram or ewe now and then to another Icelandic breeder.

"I understand those sheep were *named*," Sheriff Fred Hosselkus
said, over the phone, and I confirmed that in fact they were. "Shame,"
he said, but I wasn't sure if he meant the naming, or the killing.

"What do I do now?" I asked, sincerely.

"Why don't Billy and I go talk to Monroe," Fred said. "We'll tell him if he and Daphne get all their stuff off your property by five tonight with an officer standing by in the driveway to make sure they don't give you any trouble, you'll think twice before pressing criminal mischief charges."

I had not yet thought of pressing criminal mischief charges. But our sheriff is a good man, compassionate and moral, and in a very small town where neighbors have to depend on one another through the long and frigid winter, he likes it when conflicts get resolved along the path of least resistance.

"I'll send Billy out there right now to take some pictures," he said. "We want to keep all our ducks in a row."

Once I knew the story, it was easy to find the slaughter site. My Wüsthof cleaver over here, an empty bottle of Black Velvet over there, a bloodstained golf shirt, a Texas Rangers ball cap, an unopened can of Pabst Blue Ribbon caked in mud, an unspooled roll of toilet paper and several small pools of dark congealed blood. There were also a great many chicken feathers—apparently the ritual had involved killing one of those too.

Billy asked if he could take the hat and shirt back to town with him, but not before he regaled my private students—most of them sophisticated ladies from urban centers—with tales of cabin fever, unrequited passions, restraining order violations and dramatic winter rescues full of severed limbs and body parts frozen to large pieces of metal. Before he left he took me aside and said, "We can all be thankful that kid didn't bleed out behind your barn, Pam, or you might be in for a whole mess of trouble you don't want."

Later that afternoon, while I taught my class in the living room, Monroe and Daphne moved their things out of the bedroom, with Fred and Billy in the county's GMC in my driveway, standing by.

The day after Monroe and Daphne moved out, a friend of theirs with a Georgia area code called the house phone. "Monroe doesn't live here anymore," I said, in the most neutral voice I could muster.

The young man barked out a laugh like a dog. "Did he leave on good terms?" he said. "Or did he crash and burn like he always does?"

"You'll have to take that up with him," I said, and hung up.

What had Monroe done, I wondered, in front of or to this young man, to make him willing to say such a thing to a total stranger? And how had he hypnotized Daphne? Sweet, southern, docile, acquiescent Daphne. What was she doing with herself when the men started sharpening the knives? Did she try to talk Monroe out of killing Phoebe? Did she hide in the house with the stereo loud so she wouldn't have to hear her bleating? Did she, or anyone else in the drinking party, think for a minute, I wonder what Pam will have to say about all this when she gets home—not next week or next month or next summer, but tomorrow? I knew I was still asking the wrong questions. But I wasn't yet sure what the right ones were.

What came next was a crash course in sheep and chicken tending, which I failed, rather spectacularly, two days after Monroe and Daphne left. I still don't know how the chickens got out of the chicken run at the exact moment one of my students opened the kitchen door, but the dogs raced out of the house like competing contestants on a game show, and faster than you can say "Drop that chicken!" I had two mortally wounded birds, one in each set of handsome wolfhound mouths—Fenton, still fit and fast in 2011, breaking his bird's neck instantly, efficiently, but William, still a puppy, managing to spill the guts of the second bird without actually breaking her neck. After wrangling her out of William's mouth and getting the dogs locked back in the house, it was left to me to cut off the chicken's head.

"You can do this, Pam," my student Laura said, impressively composed, as I raised the axe and the chicken blinked at me sweetly. "But you have to do it now because she's suffering."

"What if I don't get it right on the first try?" I said. It was dawning on me that this would be the very first time in fifty years I personally killed a living thing other than bugs, and even spiders I usually took outside.

"Then you will hit her again and again until she dies," Laura said, calm as the surface of a pond in summer, and it took three tries to be sure but then she was absolutely dead. Laura and I carried the bodies a mile into the forest and left them for the coyotes.

I hated killing that chicken. I hated that it was my lack of vigilance that put the dogs and the chickens in the yard at the same time. I wasn't even done hating Monroe for getting drunk and slaughtering Phoebe and letting little Sampson wander off to get torn limb from limb by coyotes, and now I had to take a break from hating Monroe so I could hate myself. You didn't have to get raging drunk, apparently, to screw up colossally in the animal husbandry department. I was two sheep and three chickens down in a week, and at the end of the day I had no one to blame but myself.

Meanwhile, at the Tommyknocker Tavern in town, Monroe was telling everyone he couldn't understand what I'd gotten so upset about, because I had told him when we got the sheep he could do anything he wanted with them. The only thing I'd ever said to Monroe that could possibly fall into that category was that he and Daphne could keep the money from the wool sales, since they were the ones doing the sheep care and feeding. If Monroe had ever actually believed it would have been fine with me for him and his buddies to get drunk and start killing ranch animals, he'd have had no need to invent the mountain lion tracks, nor the especially loud coyotes, nor the bear last seen at Red Mountain Ranch.

I'd lived in Creede for nearly twenty years by then. I was well versed in small towns and the way people talk in them. I'd had eyebrows raised at me for being on *Oprah*, been laughed at when a friend from CBS *Sunday Morning* had lobsters FedExed in for my birthday and received hate mail for an article I wrote for *Santa Fean* magazine that I thought was a veritable love letter to Creede, but to which some people in town took exception. But I also knew this: Monroe and Daphne would be gone, as most tourists are, before the snow fell. A few years would go by and no one would remember even their (actual) names.

I also understood I had been given a wake-up call to give the ranch more attention. I was never going to be able to live my life without ranchsitters, but I would screen them more carefully in advance. I would make it my goal to never leave the ranch for more than a month without dropping in. If I ever doubted how things were going, I would cut short whatever work trip I was on and come home and see for myself. Most significantly, I would drop from three-quarters time at UC Davis to half-time.

I got better at caring for the chickens and sheep. The owner of the Far Dog sent me his humblest apologies, assured me the employee who butchered Phoebe had been fired and invited me in for a meal on him. We had more lambs, two the next spring and two the next. I lost a ewe to pneumonia the winter after Monroe and Daphne's departure, and a two-year-old ram who apparently got himself cast up (that's rancher talk for *stuck*) against the barn wall and couldn't move. He must have twisted his gut sometime in the night trying, because when we found him in the morning he was stiff as a board. Doc Howard said, by way of consolation, "You know, Pam, sheep are born looking around for a place to die."

The year after we lost Phoebe and Sampson, Jordan gave birth to a ram we named Junior because he was the spitting image of Motown, his sire, black with white spots and a white face and tail, two white legs and two black ones. Rams tend to get more rammy with age, and at six, Motown was getting to be more than I could handle. I knew the rams would clash when Junior came of age, so I sold Motown to a breeder in New Mexico. Junior stayed sweet, and sired beautiful babies until the day his third set of lambs were born. The first thing he did was try to kill them. It's not unusual for a ram to try to kill a male lamb—Motown *had* knocked Junior sideways the day Junior was born—but once it became clear both lambs were females, I feared Junior might have a screw loose.

We moved him out with the horses, where, in spite of the size differential, he found ways to terrorize them too, kicking his little hoof out—Van Morrison style—at sweet old Roany, and running him off pile after pile of hay. Junior wouldn't quit no matter how many separate piles of hay I made. It didn't seem to be about hunger or even ownership of each pile as much as the thrill of making an animal four times his size run. Deseo tried to stick up for Roany, cracking Junior in the head with a full-extension kick of both back hoofs on more than one occasion. It made a hell of a noise when his hooves hit those horns, but it seemed not to even faze Junior, as a ram's head is designed to be slammed into over and over again.

Deseo is scared of the water trough even on a good day, so that's what Junior chose to keep *him* away from. There is nothing in the universe *más macho* than an intact miniature donkey, so Junior left Isaac alone. But Isaac's brother, Simon, is shy, and let Junior chase him out of the windbreak on the back side of the barn no matter how hard and fast the snow came.

Junior rammed me often, so hard it sent me sprawling in the sheep pen, so hard that when I got done with chores and went in to take a shower, I found the backs of my legs severely abraded and the inside of my pants covered in blood.

I built a whole new pen to isolate Junior further, but by that time he'd learned that if he applied continuous pressure to the metal stakes I'd sunk in the ground he could uproot them, and when I sunk them deeper he learned that he could hook his horns into the wire fencing and eventually tear a hole in it big enough to ram through. When I bought thicker gauge wire he learned to bash his way out by hitting the gate over and over again until the wooden parts of the frame splintered. I even tried rebuilding the walls of his enclosure so they curved in at the bottom, making it impossible for him to get his body into position for ramming. That's when he started slamming himself into the outside wall of the hundred-year old barn.

You would think a fifty-four-year-old woman could outsmart a four-year-old ram, but I couldn't. By that time the lambs were almost yearlings and I knew with their mother's help they could all hold their own against him. I hoped putting Junior back in with the ewes would calm him down, and at first it did. But then Junior chose Natasha—a two-year-old ewe—as the victim of his bullying, spending so much time keeping her off her food he barely got to eat himself. Each morning, I let her out alone so she could eat her hay in the snowy yard.

It didn't take two weeks for Junior to start bashing down doors again. The third morning in a row I woke to Jordan and all the other girls standing belly-deep in snow a hundred yards from the pen, just asking a coyote to come have a feast, I decided enough was enough. If I took no action, someone was going to get killed, and odds were it wouldn't be Junior. On a ranch, I have learned, it is often the sweetest residents who die.

It was getting close to the start of spring quarter at UC Davis, and I couldn't leave a new ranchsitter with this problem, couldn't take the risk Junior might ram her as hard as he rammed me. I put Junior up on Craigslist and tried to sell him, but at that time of year no one needs another mouth to feed. My friend Sam Arnold asked her hunter son if he could make use of the meat and the cape and he said he could. He came to the house on a brilliantly sunny afternoon and told me to lure Junior out of the pen. I went into the barn and got a can of grain and Junior followed me out into the yard. Then the young man told me to step away and I did. He raised his rifle to his eye from thirty yards away and shot Junior right between the eyes.

For four seasons in my twenties I worked as a Dall sheep-hunting guide in the Brooks and Alaska ranges. It was one hunter and one guide for ten days; that's how long it took because the rams were smart and they could climb much faster than we could. Their sense of smell was about ten thousand times better than ours, so if we were upwind we had to stay put for hours. Their vision was unparalleled, and when they slept in groups in the afternoon they always left a sentry—one of the youngest rams—keeping watch. Even when we were downwind we had to find a way to approach the rams without crossing open terrain, which in the treeless high country of Alaska is nearly impossible. Even with ten days at our disposal, the hunters only killed about 35 percent of the time.

I guided sheep hunters in Alaska because I was in love with a guy who made his living that way and because I wanted, more than anything, to be out in the Alaskan bush for two months a year. I've never quite come to peace with myself for doing it, but those seasons taught me a lot about myself as a carnivore, about the relationship between meat eaters and game. Most of the hunters who killed on those hunts had great respect for the sheep and their environment, and the ones who didn't generally went home empty-handed.

Killing Junior was the exact opposite of all that. And in spite of the close range and Sam's son's perfect marksmanship he died hard, bellowing and spinning and spewing blood across the snow for twenty feet in all directions while Sam and I and all the other animals looked on, amazed. In Alaska, we'd instructed the hunters to shoot the rams, not in the skull plate, as this young man had, but through the heart.

What had sickened me most when Monroe killed Phoebe was that he'd done it in front of the other animals. I'd imagined the horses, Deseo especially, smelling the beer and blood and thinking they might be next. And now here I was, creating the same trauma a few years later, minus the booze, minus the knife, plus one head-rattling explosion.

"He was either a good bad man, or a bad good man," reads one of my favorite Toni Morrison lines, "it all depends on what you hold dear." By which I think she means longevity has a way of turning heroes into villains and vice versa. With Junior, life had delivered me an opportunity to stop holding a grudge against Monroe. It handed me a particular set of circumstances, and the next thing I knew I had blood on my hands.

There is something deeply wrong, my years as a hunting guide taught me, with anyone who can take a life lightly. For the most part, neither the hunters I guided, nor the ranchers I know in this valley, ever do. When I had to kill the chicken that William eviscerated, when I lured Junior out to the yard with a can of grain, I understood that Monroe had not been lying when he said the sheep were his friends. Sometimes, friends do terrible things to each other.

Ranch Almanac: Lambing

My shearer, Tom Barr, says Icelandics are the toughest sheep he shears, the strongest and the most unruly, but since they're the only sheep I've had, I can't compare. I find the ewes sweet and self-sufficient, if a little bossy, and I like sitting outside listening to their bleats and baas when they're grazing around the house in the afternoon.

When the sheep are out, the wolfhounds are in, or we have a hell of a rodeo. Fenton got his ribs smashed hard a couple of times when he cornered Motown down by the creek one day, and Jordan lost a pretty big clump of wool from her butt to William who was very insistent she sit down right now. *So far Livie has been smart enough to keep her distance, and there's never been any blood drawn on either side.*

Lambs are born, like clockwork, on the twenty-fifth of March every year. They come alone or in pairs, black and white, or orange and white with big white stars on their faces, and sometimes a color I'd call pure golden blond. From the minute they are born until they are three weeks old, they have the softest, tightest, most beautiful curls you've ever seen.

During lambing season mamas and babies stay in the big pen 24/7. I'm grateful when the new lambs turn out to be female, because I'm not a good enough farmer to raise multiple rams, who do as their name suggests. I raise all the lambs to respond to basic voice commands and to enjoy a scratch behind the ears, but uncastrated, all my rams eventually become unruly, and nobody has much use for an aging, castrated ram.

I've learned a lot over the years about lambing: how to recognize when a ewe is in trouble, when to step in and when to leave well enough alone. But at the first birth I attended, a year after we got the sheep, my then ranchsitter, Mary Kate, and I stood outside the pen wringing our hands and saying encouraging words to Jordan the ewe who was down on her knees panting and looking more than a little uncomfortable.

Motown the ram stood over her, calm by his standards and, we thought, protective. We'd read lots of conflicting advice on the internet and had decided to go with the "most Icelandics know exactly how to do this themselves" school of sheep ranching. Mary Kate is an RN and kept repeating the first rule of nursing, "If it is not broken, don't fix it," until one black and white little lamb popped out, leapt immediately to his feet and started to nurse. We had about thirty seconds of cooing and grinning before Motown took a few steps back, got a running start, and tossed the two-minute-old baby into the air using his giant full curl of horns. Mary Kate ran to the baby while I threw my body on top of Motown, got him in a chokehold, and pulled and pushed him out the gate. Nowhere on the internet had it said, "Get the ram out of the pen before the ewe gives birth," though we felt like idiots for not even speculating.

The baby seemed unhurt—if a little dazed—and in less than

a minute had resumed nursing. We guessed it was a little ram, more because of Motown's reaction than because of any body part we could discern, and when his horns started to come in a few days later, it turned out we were right.

The baby was nursing happily, and Jordan seemed in no distress. We decided we might leave them alone to let them bond when we noticed something else seemed to be emerging from Jordan's nether regions. "Don't worry," Mary Kate said, with some authority, "It's probably just the afterbirth." We settled back against the wall of the pen to watch. "Does an afterbirth have hooves?" I said, and sure enough, less than a minute later, a second little black and white ram was born.

PART THREE

Diary of a Fire

Diary of a Fire

Many folks visiting the Rio Grande National Forest are notic-
ing a big change in the high elevation forests as literally millions
of trees are succumbing to the spruce bark beetle. More than
600,000 acres of spruce-fir forest have been infested by spruce
beetle since 2002 and the beetles are continuing to spread. The
native spruce beetle primarily attacks mature Engelmann spruce,
although it sometimes infests blue spruce too. The tiny beetle
is killing trees down to 5 inches in diameter. Luckily, smaller
spruce and all sizes of subalpine fir will continue to survive and
they will provide the base for creating the next forest.

—From the USDA Forest Service website

On June 5, 2013, lightning strikes a dead Engelmann spruce in
the San Juan National Forest near Wolf Creek Pass in a direct
line south from the ranch, up and over the Continental Divide. The
smoke plume the resulting fire ignites is too thin and distant for me
to see from my kitchen window—probably fifteen miles as the crow
flies, so I don't know about it yet. The spring of 2013 has been the driest in more than a decade. The region has had very little precipitation
in April and none whatsoever in May. While the rest of the country
has exploded into summer activity, we've hunkered down at home,

rationed our water, watched the horizon. We've had ten red flag days since May 20 and I can feel the whole valley holding its breath.

Red Flag Warning: A designation put in place by the National Weather Service to alert land management agencies about the onset of critical weather and fuel moisture conditions that could lead to rapid or dramatic increases in wildfire activity (*USDA Forest Service Fire Terminology*).

On June 7, the West Fork Fire makes its first appearance on the internet when it is only a quarter acre in size. The Archuleta Emergency Management Website, receiving its information from the Durango Interagency Fire Dispatch, reports that the West Fork Fire, started by lightning on Monday, June 5, is burning in a rugged and remote area of heavy "down-dead and standing bug-kill timber" at 10,850 feet in elevation.

It takes the better part of a week for the West Fork Fire to grow from a quarter acre to 25 acres. We still haven't seen any smoke on our side of the Divide, but I keep my eyes trained on the mountains to the south, which are covered with tens of thousands of beetle-killed spruce trees, standing like matchsticks on the hillsides, taunting the clouds full of dry lightning.

I've probably been hiking a hundred times up on the Divide behind the ranch just north of where the fire is burning. I turn left out my driveway, away from town, and follow Middle Creek Road all the way to its end. There I follow any one of a number of elk trails through the forest until I get to the tree line, where there's a marmot trail that wraps around the backside of Copper Ridge, facing Red Mountain. From there it's a steep but short grunt up to 12,800-foot Copper Mountain, which towers over the headwaters of Red Mountain Creek.

It is glorious country, flat mesa top fringed with giant slabs of volcanic rock, tundra meadows full of purple bluebells and miniature stalks of Indian paintbrush which glow a vibrant purple-red up that high in a really wet year, and cover the tundra in a palette that includes oranges, yellows and sometimes even whites.

From the top of Copper Mountain it's a 360-degree view most people can't imagine. To the south, the tundra-covered dips and swirls of the mountains surrounding Wolf Creek Pass: Piedra Peak, Palomino Mountain, and on the other side of Porphyry Basin, the Window and Sugarloaf. To the southeast, South River Peak and Fisher Mountain stand rock-strewn and mostly bald above the relatively lush Ivy and Lime Creek drainages. To the northeast, the ranch and the rest of Antelope Park point the way to the town of Creede, San Luis Peak and the nearly always snow-dusted La Garita Range. Due north is Bristol Head, and above it, Table Mountain and Snow Mesa, a pancake-flat highland lost in the clouds. To the northwest, the headwaters of the Rio Grande and Jarosa Mesa. And to the west, perhaps grandest of all, the high San Juans: the Pyramid, Handies Peak, Sunshine Peak, the melting ice cream cone of Uncompahgre and the Wetterhorn, the last four standing above 14,000 feet, under a Colorado bluebird sky.

It's a place that literally and figuratively takes your breath away, a place where you might find yourself believing there is too much wild country ever to be destroyed. You might think climate change can't touch this, nor fracking, nor the Koch brothers, nor Trump and his cabinet of oil barons. But all you have to do is look closely at the mountainsides to know not only that those things *can* touch us, they already have.

After the pine beetle spent the 1990s decimating forests in northern Colorado, its cousin, the spruce bark beetle showed up in our part of the state in the early 2000s. Foresters blame the devastation the spruce beetle has caused on drought conditions in the southwest and consistently warmer temperatures due to long-term changes in sea surface temperature—all climate-change-related trends that are expected to continue and worsen for decades. In 2012, 183,000 new acres of spruce-beetle-infested trees were discovered in Colorado, bringing the state's total to a million acres. Many of those new acres are in the San

Juan and Rio Grande national forests—which is really all one forest, separated in name only by the Continental Divide. It is the Rio Grande National Forest that comes all the way down to my fences, that surrounds the ranch on three sides. By 2013, the only live trees left on many of the hillsides are the youngest spruce trees, which have too little diameter to make it worth the beetle's while, a few subalpine firs, and the giant stands of aspens, lime green in their early summer finery, that braid themselves through the larger groves of spruce.

The spruce/fir forest doesn't burn very often, but when it does, it burns big. Add a century of fire suppression, climate-driven high winds and low humidity, and an average temperature increase of 2 degrees, thanks to all the carbon dioxide we've pumped into the air. I'm no scientist, but my intuitive understanding goes something like this: Maybe the forest looked around at its cluttered, overheated, airless self and said, "What if I invent a beetle that will leave a million trees standing dead and crisp on top of a mountain that gets hundreds of lightning strikes each summer. Let's see you try to stop me burning then."

Dead Fuels: Fuels with no living tissue in which moisture content is governed almost entirely by atmospheric moisture (relative humidity and precipitation), dry-bulb temperature, and solar radiation (*USDA Forest Service Fire Terminology*).

By the morning of June 13, the fire has blown up to 150 acres, due, the National Forest Service's InciWeb site tells us, "to topography, fuel loading, and outflow winds from thunderstorms in the area." When I'm not looking out the window, I'm looking at InciWeb, which updates the size of the fire every twelve hours and informs us, among other things, what equipment we are being assigned. We started out with a ten-person Type 2 hand crew, one Type 6 engine and a Type 3 incident commander, and today we've added an additional ten-person hand crew, two Type 2 helicopters and one Type 3 helicopter. On the

Glossary of Wildland Fire Terminology website I learn that a hand crew is a team of eighteen to twenty firefighters assigned to construct fire lines and firebreaks using hand tools, chain saws and drip torches, and that a Type 1 resource provides greater overall firefighting capability, due to power and size, than would be found in a Type 2 resource. Firefighters are on scene, InciWeb assures me, to provide structure protection to cabins and outbuildings on private property.

Also on June 13, a second fire, one they will name the Windy Pass Fire, starts by lightning, and burns 5 to 6 acres on the south side of Highway 160, not all that far from where the West Fork Fire is burning on the north side of the same road. Twenty-seven people are at work fighting the Windy Pass Fire by Friday the fourteenth, and an additional twenty-person crew is on order.

The West Fork Fire is not the first fire that has threatened the ranch since I have owned it, and I know it will not be the last. In 2002—in another hot rainless June—the Missionary Ridge Fire burned for forty smoke-filled days and nights and devastated nearly 73,000 acres of forest, destroying forty-six houses and cabins, and costing $40.8 million to suppress. The Missionary Ridge was what is known as a crown fire, the type that moves rapidly through a forest canopy—treetop to treetop, with flames reaching 250 feet in length or height—instead of on the ground. The Missionary Ridge Fire did all kinds of things normal wildland fires aren't supposed to do. It burned downhill, for instance, when it is in fire's nature to rise. It burned right through giant stands of aspen, which sometimes can slow or stop a fire because of the high moisture content in their trunks. When the Missionary Ridge Fire started it was many miles and several mountain passes away from the ranch, but its behavior was so erratic, no one in the region felt safe.

In 2002, there were only isolated stands of beetle kill, but conditions were so hot, dry and windy that summer the fire began making weather of its own, churning up powerful winds inside its self-created vortex, sending columns of smoke and ash up to a mile wide that rose to 40,000 feet and caused birds to fall dead out of the sky. Burning chunks of wood were carried 10,000 feet high, and when the column of hot air that was supporting them cooled and collapsed, the embers fell into unburnt forests, igniting them too, burning through 10,000 acres in a day. Eighteen hundred homes were evacuated as the fire twisted and turned unpredictably, making 50 mph runs up mountain ridges and creating fire tornados with winds of more than 100 mph that turned over vehicles and blew down whole stands of trees. Firefighters stopped talking about how to contain the fire and tried instead to "herd it" away from people's homes. The San Juan Basin was designated the driest spot in the nation that year, moisture inside the conifers and ponderosa pines fell below 5 percent (boards stacked in lumberyards normally have moisture content of 12 percent), which meant if a spark hit the ground there was a 100 percent probability of ignition. The prevailing winds in southwestern Colorado are easterly, and the Missionary Ridge Fire lay directly to our west.

Then, on June 19, 2002, just when firefighters started to get the Missionary Ridge Fire into the very first percentages of containment, the Million Fire started thirty miles southeast of the ranch near the town of South Fork, burning nearly 10,000 acres and eleven homes. We were smoked in for a month no matter which way the wind blew. Longtime Creede residents packed up their belongings, put For Sale signs on their houses and headed to more watery places—Portland, Oregon, or upstate New York. In 2002, we were made aware and uncomfortable by our proximity to the fire, but we were never put on standby to evacuate. Even at its closest, the Missionary Ridge Fire never got closer than twenty-five miles from the ranch.

The West Fork Fire, however, is walking distance from the ranch—a serious day of walking, to be undertaken by a serious walker, because of the 12,000-foot mountains that make up most of the terrain between. Also, in the eleven years since the Missionary Ridge Fire, we have gained half a million standing beetle-killed trees.

A thing that sets me apart from a lot of other people on the planet, and connects me intensely to others, is that for all of my childhood and some of my adulthood, I believed if I stopped paying strict attention my father would kill me or, if not kill me, do such irreparable damage to my life I would become as miserable as he. My father was in assisted living in 2002 when the Missionary Ridge Fire was running seven miles a day toward the ranch, but I still thought, as I always think when I am afraid, Here he is, finally coming for me. In June 2013, eight years after his death, I thought it again.

An infrared flight on Friday night, June 14, reports the West Fork Fire has grown to 470 acres, mostly into the Burro Creek drainage, and is officially listed as zero percent contained. Sixty-seven people are now assigned to the fire, digging hand lines and conducting small burn-out operations, trying to secure the south flank assisted by a Type 1 and a Type 2 helicopter that are dropping water on the ridge to the west of Borns Lake, trying to keep the fire from moving on to private lands. The crew has also started reducing hazardous fuels, clearing brush and laying hose in case structure protection is needed. This afternoon, firefighters helped safely evacuate thirteen backpackers from along the West Fork Trail and Rainbow Hot Springs.

Burn Out: Setting fire inside a control line to widen it or consume fuel between it and the edge of the fire. (As distinguished from a *backfire*, or *backburn,* which is a fire set along the inner edge of a fire line to consume the fuel in the fire's path and/or to change the direction of the fire's convection column.) (*Glossary of Wildland Fire Terminology).*

On June 15, Greg, newly arrived for his summer visit, calls me into the kitchen to show me a plume out the window, a thin whisper of smoke rising behind and to the right of Red Mountain. It's innocuous, really—no wider than a contrail. We scan the internet looking for reports of this newer, closer fire, but upon finding nothing, we can only conclude the West Fork Fire is growing quickly, and growing straight toward us.

A few hours later InciWeb confirms the fire has more than tripled in size, growing to 1,700 acres by midnight. The growth was primarily northward in the Weminuche Wilderness, but the fire has also expanded east and west and has crossed the West Fork River near Beaver Creek. The Windy Pass Fire also made a significant run on the fifteenth as it raced through pockets of dead and down fuel and it has grown to 108 acres.

> For public and firefighter safety, the West Fork Trail has been closed. Please do not call 911 to report an outside smoke haze or an outside smell of burning wood, especially if it is occurring in the morning. If you see a smoke column (that is not up near Wolf Creek Pass) at any time please call 911 (*The Pagosa Springs Sun*, June 15, 2013).

Spanning the Continental Divide and accounting for huge portions of both the San Juan and the Rio Grande national forests is the Weminuche Wilderness, which, at two-thirds the size of Rhode Island, is the largest wilderness area in the state (780.9 square miles). Both the Colorado and Rio Grande rivers make it all the way from their headwaters in the Weminuche to the Pacific and Atlantic oceans, respectively. The average elevation inside the wilderness is 10,000 feet. It contains three peaks that rise over 14,000 feet (Eolus, Sunlight and Windom) and many others that rise above 13,000 feet. The Weminuche is among the most rugged country in the Continental United States and, as the spruce beetle has proven, some of the most fragile. I can walk easily into the Weminuche right from my back fence.

Wilderness is the highest form of protection of any U.S. wildland and there are currently 110 million acres with this designation. No roads, vehicles or permanent structures are allowed in a wilderness, nor mining, nor logging. As far as I am concerned this is all good news. But because the Weminuche is a designated wilderness, there are restrictions on how the forest service is allowed to fight any fire inside its borders.

On June 16 I'm scheduled to leave the ranch and drive to Aspen to teach for a week at the Aspen Summer Words writing conference. From there I'm scheduled to fly to Oregon for another week of teaching, and another week teaching in Big Sur after that. Greg will stay and tend the ranch. We talk about worst-case scenarios. He will keep the dogs with him at all times. As long as we are given notice before evacuation, we have friends with stock trailers who'll help us evacuate the equines. If there's no time to come back a second time with the trailer, Greg will turn the sheep loose and let them fend for themselves.

"I'm not leaving," Greg says. "I'll be the crazy guy on the news, here with the hose trained on the roof."

"Please leave," I beg, numbly throwing my teacher clothes into a suitcase, "if they say you have to. But if you stay, give the barn roof a squirt too."

The West Fork and Windy Pass fires are now being managed as a complex called the West Fork Complex. A National Incident Management Team (NIMO) has been ordered with a Type 2 configuration. The structure of the NIMO teams allow them a great deal of flexibility in terms of ramping firefighting resources up or down as needed. NIMO teams are also structured to allow for management of longer-term incidents and free up the Type 3 team to be available for new starts in southwest Colorado.

Forest Service campgrounds at West Fork and East Fork are both open as are the private campgrounds in the West Fork area (*The Pagosa Springs Sun*, June 16, 2013).

On June 16, as I drive over Independence Pass to Aspen, the West Fork Fire grows from 1,700 acres to more than 2,500. As I put more and more miles between myself and the ranch, the winds are pushing the fire straight toward it, up the Beaver Creek drainage and all the way to Elk Creek. As I am unpacking my clothes into sleek white drawers at the world-famous think tank known as the Aspen Institute, firefighters are seeing "extreme behavior" with embers traveling up to a mile ahead of the main fire. As I am eating stuffed mushroom caps and puffed pastries at the conference's opening soirée, helicopters continue to make drops to cool the south flank of the fire (which is not my flank of the fire), and firefighters are putting in more structural protection around cabins.

On the other side of Highway 160, the Windy Pass Fire grows to 129 acres in such steep terrain it can be fought by helicopter only, while ground crews put in structural protection at Wolf Creek Ski Area in case the fire decides to make a sudden run.

On the morning of June 17, as I walk through the heavily watered and landscaped grounds of the Aspen Institute on my way to class, the total acreage for the West Fork Complex has reached 3,280 and the transition to the NIMO team is under way. The total cost for the two fires so far is estimated at $411,000.

By the time I am done with class on Tuesday the eighteenth, the complex has grown to 4,070 acres, moving north toward the ranch and making some short runs, InciWeb reports, up to the 11,000-foot level.

The Divide behind my house will, I pray, provide some protection. It is higher than 12,000 feet in most places, and 12,000 feet is where the trees run out. There's a lot of tundra meadow up there that should slow the fire down, as well as a lot of rock. The fire should run out of both oxygen and fuel before it has a chance to cross over. But just to the east of Red Mountain, up at the top of Ivy Creek drainage above Goose Lake, there is a relatively low spot where the trees climb all the way to the top.

Greg reports the last two days have been less windy with more cloud cover and more moisture in the air, but if it dries out again and the prevailing winds kick up from the southwest, if sparks start traveling again, a mile or more ahead of the fire, what would keep a few of those sparks from sailing over the Divide and landing in the dead trees up Copper Creek Basin on our side? And if it does cross over, with a southwesterly wind behind it, there will be virtually nothing between the fire and the ranch but a few tens of thousands of trees, most of them beetle-kill spruce.

On Tuesday night in Aspen, after giving a reading in a state-of-the-art theater and being taken out for some of the most expensive sushi in America, I sit up all night refreshing my computer, waiting for InciWeb to update the perimeter of the fire after their nightly infrared photography flight. Even though my laptop is small and the topo lines are blurry and in some cases, I believe, inaccurate, I have memorized the map on the site with the red burn border that has been spreading like the albumen of an egg on a skillet.

When I ask myself why I am doing this, rather than sleeping in my sleek white bed with a quality mattress and high-thread-count sheets, the only answer is I want to know the moment the fire jumps the Divide. I want to catch it at its jumping. I want to know precisely when the flames become visible outside my kitchen window. I want to be awake when the fire starts altering my personal landscape forever.

Any reasonable, self-caring person scheduled to teach twenty-one full days in a row without a single day off would take themselves the hell to bed. To say nothing of the readings, and panels, and the endless infernal mandatory cocktail parties. But in every picture that exists of me as a child I have rings around my eyes so dark I look anemic. Staying awake all night never kept my father from hurting me, but I wanted to know in advance when it was going to happen. I couldn't bear it if it took me by surprise.

So tonight, I'll stay awake and be with my ranch, with my barn, and with Greg—virtually—to help them face the fire. I know I can't keep sparks off my barn roof all the way from Aspen, any more than I can raise a horse's body temperature by watching the plummeting numbers on Weather Underground, but that does nothing to assuage the fear that if I take my eyes off this computer, all freaking hell might break loose.

Extreme Fire Behavior: "Extreme" implies a level of fire behavior characteristics that ordinarily precludes methods of direct control action. One or more of the following is usually involved: high rate of spread, prolific crowning and/or spotting, presence of fire whirls, strong convection column. Predictability is difficult because such fires often exercise some degree of influence on their environment and behave erratically, sometimes dangerously (USDA Forest Service Fire Terminology).

Spotting: Behavior of a fire producing sparks or embers that are carried by the wind and which start new fires (spot fires) beyond the zone of direct ignition by the main fire. A cascade of spot fires can cause a blowup (Glossary of Wildland Fire Terminology).

Eleven years ago, on June 8, 2002, a forestry technician named Terry Barton started a fire in a campfire ring in the Pike National Forest between Colorado Springs and Denver, thereby starting the largest wildfire in Colorado's recorded history, burning 138,114 acres and 133 homes. One resident and five firefighters died as a result of the blaze. The fire cost $40 million to suppress and caused another $40 million in property loss.

When questioned, Barton claimed she started the fire, in spite of a total burn ban that was in effect, attempting to burn a letter from her estranged husband. One of her teenaged daughters eventually testified the letter was actually written by Barton herself. A psychology teacher had told Barton to write her feelings towards her ex-husband into a letter and burn it. Apparently, the teacher did not specify a locale.

Professional firefighters suggested Terry Barton might have set the fire on purpose, so she could fight a local fire instead of being called away from her family to fight fires in other states. Psychiatrists speculated Barton started the fire so she could heroically put it out and save the forest. But I like the daughter's version best, where she burns her own letter and then lies about it, because of the precise gut-punching combo of empathy and disgust it evokes in me. Who ever thinks they are going to start the largest fire in Colorado history? *Nobody.* But I have been encouraged to write and to burn such a letter. I have been compelled, in the face of calamity, to tell a tiny, face-saving lie.

On Wednesday morning, June 19 at 8:00 a.m., a red flag warning is issued for the area containing the West Fork Fire. Drier air has moved into the area, and warm and windy conditions are predicted for at least four days. Stage 1 fire restrictions are put into effect, though InciWeb assures us there is no immediate danger to Highway 160, Wolf Creek Ski Area, nor the towns of South Fork and Creede. Also today, NIMO will assume management of the fire. Curtis Heaton, the NIMO incident commander, thanks the Durango Interagency Zone Type 3 team for the great work they did. In other words: "Step aside, locals, the big guns from National are here!" The arrival of the NIMO team means more money, more firefighters, more helicopters, more engines, more technology and more and more professional updates.

By the time I finish teaching my class on the afternoon of the nineteenth, Greg has sent me the first pictures of what looks less like a fire and more like the detonation of a nuclear bomb over the Continental Divide between the ranch and the town of Creede, several miles east of where we saw that first wisp of smoke. To say the fire has grown today would be like calling Hurricane Katrina a really hard rain. The 6:30 p.m. update confirms the afternoon's red flag conditions have caused extreme fire behavior and the West Fork Fire has, in one day, tripled in size, growing from 3,879 acres to 12,001. It has moved deeper into the Weminuche Wilderness, running farther up the West Fork and Beaver Creek drainages where in many places it has run into rock. A smoke plume has risen to 30,000 feet above sea level and is visible from communities within a 75-mile radius. Flames are leaping more than 100 feet above the trees and communities 150 miles away are filling with smoke, including the city of Pueblo. As of six thirty, the fire has still not jumped the Continental Divide.

Meanwhile, on the south side of Highway 160, the Windy Pass Fire gains 500 acres, coming within a quarter mile of the buildings at Wolf Creek Ski Area. Firefighters are trying to hold the fire west of the Continental Divide there too. Highway 160 is still open, although smoke is limiting visibility. Total acreage for the West Fork Complex is now 12,710, though heavy smoke is making it difficult for aircraft to accurately assess the exact perimeter of the fire.

Large Fire: 1) For statistical purposes, a fire burning more than a specified area of land e.g., 300 acres. 2) A fire burning with a size and intensity such that its behavior is determined by interaction between its own convection column and weather conditions above the surface (USDA Forest Service Fire Terminology).

Convection Column: The rising column of gases, smoke, fly ash, particulates, and other debris produced by a fire. The column has a strong vertical component indicating that buoyant forces override the ambient surface of the wind (USDA Forest Service Fire Terminology).

At 8:00 a.m., on the morning of June 20, as I'm getting ready for my last class in Aspen, I find out the West Fork Fire has crossed the Continental Divide ("spotted across the Continental Divide" is the language on InciWeb), not right behind the ranch, but several miles east near the Big Meadows Campground. InciWeb reports that a crew from the Rio Grande National Forest team is on their way to the "spot fire." I understand these words have been chosen consciously, to make this new fire sound small, manageable, *occasional,* even. But I am two long weeks into this party by now, and I know better.

There are certain words I always miscapitalize in a first draft, and sometimes I don't catch them, even in revision. Elk, Paddleboard, Monsoon, Sushi. When my late editor Carol Houck Smith wrote in the margins of my otherwise clean manuscript, "Pam, why?" all I could think to tell her was I tended to capitalize things I really liked. In other words, Elk, Paddleboards, Monsoons and Sushi were the Gods of my Universe.

Big Meadows Campground sits on the border of the Weminuche Wilderness close to the Divide. I have taken the dogs for walks up that road during the spring runoff, photographed July's embarrassment of wildflowers, listened to the elk bugle in September. The thought of all those elk being burned alive nearly bends me in half.

I find a website that says animals are smart about forest fires, can get out ahead of trouble and do, that the elk mortality rate during the 1988 Yellowstone fires was only 1 percent of the 31,000 elk who live there. But, it continues, when the fire fronts are wide and fast moving, when the fire is crowning and there is a lot of smoke on the ground, elk can die of asphyxiation just as a human can, or a deer, or a mountain lion, or a bear.

At 8:30 a.m. that same morning of June 20, Sheriff Hosselkus issues pre-evacuation orders to residents and visitors on West Fork Road, as well as private landowners in the East Fork drainage area on the south side of Highway 160, many miles to the south of the ranch. The website is quick to add that a pre-evacuation order does not mean an evacuation is imminent; however, residents and visitors should be prepared to leave within an hour if an evacuation order is issued.

By 11:00 a.m., "just as a precaution," InciWeb insists, the Forest Service is closing Big Meadow and Tucker Ponds campgrounds as well as Forest Roads 410 and 430. It is hard to ignore the quaver in the voice, even on the screen, even in the bureaucratese. And sure enough, by 2:30 p.m. they post an update that the fire is now fully established in the Rio Grande National Forest on the east side—*our* side—of Wolf Creek Pass.

Extended Attack Incident: A wildland fire that has not been contained or controlled by initial attack forces and for which more firefighting resources are arriving, en route, or being ordered by the initial attack incident commander (USDA Forest Service Fire Terminology).

At this point, everything slows down to that filmstrip quality of trauma, and simultaenously starts moving very quickly. The Lake Humphreys and 4UR areas are evacuated, as well as the Metroz Lake area. Now all the place-names are on my side of the mountain. I know the people who have been evacuated. My ranch, like all of these properties, sits on the northern border of the Weminuche Wilderness. How long, I wonder, until we are added to the list.

Every structure along Highway 160 west of South Fork and every structure on 149 north of South Fork is on pre-evacuation, all the way to Wagon Wheel Gap: Park Creek, Wolf Creek Ranch, Fun Valley, Elk Creek, Masonic Park, Trout Creek and Riverbend. This time InciWeb insists residents should be prepared to leave at a moment's notice (*what happened to that hour?*). They should gather medications, important documents, pets, etc., and wait to be notified by a sheriff's deputy.

Effective immediately: Highway 160 will be closed to traffic in both directions at the chain-up areas on the east and west side. The highway will be open to fire traffic only (NFS InciWeb).

In the three hours it takes me to drive from Aspen to Denver so I can fly to my next job, at Pacific University near Portland, the fire makes a seven-mile run in a northeasterly direction. At 5:49 p.m. on June 20, Eric Norton, fire behavior analyst for the NIMO team, calls the fire behavior "so extreme, it is undocumented and unprecedented." It rips through Big Meadows and Metroz Lake, burning downhill to within a quarter mile of Highway 160. By the time I land in Portland the fire has more than doubled in size, from 12,710 acres to 29,000, but for the moment it's racing northeastward, away from the ranch and straight for the town of South Fork. There is now a mandatory evacuation in place from the top of Wolf Creek Pass to the city limits of South Fork, and shelters have opened in Del Norte High School for people, and the Sky High Complex in Monte Vista for RVs and large animals.

You are wondering, at this point, why I don't go home, and I guess the honest answer is I am the sort of person who always shows up where and when I am supposed to. Greg is also that sort of person and he talks me into staying. "In the first place," he says, "nobody who's spent their life in the Oregon rain is going to be able to picture what is happening here. In the second place, the fire made a big run, not at us but parallel to us. It would have to do a hard 180 to come at us now, and the Divide seems to be holding whatever fire there is to the south." South Fork is nineteen miles southeast of the town of Creede—about twenty-five miles, as the crow flies, east southeast from my ranch. Because of the prevailing westerlies, the fire is eating up much of the mountains between us. What burns and how fast depends on how hard and which way the wind blows.

Meanwhile, on the other side of the Divide, firefighters are combating the Windy Pass Fire with indirect containment as it continues to threaten to burn down Wolf Creek Ski Area. Wolf Creek is family owned, a homey resort with chairlifts instead of gondolas and tickets regular people can afford. It would be sad for everyone in the region to lose it. It also happens to get 400 inches of snow in a good year, the most of any ski area in the state. That is if we have a good year. That is if we ever have a good year again.

In Oregon, I don't get to campus until two thirty in the morning, so it seems like not such a bad idea to stay up hitting refresh all night. At 8:00 a.m. Mountain Daylight Time, InciWeb reports this will be the third red flag day in a row and that because of the abundance of volatile fuels, the fire is expected to make significant runs.

My first class starts at 10:00 a.m. MDT, and at 9:52 I get word the entire town of South Fork is under mandatory evacuation and all residents must be out by ten. Highway 149 has been closed between South Fork and Creede; 160 remains closed over Wolf Creek Pass, and there is no estimated time for reopening. Fire resources from across the state and all over the country are headed to and arriving in South Fork. For the first time this morning, our fire makes the national news, CBS reminding its national viewers by point of reference that the fictional Griswold family was camped in South Fork in 1983's *National Lampoon's Vacation* during the famous scene where a dog urinates on a picnic basket.

I go off to teach in a daze, hitting refresh on my phone under the desk while the students are writing. At noon, all Denver news channels report a high probability the entire town of South Fork will be lost. Its mayor, Ken Brooke, who took his family to safety and then came back to help the firefighters, is quoted as saying, "I just tell them it doesn't look good. I tell them the truth; that the fire is coming. I just tell them to keep themselves safe, evacuate as need be and don't come back." One Denver TV station claims the town *has* been lost already.

It is easy to tell, even from the government speak on InciWeb, this fire is blowing everybody's mind. Even the experts. Especially them. Forest fires, in the time of climate change, are forest fires on steroids, and beetle kill is demanding a whole new approach. The standing dead trees are so moistureless they are exploding into Roman candles, starting new fires in all directions, which are quickly engulfed by the big fire, which wants to eat everything in its path.

Candle: A standing tree with a broken top which often continues to burn after the main firefront has passed. Candles usually send up a fountain of sparks and burning embers which may travel some distance and be of concern if near the unburnt side of a control line (Glossary of Wildland Fire Terminology).

"Prevailing winds are easterly," Greg says on the phone, "at about 50 mph at the moment. Everyone's saying South Fork is history—it looks like the H-bomb is going off continuously over there—but now we are straight upwind." I finally get the nerve to tell Shelley, who runs the residency in Oregon, that if the wind changes direction, I'm going to have to go home.

I picture driving five hours home from the airport, getting to the place where South Fork was (I'm in the home stretch! I always think when I get there), and seeing it vanished, incinerated, burned off the map. Colorado fires have taken out subdivisions in recent years, but no actual towns. Creede burned to the ground a few times in its boom-town days, back in the 1890s, but that was because the miners built their shacks out of plywood and there was always somebody drunk enough to kick over a lantern.

At 3:05 p.m., Colorado time, InciWeb reports the leading edge of the fire is between two and three miles west of South Fork and still approaching, but air tankers have been able to fly for the first time in forty-eight hours and are dropping retardant on the fire, cooling it and slowing it down. Power has been turned off in town and all the surrounding areas. Thirty-six fire engines have arrived from all over the state and are standing ready to try to protect the town.

Late that night, when I make it back to my room after the readings, Greg calls and with a not quite imperceptibly shaky voice says he thinks he has seen another smoke plume, just before sunset. This one is immediately to the west of us, behind the mountain we call Baldy, where no smoke plume related to the West Fork Fire should be.

"I'm not positive," he says. "It could have been a dust devil or maybe some trucks up there kicking up a whirlwind."

My skin prickles and I get that same wash of cold through my veins I got whenever I could feel my father turning his rage in my direction. We are precisely down the prevailing winds from Baldy. If Greg is seeing what he thinks he is seeing, the ranch will soon be surrounded by fire on three sides.

"Honestly," he says, "this is the second day in a row I have seen it. But it is so small and inconsequential compared to the mushroom clouds to the east of us, I didn't want to scare you anymore."

No matter how I twist my logic, I can think of no scenario in which there would be trucks up on Baldy, two days in a row, kicking up a similar plume of dust. It is not, for one second, lost on me that our luck has apparently run out on June 21, the solstice, my favorite day of the year.

———

Back in my early days on the ranch, in the time of life when throwing a party sounded like a good idea, I'd throw one big one a year on the summer solstice. My friends would come from all corners of the country—Seattle, Portland, San Francisco, Chicago, New York—and even England. We would play music and sing, put my rafts in the Rio Grande and float down the river, play epic games of horseshoes and darts. Paul Stone, a local inventor, would come out and shoot his black-powder-fired bowling ball cannon into the national forest beyond my pasture, and the horses—so much younger then—would come dashing toward the barn at the sound of the explosion, manes and tails high, eyes wild.

Because I am a prose writer, I'm compelled to find meaning in the fact that the West Fork Fire has its biggest and most dangerous day so far on the only holiday in the whole year I ever feel like celebrating. In two weeks and after twenty years, I'll be taking my final ranch payment to Dona Blair. What message if it burns down the very same summer I make it mine? What message if the very same day? And even if the house and the barn are saved, what will I be left with? Charred mountains on all sides of me to look at until I die. And what if the elk are gone, the mule deer, the bears and the birds? No more giant stands of aspen quaking gold in the third week of September, no more fresh scent of living spruce forest on my daily cross-country ski.

Another lesson from my childhood: once the thing I fear most happens, there's no place to go but up. Being cut out of my father's Cadillac with a chain saw by highway patrollers on Christmas Eve, for instance, was so much better than sitting in the bar with him while he had his fourth martini knowing black ice was forming on the road outside. Being in the safety of the hospital while they applied my three-quarter body cast with all of the nurses making a big fuss over my four-year-old self was so much better than knowing my father was about to pick me up and throw me across the room.

Waiting is terrible, but soon, maybe *very* soon, the bad thing will have already happened, and I'll be able to start from whatever I have left. The forest has needed to burn for a long time, I say to myself, before turning off my computer for the first time in days, putting my head down, closing my eyes. If the worst happens, I will spend the rest of my life watching it recover, one stalk of fireweed, one tiny aspen shoot at a time.

By the morning of June 22 at 8:00 a.m. Colorado time, Greg's smoke plume has been given a name—the Papoose Fire—and added to the official literature on InciWeb. Started by lightning on June 19, it has grown in three days to 4,000 acres, bringing the total of the West Fork Complex to 66,200 acres. The Papoose Fire is threatening to close Highway 149 in the other direction, up and over Spring Creek Pass toward Lake City. Because this closure would effectively seal the valley off from the rest of the world entirely, InciWeb assures us that in the event of closure, police will escort people with medical emergencies over Spring Creek Pass.

Greg sounds the shakiest on the phone he has so far. The valley is filled with so much smoke he can't see the mountains. There is some kind of setup on Middle Creek Road, not far from the bottom of the driveway, which he thinks may be a roadblock. He hasn't received an evacuation call, but he's afraid if he leaves the house, they might not let him come back. It's a whole different thing, he says, when you can't see the fire that's coming at you. He is worried about, among other things, my elderly horses' lungs.

I call my friend Becky Barkman, who has horse property a hundred miles away in Gunnison, and ask if she'll come get my equines out of the valley. Owner of the Lucky Cat Dog Farm kennels as well as a handful of long, leggy Thoroughbreds, Becky is a force of nature. She spends her winters taking tourists on winding dog sled runs through the canyons and sometimes, over the holidays when she gets too busy, I get to drive an extra sled. It's my favorite way of all to move through space, clinging to the back of ten pounds of wood and a canvas bag stuffed with tourists wrapped so tightly in blankets they look like dolmades, twelve wagging, laughing dogs pulling the sled for all they are worth—20 mph on the downhills—as I steer it though the snow. Becky wears the same bright red one-piece snowsuit all winter—she's one of those flinty, lean horsewomen, and with her short shock of white hair, Top Gun sunglasses and full-on attitude, I think of her as the Annie Lennox of mushing.

To get to the ranch from Gunnison, Becky will have to talk her way through one or possibly two roadblocks, but if anybody can do it, she can. It's a five-hour round trip from Becky's house to my house in the best of conditions—six hours minimum with a livestock trailer, but by four thirty that afternoon, Becky texts me a photograph showing Roany, Deseo, Simon and Isaac standing knee deep in green grass in Becky's pasture, a blue, smokeless sky behind them.

Months from now, when this is all over, Becky will tell me when she came over the top of Spring Creek Pass and hit a wall of smoke blacker than anything she had ever seen, she thought about turning back. "It looked like the end of the world," she'll say, "but I knew in the same situation if it were you, you would drive straight into that wall and rescue my horses."

On the afternoon of the twenty-second, the winds shift from the west to the south, sending the Papoose Fire north, up toward the Rio Grande Reservoir and the Ute Creek and Squaw Creek trails, some of the best hiking in the state. If the infrared map weren't so frightening, it would almost be funny. My ranch is sitting in the center of a deep bowl made of burnt and burning trees. For two decades I have felt protected by my position, protected by these mountains. I have felt vulnerable only (I would admit if pressed) on the northeast—a small window that opens to the valley, to Middle Creek Road, and the state highway beyond. But even to the north, on the relatively "mountainless" side, the Rio Grande snakes past, a softer barrier than the mountains, and beyond the river, and the state highway, the cliff called Bristol Head.

Now my horseshoe of good luck is on fire. And still, it seems unaccountably lucky to have three fires raging with zero percent containment, all of them only a few miles from the ranch and none of them, at least for this moment, bearing down on the ranch itself. The leading edge of the Windy Pass Fire is safely to the south of us, still on the other side of the Divide; the leading edge of the West Fork is running hard away from us to the east, and the Papoose, which started precisely up the prevailing winds from the ranch, is all of a sudden moving on a longitudinal line, hell-bent for leather north.

I also know conditions can change in a heartbeat. Even a forty-five degree shift in wind direction could bring the fire back toward my pasture, my sheep and my beautiful barn. Every day since June 18 has carried a red flag warning, and every day forward predicts the same. The complex, InciWeb tells us, is now big enough to make its own weather. Convection columns are rising to 30,000 feet above sea level, then cooling when they finally hit cold air aloft. They collapse, sending all that hot air rushing back toward the ground, spreading embers outward and exploding the fire into even bigger and more ferocious flames, which send up new convection columns and so on. Even the scant amount of moisture produced inside the columns turns out to be bad news, because if that moisture condenses in the rapid rise, it can create pyrocumulus thunderclouds, which can produce lightning, which can start new fires. Tomorrow they're calling for 10 percent relative humidity and wind speeds of 50 mph on the ridge tops, which is where the worst of the flames always are.

Fire Whirl: Spinning vortex column of ascending hot air and gases rising from a fire and carrying aloft smoke, debris, and flame. Fire whirls form from the stretching of the vorticity due to upward

flowing air and can range in size from less than one foot to more than
500 feet in diameter and have the intensity of a small tornado (USDA
Forest Service Fire Terminology).

At bedtime InciWeb reports that in South Fork firefighters are still
holding the West Fork Fire two miles west of town, though it made a
run up Sheep Mountain to the east and is burning above Highway 160,
which is still closed. The northern flank of the West Fork Fire, the
closest flank to the ranch, has put up a significant column in the area of
Wagon Wheel Gap, very close to the house where Dona Blair and her
new husband, Dick Smith, spend their summers. I've been keeping my
eye on them on the InciWeb map, but today the site says heavy smoke
has prevented fire managers from determining the full extent of fire in
that area.

The next morning, the twenty-third, Greg calls to say the Papoose
Fire ran all the way north to the Rio Grande Reservoir on the back
side of Baldy, and then made a sudden U-turn. It's coming back south
on the front side of that same ridgeline, which, if it wraps all the way
around the back of Antelope Park, puts the ranch right in its path.
"This is the first time I can see actual flames from the house," Greg
says, "but most of the time the smoke is too bad to see anything."

InciWeb reports firefighters were up all night protecting twenty-
five residences just west of the Rio Grande River at the foot of Baldy.
I know those houses and the people who live in them. On a clear day,
I can see those houses from the ranch. A red flag warning has been
issued for the fifth day in a row with a Haines Index of 6. The Haines
Index measures the stability and dryness of the air over the fire in order
to predict "large plume driven fire growth." A score of 2 to 3 is very
low potential, 4 to 5 is moderate potential and 6 is the top of the chart.
Teaching commitment or not, it's time to go home and do what I can
for the remaining animals: the man, the dogs, the sheep, the chickens
and Mr. Kitty.

I teach my class at Pacific from nine to noon and make a reservation on a 3:30 p.m. plane. A conference volunteer is assigned to drive me in a nineteen-passenger van the forty-five minutes from campus to PDX. We plan to leave at twelve thirty, which should give us time to spare. As we head toward Portland, not on the highway but on sur-face roads, hitting light after light after light, I say to the driver, who is probably twenty but looks fourteen, "I've never gone this way before," and she says, "Oh, I'm *way* too scared to drive on the highway." I decide not to ask how she got the job driving the airport van.

Most of the roads we take are highwayesque, as in, they have two lanes in both directions, but no matter how slow the car in front of us is going, we do not engage the turn signal nor power the big van out into the fast lane and around it. We pass sign after sign telling us how to access the actual highway. We go straight through the middle of downtown Portland, a red light at every intersection for more than a hundred blocks.

We head out the other side of the city toward the airport on the slowest road so far, this one starting to back up with afternoon traffic. I fidget in the back of the van, eventually saying, "It's only an hour until my flight time, and I'm sure there is some kind of luggage cutoff. Any chance we could get on the highway for these last five miles?"

"Oh, we're almost there now," she says, vaguely, though my phone is telling me the airport is precisely 5.7 miles away, a distance that would take us six minutes if we would just *for the love of God* get on the highway designed for such a purpose. When the light rail stops alongside us, I consider leaping out of the van and making a run for it.

When she finally runs out of surface road and has no choice but to get on the highway, she takes the wrong ramp and the cloverleaf turns us back toward Portland. "You're going the wrong way," I say, my voice suddenly shaking with rage.

"No, I'm not," she says.

"Yes, you are," I say, starting to wonder if there is some reason I am not meant to get to Creede today.

"Oh, sorry," she says, and in that same slow motion she has done every other thing since we left the University, she flips on her turn signal and makes for the next exit.

"You have to go faster," I growl, close to tears. "There is a wildfire bearing down on my house and I have to make this flight." I know she has been told this is why I am leaving early. I jump out of the van before she has come to a complete stop at the curb, dragging my too big for carry-on suitcase with me.

"I'm sorry!" she yells, and it's clear she really is. I am instantly ashamed that I growled at her. I arrive at the counter exactly thirty-one minutes before flight time. The agent squints her eyes hard at her watch, then takes my bag.

The plane lands in Denver a little after seven, and I'm both eager and terrified to get back to my valley. I drive straight to Target and buy five room-sized air cleaners with replacement filters. Then I stock up on good fresh groceries. (By now you are sensing a theme with me and calamity.)

Even with four-wheel drive, there are only two ways into or out of Creede: Highway 149 south, from Lake City, or Highway 149 north, from South Fork. Because of the shape of the mountains, neither of them is what anyone would call direct. My normal route from DIA is 285 southwest out of Denver for four hours—until I hit Del Norte, wrap around the mountains to South Fork, and follow the Rio Grande back up the canyon. With 149 closed between South Fork and Creede, my only choice is to leave 285 in Poncha Springs, climb over Monarch Pass to Gunnison and from there take 149, which climbs Slumgullion Summit and Spring Creek Pass before dropping down to the Upper Rio Grande Valley and eventually Creede. The mountains are so twisted up in this part of Colorado the Continental Divide makes a turn as deep as a river's oxbow. My ranch, for example, is twenty-five miles east of the Divide at Spring Creek Pass, and yet longitudinally, it is west (by more than twenty-five miles) of the Western Slope town of Gunnison.

This is the route Becky used to get my horses yesterday. I call it the back door, because it is both the long way around and the foolproof route no matter the conditions. In twenty-five years of living here, the highway department has never closed Spring Creek Pass because of weather, even when every highway in southwestern Colorado is closed because of snow or ice or avalanche. It's as if the Colorado Department of Transportation has decided if you *know* about Spring Creek Pass you are probably a local, and if you are crazy enough to try it in a big storm, you've probably had some practice slalom skiing your car through a couple of feet of powder to get home.

I've heard mixed reports about 149 being closed just below Spring Creek Pass, but Becky wasn't stopped so I hope I won't be either. It's 1:00 a.m. by the time I get on top of Monarch Pass and from there I can see the orange glow to the south, lighting the mushroom clouds that are still rising, even at that hour. As the crow flies I'm seventy-five miles away from actual flames here, and the fire has the sky lit up like a carnival.

As I roll into the town of Gunnison a wave of exhaustion hits me, and I don't know how much luck I'll have talking my way through a roadblock at three in the morning. Maybe some part of me is just too afraid to see the burning mountains at that most vulnerable of hours. I pay for a room at the Best Western and go to sleep in my clothes until first light. I take a thirty-second shower and check the internet, which tells me as of last evening's infrared flight, the West Fork Complex has grown to 76,000 acres and is zero percent contained. We are now the number one priority incident in the country, which means we have nine new helicopters and another thousand firefighters on the way. The Papoose Fire has grown to 20,000 acres and is currently the most active fire on the complex. Firefighters spent yesterday trying to keep the Papoose from crossing Highway 149. If it does, and starts running along the top of Bristol Head, the town of Creede is ten miles downwind and directly in its path. Because of the volatility of the Papoose Fire, NIMO has ordered a spike camp set up nearby at Freemon's Ranch.

The West Fork Fire is now more than 50,000 acres and has been divided (by the Continental Divide, as everything is divided around here) into an East Zone (our side of the divide) and a West Zone (the Pagosa side). On the East Zone today, firefighters will "evaluate and provide structure protection" (that means place giant portable water bladders in close proximity to houses) in the area between South Fork and Creede, and "will remove fuels adjacent to structures to provide additional protection" (that means cut down the trees). Firefighters have managed to stall the fire two miles outside of South Fork, and they are looking for natural firebreaks they can "reinforce" (that means bulldoze) and use as a control line. Containment lines on the Windy Pass Fire put in place to protect the Wolf Creek Ski area are holding. *Incredibly* (InciWeb does not say but must be thinking), no structure loss has been documented at this time.

This will be the sixth red flag day in a row with a Haines Index of 6. Winds are predicted to reach 15 to 25 mph out of the southwest, gusting to 35, but gusts could reach 50 mph on the ridge tops. Relative humidity will be 11 percent.

I am out of the hotel room and moving toward home before sunrise.

When I hit Becky's black wall of end-of-the-world smoke, I slow down and try to comprehend what I'm seeing. My river valley, usually so blue and green at this time of year, looks like the aftermath of a war zone— the word "Beirut" jumps to mind, unbidden. Charred, smoldering, the sun a sickly orange ball in the sky. The entire mountainside, to the west of 149—miles of it—is nothing but blackened stumps and rubble. Firefighters line the edges of the giant meadow, where just last winter

I watched a herd of three hundred elk gallop through chest-deep snow. They are putting out spot fires that have spilled from the trees onto the grass, working to keep the fire west of the highway. Even the Rio Grande, that glistening, serpentine jewel, is muddied and dull with ash and charcoal runoff.

As I approach Freemon's Ranch, I see four cowboys moving a herd of horses across 149, in an attempt, I suppose, to get them to safer pastures. The horses are wild eyed, red rims flashing around brown pupils, their nostrils crusted with snot. I want to get home, but I stop to take pictures. What will it be like to live in this valley from now on?

In the first big meadow beyond Freemon's, I see Camp Papoose has been established, and it is filled with beautiful, dirty, exhausted women and men. I read this morning that by tonight there will be 895 firefighters in town, which is more people than live in this county. And here are a whole mess of them, our literal heroes, sitting in folding chairs outside of tents, eating cans of whatever with plastic forks, half-melted boots still on, suspenders loosened, charcoal-scarred arms coming out of filthy T-shirts, deep fatigue visible through the ash-exaggerated lines on their faces.

I thought the sight of the burnt forest would make me cry, but in fact it's the sight of these off-duty saviors that bring tears. I'll go home, I think, and make the biggest sign imaginable and hang it on the front gate. THANK YOU FIREFIGHTERS! WE ♥ YOU! There's nothing that undoes me like the possibility of rescue.

Everyone greets me enthusiastically when I get home, but the dogs know there's trouble and are looking to me, their alpha, to fix it. The first thing I do after petting them and hugging Greg is check on the sheep and chickens. All of the sheep have black and green goop in their eyes and crusted around their noses, but no one is coughing, and when I give them their hay it's clear there's nothing wrong with their appetite. Their water trough has a slightly ashen color to it, so I dump it and refill.

It looks to me like Sheryl Crow has been pecking Martina's head. I have been told chickens do this to each other when they're under stress or sometimes just out of meanness. I pick up Martina, pet her feathers and smooth what's left on her head. I tell her everything will be all right, but I don't think I have the wherewithal to convince anyone of that, even someone with a brain as small as a chicken's.

I'm out in the sheep pen a total of twenty minutes, and when I come inside my lungs ache worse than when I had pneumonia. I set up all the air cleaners—one in each room—then make buffalo burgers for lunch. Even with all the air cleaners running it's smokier than hell in here, but it's so much worse outside I decide the dogs can only go out for five-minute runs. I get to work making my THANK YOU FIRE-FIGHTERS sign.

Criteria Pollutants: Pollutants deemed most harmful to public health and welfare and that can be monitored effectively. They include carbon monoxide (CO), lead (Pb), nitrogen oxides (NOx), sulfur dioxide (SO2), ozone (O3), particulate matter (PM) of aerodynamic diameter less that or equal to 10 micrometers (PM10) and particulate matter of aerodynamic diameter less than or equal to 2.5 micrometers (PM2.5) (Glossary of Wildland Fire Terminology).

After lunch, InciWeb reports the Papoose Fire continues to threaten structures along Highway 149. On the northwest side the fire has slopped over Rio Grande Reservoir Road, and firefighters are working to improve Forest Road 521 so it can be used as a control line. Newly arriving firefighters have been assigned to the area in an effort to keep the fire from moving north.

Meanwhile, down in South Fork, a dozer line has been created between the edge of the fire and the town, and sprinklers have been put in adjacent to immediately threatened houses. An air quality monitor has been set up in Del Norte and we are invited to consult the Colorado state website to learn more about health issues associated with smoke. As of 6:00 p.m. this evening, no structures anywhere on the West Fork Complex have been damaged or destroyed.

Slop Over: A fire edge that crosses a control line or natural barrier intended to contain the fire (USDA Forest Service Fire Terminology).

On the morning of June 25, I walk down my long driveway to check out the roadblock. There are a couple of guys in T-shirts—suspenders holding up their bright yellow fire-resistant bottoms—sitting in folding chairs with their big booted feet splayed out in front of them. The guy with the radio chirping on his belt tells me everyone on Middle Creek Road has been evacuated, and everyone on the Spar City Road to the east of me as well.

"I didn't get a call," I tell him, and when he squints at me I realize he's a kid, maybe not even eighteen. "It's okay," he says, "the people at the Soward Ranch decided not to leave either."

"No really," I say, "I didn't get a call."

He looks down at his soot-blackened forearms and then turns his palms to me, which are startlingly white by comparison.

"I don't know what to tell you," he says. "But I reckon we can keep a pretty good eye on you from here."

Back at the house, Greg and I speculate about why we haven't been called. Does my pasture give us some magic amount of defensible space, or is it because the firefighters can see my house from this new checkpoint? Or is it simply an oversight? I imagine a fingernail running down the list of people to call and skipping over Houston, moving on to Huntzinger or Jackson or James. As long as the phone doesn't ring, we decide, we are not going to try to find out.

The thing about evacuation is they can't physically force anybody to leave their homes, but once you agree to leave, they *can* physically restrain you from coming back. The people in South Fork have been out of their houses for six days now, with the power turned off. I imagine fish tanks full of floaters, science projects in refrigerators. I imagine my own sheep, my chickens, surviving the fire and then dying four days later, of thirst.

For the first time in a week, we are not under a red flag warning, though the strong winds, InciWeb warns us, will continue (yesterday's were measured at 62 mph on the top of Wolf Creek Pass). As of this morning there are 1,313 personnel, 68 engines, 1 dozer, and 11 helicopters on the fire, which last night's infrared flight measured at 79,182 acres. The latest worry on the northern flank of the Papoose is that the fire will cross Squaw Creek and threaten the Rio Grande Dam.

Under the command of Phoenix National Incident Organization Commander Curtis Heaton and Rocky Mountain Incident Management Team Commander Pete Blume the East Zone of the West Fork Complex now includes the Papoose and the Eastern Part of the West Fork Fires. As of tonight, a night shift will be established for this fire (NFS InciWeb).

On the morning of the twenty-sixth, when I take a thermos of coffee and a blender full of peach banana smoothies to the firefighters at the bottom of my driveway, I learn that late yesterday afternoon, right about shift change, the Papoose Fire made a run down into Crooked Creek, and it required all firefighters from both shifts to protect the structures in that area. The night shift fought the fire hard all night, and when the wind finally stopped and the light finally dawned, there was still no structure loss on the West Fork Complex.

Also on June 26, the Colorado National Guard arrives in Creede to provide staffing for security and roadblocks. What kind of security, I wonder. Would anyone in this county, under these conditions, break into somebody's evacuated home? Most people around here don't even have a set of keys to lock their door. My ranch, in fact, did not come with any. Or has the National Guard arrived to keep people from breaking back into their *own* houses, to feed their fish, throw away their rancid cottage cheese, make sure they turned off the oven? Also, the Army Reserve Space Support Team (ARSST) arrives to see if they can help by providing satellite imagery data to fire managers.

By the morning of the twenty-seventh, there are 1,436 firefighters, 82 engines, 7 water tenders, 12 helicopters and 2 single-engine air tankers working on the fire, but it is still zero percent contained. There is a red flag warning today for dry thunderstorms developing in the afternoon. Little if any moisture is expected from these storms, but there will be gusty winds and dry lightning.

We didn't sleep at all last night for choking on smoke. I turn the air cleaners to their highest setting and start chopping vegetables for a hearty beef stew. Out the kitchen window, the little stand of aspen at the back of the property quakes in a light wind. If every tree burns except those, I think, I will be okay. *You have to be okay even if they burn too,* says the voice that is always in my head, and I know it's the only answer.

I'm just about to put the stew into the oven when I hear Greg say, "Pam, come look at this." There is something strange in his voice, so I put the pot back on the counter and go down the hall to the bedroom. Out the bedroom window the fire is running southward, straight for us, across the east-facing slope of Baldy. And it's moving fast, engulfing huge swathes of forest at a time. Winds, which are suddenly out of the northeast (those goddamn winds!), are pushing the fire into and back out of Trout Creek Canyon, which is straight across the valley floor from my bedroom. The average tree in Trout Creek Canyon is probably eighty feet tall, and the flames are leaping another hundred feet higher than that.

We watch silently as bunches of ten and twenty treetops explode, rocket into the air sending sparks in all directions, setting new trees on fire in a geometric arc, which in seconds becomes engulfed in this sizzling mountain of flame, this wall of moving chaos. When we open the window we can hear the explosions, the electric pop and hiss of the fire, not unlike the sound when lightning takes out a telephone pole, except continuous. It is beautiful, in its way, and terrifying, and as powerful a thing as I have seen in my life.

"I've been standing here thinking about Milton," Greg says, because what else does a poet think of in the presence of a paradise lost. "I guess he must have seen fires like this in his lifetime—maybe up north somewhere in Europe. Would they have still had big forests in England in his time?"

I've been watching the map so carefully, measuring with the width of my fingers the distance between the fire and the property line, the fire and the barn, the fire and my little stand of aspen. I've been measuring that shrinking mileage against the number of days until the monsoon comes, *should* come, praying (not that I was ever very good at praying) that in a week or even less it might start raining. Unless along with everything else, this fire finds a way to presuck the monsoon moisture right out of the sky.

On average, the Papoose fire has moved a mile every twenty-four hours, though there was one day when it ran several miles, up the backside of Baldy, and another when it moved almost not at all. I've managed each night to run the numbers in such a way as to convince myself there's at least half a chance the ranch will be saved by the monsoon. It's been the only way I can get any sleep.

As hard as I know it's been for Greg to be at the ranch in all the smoke and worry, it's also been hard to be away, relying on maps and charts and the crazy doublespeak of InciWeb, which often seems constructed only in tautologies ("Priority Number One: Facilitate cooperation with the cooperators") and jabberwocky ("Ensure the risk analysis process continues to be utilized to mitigate risk and provide for the flexibility to apply the right resource to the right task at the right time"). Now I'm home and this day is blowing all of those averages out of the water. The fire has run six miles since this morning, it isn't even two in the afternoon and the wind is only getting stronger. The very air between us and Baldy feels charred. Am I such a devoted environmentalist that I'll be willing to live in this big a scar in the name of sitting at the bedside of the ravaged earth, without it breaking my heart to pieces each morning when I open my eyes?

As we stand at the window contemplating seventeenth-century poetry and a two-hundred-foot wall of fire less than a mile and a half away, at least 35 of the (now) 109 engines that have answered our call from all over the West come barreling up Middle Creek Road without even hesitating at the checkpoint, lights blazing in the burnt orange and charcoaled light of that terrible afternoon. About ten minutes later, the folks who live at the Soward Ranch come tearing down the other way, having decided, apparently, to evacuate after all. There haven't been this many vehicles on Middle Creek Road all at one time in the twenty years I've lived here.

Greg and I run out into the yard and ash balls the size of lemons are hitting the house, landing in our hair. Here, the pop and the sizzle of the fire is louder, more like the noises a woodstove makes, but on a much grander scale. This unprecedented run must be sending up one of those nuclear-looking clouds like the West Fork did last week, but now we are too far inside the cloud to see it. The sky is the color of steel, the color of Armageddon. This, I think, might really be the end of the world.

Torching: The ignition and flare-up of a tree or small group of trees, usually from bottom to top (USDA Forest Service Fire Terminology).

Blow-up: A sudden increase in fire intensity or rate of spread strong enough to prevent direct control or to upset control plans. Blow-ups are often accompanied by violent convection and may have other characteristics of a firestorm. (See Flare-up) (USDA Forest Service Fire Terminology).

Firestorm: Violent convection caused by a large continuous area of intense fire. Often characterized by destructively violent surface indrafts, near and beyond the perimeter, and sometimes by tornado-like whirls (Glossary of Wildland Fire Terminology).

We all go around saying Mother Nature bats last—and I say, we can only *hope* so. Back at my bedroom window, watching acre after acre of trees explode into flame, I have to conclude she's seeing the ball pretty well with runners in scoring position. I picture her in the batter's box with the bat on her shoulder and a gleam in her eye, her hair all spiked out like Becky Barkman's. *Suppress this, motherfuckers!* says the thought bubble next to her mouth. Seeing her power up close like this makes me believe she may find a way to survive us still.

The leading edge of the fire is fully back out of Trout Creek now and starting to make its way around Antelope Park, the home stretch between it and my little stand of trees. "Okay," I say, and Greg looks a question at me. "If the forest is going to all of this trouble to save itself, then the least I can do is spend the rest of my life watching it come back to life." It feels good in my heart to have one thing settled.

At five, the phone rings and it's Dex, who volunteers for Search and Rescue, telling us we're on standby now and will likely get the call to evacuate within the hour.

I would have guessed packing for evacuation would be scattered and nervous and haphazard, but in fact it puts me, for two hours, into a state of razor-sharp eye-opening clarity. Before today, I would have said my three thousand books were my most valued possessions, but I quickly realize they actually fall into three clear categories: books I love by people I don't like, books I don't love by people I like okay, and books I adore by people I adore, which are the only ones worth saving. I get out to the car with one largish produce box and call it good. I have enough photo albums of my adventures from the predigital days to fill a medium sized U-Haul, and they won't all fit no matter what I do. So, yes to Bhutan and Bolivia, both of which changed my life, no to Patagonia, which was beautiful but bleak. Yes to Laos, where I watched the saffron-clad monks line up in the misty dawn with their begging bowls while the women of Luang Prabang fed them; no to Cambodia—where a man tried to sell me his teenaged son for ten dollars. Yes to my signed Todd Helton jersey, because there will never be another Todd, yes to the pelican woodcut print my grad students bought me, yes to the Christmas present Greg got me the first year we were together: a whole series of little boxes filled with tiny talismans. Yes to my lime green ultralight Marmot sleeping bag because they finally made one I don't sweat in, and it would be too sad to use it a total of once. Yes to a pretty silver and green rock I can't for the life of me remember the name of. Years of back taxes? Not so much. I face my closet and can't find one single stick of clothing I care whether or not I own. If I ever have to evacuate again, I believe I'll make more or less the same decisions, with a possible 25 percent reduction. Even as I'm filling boxes, I'm already planning—if what I'm leaving behind still exists when the fire is over—to make a dozen trips to Goodwill.

A little while later, carrying a box through the smoky air to the car, I stop for a minute to stare at my lovely lopsided barn, raised in 1920 by Bob Pinckley. I would burn every single object in these boxes myself to save it. But I would trade even the barn for the forest, maybe not the ravaged beetle-killed forest, but the all-green one, the one that was here twenty years ago when I moved in.

I set my box in the 4Runner and check on the sheep and chickens. When we evacuate, I'll turn the sheep out to pasture with a couple of bales of hay. It's hard to picture the fire running across what little stubble there's left out there, and they would have creek water, and some pockets of dried-up grass to eat if they keep us out of the house until next week. Mr. Kitty, the Mad Max of cats, will also stay behind. He's feral and won't let himself be picked up or carried. For the first several years he lived here, Mr. Kitty wouldn't touch his cat food, intimating he preferred his food fresh and still warm. If any living creature can survive an environmental disaster, it's him.

The chickens, on the other hand, won't last five minutes in this land of coyotes, bald eagles, mountain lion and lynx. The only thing to do is put them into our one cat carrier—together—take them with us wherever we go, and hope for the best.

And where will we go? I haven't gotten that far in my figuring. Becky says we are welcome in Gunnison—she has a bunch of little outbuildings. But she also has thirty sled dogs and ten horses, not counting my equines. It might be a bit ungrateful to show up with two 150-pound dogs and a couple of pissed-off birds.

There are shelters, of course, in Del Norte and Monte Vista, but I'm thinking more along the lines of a dog-friendly spa. It's hard to imagine a spa—or for that matter, a shelter—being chicken friendly. We can't go too far, because as soon as the evacuation lifts, I'll need to come home and check on the sheep.

It's three hours since Dex called, the 4Runner is one-third full, and Greg has loaded his guitar equipment and a couple of boxes of books into the back of his truck. Still no evacuation call. I walk back into the house and say to Greg, "That's all I'm taking. This has been enough time. I don't want to think about it anymore."

Meanwhile, to the east of us, the fire continues to be active near Metroz Lake and Elk Mountain, which would be plenty close enough to strike the fear of God in us, if we didn't have Dante's inferno going on immediately to the west. Firefighters are using a combination of hand line, dozer line, hose lays and aircraft drops as delaying tactics to slow the fire as it moves toward a more defensible position on the lower slopes. For the first time, near sunset, the smoke lifts enough for us to see the flames of both fires at the same time. The fear that the Papoose and the West Fork will join forces is palpable under every phrase and clause on InciWeb. At this moment there is very little between the two fires other than the Soward Ranch and us.

Convergence Zone: The area of increased flame height and fire intensity produced when two or more fire fronts burn together (Glossary of Wildland Fire Terminology).

At nine o'clock that evening, InciWeb reports extreme fire behavior moved the Papoose Fire almost five miles in less than two hours, spotting of one-quarter to one-half mile occurred and the fire is now well established in Trout Creek, which is where all those engines on Middle Creek Road were heading. Firefighters burned out brush around homes there, and night shifters are currently en route to help with structure protection. Portable retardant plants are being installed at several locations along the corridor where the Papoose and the West Fork are threatening to come together. This will allow aerial resources to respond more quickly to support the forces on the ground. All power has been shut off to residences in Trout Creek, and there is still no known structure loss. There are currently 1,561 people, 113 engines, 4 dozers, 10 water tenders, 16 helicopters and 2 single-engine air tankers working on the fire, which has grown to 83,004 acres. We are told to expect heavy smoke overnight and into the morning.

Bambi Bucket: A collapsible bucket slung below a helicopter. Used to dip water from a variety of sources for fire suppression (USDA Forest Service Fire Terminology).

Lining: Activity related to burn out along a fireline, using drip torches, fusees or other flammable material (Glossary of Wildland Fire Terminology).

Drip Torch: A hand-carried fire-starting device filled with flammable liquid that is poured across a flaming wick, dropping flaming liquid onto the fuels to be burned (Glossary of Wildland Fire Terminology).

Fusee: A colored flare designed as a railway warning device, widely used to ignite backfires and other prescribed fires (Glossary of Wildland Fire Terminology).

Many more hours and then the whole night passes and still we are not evacuated. In the morning it is impossible to breathe, but by afternoon, the smoke lifts a bit and we take the dogs for a walk in the cracked and dried-out pasture. The wind seems to have simmered down. The fire stops running so hard and goes about consuming what's left of the trees on Baldy, the mouth of Trout Creek and Copper Creek Canyon. It is still crawling steadily—if much more slowly—around the back of Antelope Park toward the ranch.

Today there's an article on InciWeb with photographs showing how, in many places inside the West Fork Fire boundary, living aspen stands have slowed or stopped the fire, because they are much more resistant than the beetle-kill spruce. I look out the window at the mountain, and the sickle of aspen between me and the leading edge of the fire, and think, This is the first good news I've heard in three weeks.

The multi-agency/multi-jurisdictional incident command team is working towards a possible opening of 160 over Wolf Creek Pass on Saturday June 29th. Please note: this opening is dependent upon three main events: the local fire evacuation orders must be lifted prior to the highway opening; the comprehensive traffic control plan details need to be finalized (for safe escort of motorists); and the fire behavior must remain moderate (NFS InciWeb).

For the first time, at six on the evening of June 28, the West Fork Fire is not reported at zero percent contained. It has consumed 90,806 acres and is 2 percent contained. At a town meeting that evening, which takes place in the gym of the old asbestos-ridden, mold-infested

K–12 school (the very next year, having survived the fires, Mineral County residents will vote almost 75–25 to raise taxes in order to build a newer, safer state-of-the-art energy-efficient school, which will open its doors to students in September 2015), Incident Commander Pete Blume keeps reiterating that we must not "get our hopes up" about containment and we must "give up our attachment" to containment numbers. They are no longer looking to contain, but to control the direction of the fire, and a fire this big, in these fuels, might well keep burning until the snow flies.

I can tell by the energy in the room that we, the people of Mineral County, feel almost insanely attached to our containment numbers. We haven't had any containment numbers to get attached to at all until today; we are inordinately attached to our measly 2 percent, and we don't feel like giving it back.

If nothing else, in the last month, I have learned to speak the language of the United States Forest Service. When Pete Blume tells us "authorities will continue to minimize suppression impacts to cultural, historical, and natural resources through consultation with resource advisors and provide point protection to defend structures and private land using designated protocol," I find I know exactly what he means.

During the past week, six members of the Honolulu Fire Department have been shadowing members of the Incident Management Teams here on the West Fork Fire Complex. They are particularly interested in the management of long-term incidents since the majority of incidents they deal with in Hawaii last only a day or two (NFS InciWeb).

Years ago, while mountaineering with bronchitis in the Bhutanese Himalayas, I scarred my lungs, so when the fire is still stalled out on June 29, Greg encourages me to get out of the smoke and go back to Oregon for the last day of residency to see my favorite student, Sherri

Hoffman, graduate. After that, we'll reevaluate and decide whether I should go on to Big Sur for five days of teaching at Esalen. If the fires join forces, or we get evacuated, I'll drop whatever I'm doing and come straight home.

Founded by hippies in 1962 to explore alternative methods of human consciousness, Esalen has no cell-phone reception and extremely limited internet service and likes it that way. I call to see if they can put a landline in my forest yurt under these circumstances, and they are happy to. All of my favorite possessions, such as they are, are still in the 4Runner, so I take them with me to the airport, and after considering parking them in the $22-a-day garage, leave them out in Long Term instead.

The FAA is installing a portable tower at the Durango Airport due to the volume of aircraft flying in the area in support of our fires. Also, the Rocky Mountain Type 1 NIMO has added a swing shift to their operations. Adding the third shift allows for an on-time transition between day and night forces and for adequate staffing during the times when the fires are most likely to be active.

Please do not call 911 unless it is an actual emergency. Smoke monitors are now in place in Pagosa Springs, Freemon's Ranch and Creede. These monitors are identified as #78, #69, and #65 and can be accessed through the map located at: **** (NFS InciWeb).

By the time I make it back to my Oregon dorm, InciWeb reports that CODOT intends to reopen Highway 160 over Wolf Creek Pass tomorrow morning at 6:00 a.m. Highway 149 remains closed between Creede and South Fork, but traffic is now being escorted in and out several times a day. This morning, most residents of South Fork are allowed to return home. Anyone west of Highway 149 and/or the Rio

Grande River (whichever is closest) remains under mandatory evacuation. In Oregon, in the relatively clean dormitory air, I put my head on the pillow and sleep like a stone.

On the morning of the thirtieth, as I'm pulling out of the rent-a-car facility at SFO, Greg calls to say Sheryl Crow has attacked Martina and injured her badly, that he has wrapped her in a towel and put her in the garage, but he doesn't expect her to make it. By the time I hit the Monterey Peninsula, Martina becomes the first official casualty of the fire. I loved Martina, inasmuch as a person can love a chicken, loved especially the way she came running out of the chicken house to greet me whenever she heard my voice, and I'd like to cry for her but the truth is I'm too numb with fear and worry. There will be the question of what to do with Sheryl Crow (who Greg is calling Sheryl Crow née Manson) because nobody keeps just one chicken, but there are so many more pressing questions, I just can't deal with that one.

By the time I get to Esalen, and walk up to the secret internet hot spot behind the physical plant, I find, for the first time, the words "Red Mountain" on InciWeb. Red Mountain is the mountain out my kitchen window. It is the mountain that frames my barn. Two new fires started yesterday by spotting near Red Mountain, but they are being controlled, I am assured, with helicopter drops of water and retardant. Red Mountain and the entire Papoose Fire are experiencing wind gusts of more than 50 mph, and so far this afternoon, Papoose crews have successfully contained four spot fires that started as a result of rolling debris and embers that blew across the fire line. There have been several blow-ups inside the Trout Creek drainage and fire behavior will continue to be extreme. As I feared, the fire has burned all the way around the back of Antelope Park, but it is staying up high in the spruce forest. At least for now, it does not seem to want to burn downhill into the groves of aspen, like the one that marks the back of the ranch.

InciWeb promises the night shift will be on patrol to extinguish any hot areas near Red Mountain. Structure protection is in place at Spar City (three miles southeast of the ranch) and Red Mountain Ranch (three miles due south of the ranch), as well as at Bristol Head Acres (three miles northeast of the ranch) and the Soward Ranch (less than a mile west.) The fire has now consumed 92,176 acres and is 4 percent contained.

After reading every word on InciWeb four or five times, I am given to understand that every single property on both Middle Creek Road and Spar City Road now has structural protection in place *except my ranch*. Is this good news, or bad? Has my address been deleted from some all-important database? I understand about chains of command, but it still seems like one of those guys a hundred yards from the bottom of my driveway would have, in all this time, glanced over at our house and said, "Hey maybe those guys need structural protection too."

"I've got the hoses all hooked up and I'm ready to spray the roof if I need to," Greg says on my contraband landline that evening, "and we have the creek right here which I figure is just as good as one of those temporary tanks. We got a few thunderclouds this afternoon. I don't think any rain fell out of them, but I'm hoping it's a sign of things to come." Nothing about this summer has been like any other summer, and yet this could be the monsoon, working itself up as it always does, just in time for the ten thousand tourists who arrive on the Fourth of July.

During the Missionary Ridge Fire, I spent the last week of June and the first several days of July watching the big dark clouds form over Red Mountain, standing on the dog porch and willing them toward the ranch with my mind, my heart, every part of me. "Please," I implored the sky, "please."

Several wells in the area ran dry that summer. I stopped washing clothes, barely washed dishes, and took thirty-second showers no more than twice a week. Whether or not I helped with my conservation methods, I don't know, but my well never even sputtered. Once the monsoon kicked in I put a five-gallon bucket under my roof gutter's drainpipe, and if the roof collected enough to overflow that bucket, then it counted as a real rain. I would mark it on my calendar as such and carry the water to my thirsty pines. I picture Greg watching those same clouds now, willing them to open and drop their rain on Red Mountain, and the ranch, and all of the forest, spruce and aspen, in between.

The Red Cross Shelter in Del Norte will close Monday, July 1. The Salvation Army will provide a continental breakfast from 8–9 tomorrow for the last of the Red Cross clients.

Please use caution when travelling along Highways 149 and 160. Heavy fire traffic can be expected along the highways and within the communities of South Fork, Creede, and Del Norte. Please do not stop along roads to take pictures of the fire or firefighters as doing so could impede fire operations (NFS InciWeb).

On July 1, everyone wakes up to the news that nineteen firefighters have been killed in the Yarnell Hill Fire in Arizona. The Granite Mountain Hotshots are one of the most storied and highly trained groups of firefighting professionals in the world, and yet a fast-growing fire started by lightning overran nineteen of its members. When they realized the fire was upon them, the firefighters deployed their safety shelters, but the shelters were not protective enough to withstand the intense heat of the blaze. The Yarnell Hill Fire has the highest death toll of any U.S. wildfire since the 1991 East Bay Hills fire killed twenty-five people. It is the sixth deadliest American wildfire and the deadliest wildfire ever in the state of Arizona. Starting today, the Colorado Rockies baseball team will wear 19 on all of their jerseys to honor the fallen firefighters.

In light of the sad news associated with the loss of 19 members of our firefighting family from Granite Mountain

Hot Shots on the Yarnell Hill Fire in Arizona, the morning update was delayed by a two-hour stand down issued by Incident Commander Pete Blume along with a moment of silence. The stand down was a safety precaution provided to firefighters to debrief the situation and honor those firefighters lost on the Yarnell Hill Fire. Incident personnel were given several options to meet their emotional needs. A Critical Incident Stress Management Team is available to those needing additional assistance. It is with a heavy heart that we continue our operations today on the West Fork Complex.

The emergency response community mourns the loss of the 19 firefighters that perished in the Yarnell Hill Fire in Arizona. The Rocky Mountain Type 1 Incident Management Team and firefighters working the West Fork Complex extend their deepest condolences to those affected by the tragic events of the Yarnell Hill Fire. We are keeping the firefighters who died, those that continue to work on incidents, and the families of all the firefighters in our thoughts.

Out of respect for our colleagues, the West Fork Complex will not issue any further statements on the Yarnell Hill Fire. The morning briefing occurred at 9:00 am and operations will continue as planned. We believe the best tribute we can give at this time is to continue to focus our efforts on maintaining public and firefighter safety in honor of those who have fallen. We thank you for your understanding in regards to the delay this morning.

With the 4th of July weekend ahead, motorists can expect to see firefighting traffic along Highways 160 and 149. Please watch your speed (NFS InciWeb).

Fire Shelter: An aluminized tent offering protection by means of reflecting radiant heat and providing a volume of breathable air in a fire entrapment situation. Fire shelters should only be used in life-threatening situations, as a last resort (USDA Forest Service Fire Terminology).

Aramid: The generic name for a high-strength, flame-resistant synthetic fabric used in the shirts and jeans of firefighters. *Nomex*, a brand name for aramid fabric, is the term commonly used by firefighters (USDA Forest Service Fire Terminology).

Into the Black: Moving from outside the fire front to inside the burned area, which is sometimes the safest place to be in a flare-up (Glossary of Wildland Fire Terminology).

Later today, as I give a lecture in a large white circus tent on the edge of the Pacific, rain falls for the first time in two months, not on or near the ranch, but on the eastern part of the West Fork Fire, slowing it considerably. According to the infrared photos, some areas of that fire have not moved significantly in more than six days. The Papoose only received a tiny amount of rain, and that only on its northern extremity, almost twenty miles from the ranch. There are thunderstorms in the forecast for the rest of the week, but the percentages decrease as the temperatures rise. By the end of the week there's only a 10 percent chance any moisture will actually hit the ground. Firefighters on the Papoose will take advantage of the moisture that fell to secure the northwest area of the fire, using a combination of dozer lines, hand lines and water drops to construct secure lines around structures. As of 8:00 p.m. there have been no known structures lost on the West Fork Complex.

By July 2, the tone on InciWeb changes from the cautious optimism of the last few days to something you would almost call a swagger:

With the West Zone of the West Fork being essentially secure, aviation resources will be repositioned to other areas of the fire and will be available to support ground resources when requested. In areas where structure protection has been completed, firefighters will test pumps and sprinkler systems to ensure they are still operational. During structure protection, limbs, branches, and other vegetation was removed from around homes, propane tanks and other structures. Firefighters will begin to chip this material so that it is not creating a fire hazard. The strategies for operations on the fire include continuing protection for structures and high value resources, as well as confining the fire to areas where it will not pose an issue for the local area during the remainder of the summer (NFS InciWeb).

I wonder if the Forest Service considers my barn a "high value resource." I wonder if you are in possession of a *low* value resource, how you would ever know. Just today, for the first time, I can feel my humor returning. I am starting to believe, against my worst-case-scenario-prone nature, that the ranch is not going to burn down after all.

Evacuations in several areas of Mineral County are being lifted. Residents are warned "to remain vigilant and be prepared to evacuate at a moment's notice in the event that fire activity changes." I find it odd that InciWeb fails to comprehend that most of us will be prepared to evacuate at a moment's notice for many years, if not the rest of our lives.

Finally, at two o'clock in the afternoon on July 3, while I'm walking past the physical plant at Esalen, a rogue strand of internet buzzes in and on Weather Underground I see a green blob over the ranch that indicates rain.

"Lightly at first," Greg says, "and then hard enough to run in rivulets off the roof, and then for about six minutes right before it quit it was *a real frog strangler.*" I can hear in his voice he has been both laughing and crying.

"It isn't enough to put out a hundred-thousand-acre fire," he says, "but it's enough to clean the air and enough to go out and smell and taste and dance around in, enough to make me believe Mother Nature might not hate us so much after all."

The Joint Information Center closed as of last evening due to call volume slowing down. For fire information, please contact the appropriate zone office. Isolated thunderstorms are forecasted with winds from the northwest. Increased moisture will slightly improve chances for wetting rains. True monsoonal moisture still appears most likely to arrive at the end of this week, which is near average timing for southern Colorado (NFS InciWeb).

Six minutes of frog strangling notwithstanding, on July 3, the fire grows beyond the 100,000-acre mark to 106,637, with nearly all the new growth coming on the Papoose, burning heavily in beetle kill and old logging slash. Sustained winds of 20 to 25 mph push the fire farther into Trout and Copper creeks, just west of Red Mountain

The last time I was in Copper Creek Canyon, I was shocked at the density and sheer volume of the standing dead spruce. Even that day my thought was, *this forest needs to burn*, and today, standing here next to the physical plant at Esalen, looking across a sea of bright red opium poppies and giant moss-covered oaks to the giant kelp beds rising and falling with the Pacific, I feel, all the way to my core, that what in the smallest frame has been a summer of total devastation in my corner of the Rockies, has in a larger frame been Mother Nature bravely and tenaciously trying to save herself.

In anticipation of the Fourth of July, fire restrictions for the Rio Grande National Forest have increased to Stage 2. Fourth of July festivities in Pagosa Springs are bringing up to 10,000–12,000 visitors over the weekend. Please be cautious of fire traffic and come visit us at the town park booth. Tonight will be the last night shift for this fire. Starting tomorrow we will publish the daily update once a day at 9AM, with tweet and blog entries throughout the day (NFS InciWeb).

I arrive home on the morning of the Fourth of July. Neither the West Fork Fire nor the Windy Pass Fire is growing at any significant rate, but damned if our Papoose Fire isn't still running. Today it burns up the rest of the trees in Copper Creek and pops out the other side, and now it's eating up the trees we can see at the base of Copper Ridge, the very place I hike every summer on my way up to Red Mountain. InciWeb reports that high afternoon winds will heighten the potential for spreading and spotting. I stand in my kitchen watching the flames outside my window. The fire is as close, at this moment, as it has ever been to the ranch, to my pasture, to my barn, to my little stand of aspen: well under a mile.

We are no longer the number one priority in the country and firefighters are leaving the area at the rate of fifty per day, along with several fixed-wing planes and helicopters as they are reassigned to other fires. I try to make my brain experience this as good news.

On the night of the Fourth, the smoke clears and the stars come out. Scorpio, Cygnus, the Summer Triangle, Cassiopeia, Cepheus, the whole Milky Way. It's better than fireworks, which have been cancelled, thank God, all over the state. I go to sleep with all the windows open and wake at first light choking; Bristol Head has disappeared behind a layer of heavy smoke. But the chance of precipitation this morning had been raised from 20 to 40 percent. These are the kinds of numbers I have begun living for.

A report of a small pump house that burned just east of the Rio Grande Reservoir has been confirmed. There had been rumors of a bunk house burning, but after further investigation, it was determined it was a pump house which burned during earlier fire activity. The Hinsdale County Sheriff has made landowner notification. This is the only known structure that has burned in the fire to date (NFS InciWeb).

Life begins to return to normal, though I continue to check InciWeb daily. Most mornings we are smoked in terribly, but by early afternoon, the wind picks up, the valley floor clears and it's even possible to take a pasture walk. The fire has consumed 110,028 acres, which equals almost 172 square miles. Personnel has been reduced to 1,169 and we are down to 56 engines and 17 water tenders, and for some reason back up from 10 helicopters to 12. Containment is listed at 20 percent.

On July 6, the number of buildings threatened by the West Fork Fire is reduced from 441 to 261. This is a statistic we have not had before, and I wonder whether either of those numbers includes mine. Moisture is predicted to increase steadily each day as far as the forecast reaches. The monsoon has come to save us, like a clock, right on time.

Incident Commander Beth Lund of the Type 1 Eastern Great Basin Incident Management Team assumed command of the West Fork Fire East Zone from Rocky Mountain Incident Management Team (Type 1) from Commander Pete Blume at 6:00 am this morning (NFS InciWeb).

The new incident commander (the first woman's name InciWeb has mentioned since this whole thing began) has been put in charge of—I try not to react—"mop up." She calls a town meeting and reminds us containment is not and never has been the goal of this firefighting effort; management is. Their number one priority, she says, has been to protect structures, and they have lost only one outbuilding. "So far," she adds—though whether this is a joke or an afterthought, I find impossible to tell by her tone. She repeats Pete Blume's warning that the fire most likely won't go all the way out until the snow flies.

Firefighters are transferring by the hundreds now to blazes in Oregon and California, our monsoon seems to be building steam, and the faces of my neighbors have softened since the last town meeting. Commander Beth Lund's whole team is considerably more relaxed than Pete Blume's. And yet, each night, the infrared photography still shows the hottest part of the fire being the swathe of forest right up behind the ranch, below Copper Ridge as it wraps around to Red Mountain.

When I ask Beth Lund what will keep that finger of fire from backing down the hill toward the ranch when the winds clock around to the south, she knows exactly who I am and where I live. "Your little aspen grove at the back of your property will save you," she says. "Aspen trunks are all full of water. I'd rather have a 100-acre stand of aspen between me and a fire than a line of the best hot shots in the business."

It's all I can do not to hug her. It's all I can do not to burst into tears.

Duff: Layer of decaying forest litter consisting of organics such as needles, leaves, plant and tree materials covering the mineral soil. Duff can smolder for days after a fire. Extinguishing smoldering duff is key to successful mop-up operations (Glossary of Wildland Fire Terminology).

Pulaski: A combination chopping and trenching tool, which combines a single-bitted axe-blade with a narrow adze-like trenching blade fitted to a straight handle. Useful for grubbing or trenching in duff and matted roots (USDA Forest Service Fire Terminology).

If this fire ever goes out, if this summer ever ends, I will never be afraid for the ranch in the same way again. I have seen a wall of fire two hundred feet high stopped dead in its tracks when it hit the big meadow at the base of Baldy. I have witnessed the expertise and tenacity of firefighters when they are determined to keep a fire from crossing a road, or a dozer track, or a river. I have seen a veritable army of men, women and machines descend upon our valley, and save every single structure within a 110,000-acre fire, except for one tiny pump house that probably hasn't been used since the silver-mining days. I understand now the ranch *does* have defensible space, and a lot of it. For my lifetime at least, the ranch will have a natural fire line—that horseshoe of burnt forest will turn back into a horseshoe of protection, with my little aspen grove providing backup, if a fire ignites in the unburnt trees and somehow pops through.

There will be many more fires in Colorado in my lifetime. And floods and droughts and every other outcome of climate change, every consequence of how carelessly we have treated—how carelessly we continue to treat—this planet that is our home. But I have a different relationship to fire now, which is at least equal parts fear and knowledge. Scary as it was, there wasn't a single day of the West Fork Fire that wasn't deeply interesting. And because I have studied the fire as if I were about to take a preliminary examination in it, I will never be afraid in the same way again.

Safety Hazard Alert: The Eastern part of the West Fork
fire received nearly three quarters of an inch of rain yesterday

afternoon. Ash and mudflows will be a concern but plans are being developed for mitigation.

On the Papoose Fire, a hand line has been constructed south of Red Mountain Ranch to prevent the potential for the fire to spread north back towards Highway 149.

Containment is up to 25% (NFS InciWeb).

By July 7, people start moving around the valley again in earnest, and I load up the dogs and drive to Dona Blair's house. It no longer seems ironic to me that I will give Dona my final mortgage check with the fire still burning a half a mile from my kitchen, with Dick and Dona's trees still marked with the orange blaze flagging of imminent doom. Now it's impossible to imagine the story otherwise.

"I might have been tempted," I say, "if I were you, to go out in the dark and pull a few of those markers off your trees."

Dick is ninety-five and sharp as anyone you'll ever meet. He's been to war, a couple of times, and still owns and flies two airplanes—one he built himself from a kit. Now he gives me a look—not an unkind one—that says, "Darlin', if you'd seen half the things I've seen, you wouldn't worry too much about a goddamn tree." He cared about those trees enough to compromise the shape of his home to save every last one of them, but had he lost them, he'd have found a way to adjust.

"I try to nap every day," he says. "I believe it will keep me alive a little longer." He winks, which I know is my cue to leave. "Just a little," he adds, as he shuffles off down the hallway.

I write Dona a check for the final ranch payment. When I pull out of the driveway, the place I've lived for twenty years will be mine.

"I have to tell you," Dona says. "This has been one of the most satisfying business transactions of my entire life."

Tears spring to my eyes. "You didn't think I was going to pull it off," I say, grinning back the emotion.

"You're wrong about that," Dona says, "but that doesn't mean I'm not proud of you."

———

On July 8, sadly and confusingly, containment is reduced from 25 to 19 percent. InciWeb talks less about fire now and more about the increased risk of flash flooding and debris flow with the onset of monsoonal rains. We are urged to stay aware of our surroundings during "rain events" and not to drive or walk through areas that are flooded. We are also warned there are spruce and aspen snags all across the fire, trees with weakened or burned stumps that can fall at any time. InciWeb offers a rare scenic moment, reporting that at this morning's daily briefing Safety Officer Paul Gauchy cautioned his remaining firefighters that "those snags are weaker today than they were yesterday, and a lot weaker than they were last week."

Correction—Earlier update listed Crooked Creek Subdivision as still under mandatory evacuation. It is not. It is the Wilderness Ranch Subdivision which remains evacuated (NFS InciWeb).

I pause over the words "Wilderness Ranch Subdivision." What in the fuck, I wonder, what in the fuck is wrong with us anyway.

On July 9, the active part of the Papoose Fire moves back up into terrain so steep and inaccessible, so full of burnt beetle-killed timber, they pull the line crews back from direct attack and begin using only water drops from helicopters. To everyone's dismay, our old friend Mr. Red Flag Warning is back, due to suddenly dry air, dry fuels and maximum relative humidity from 1 to 8 percent. Nobody pays that much attention. We are all pretty much over it. Now we just want the smoke to go away.

Somehow, the size of the fire has shrunk to 109,100 acres (more accurate infrared flights, I imagine) and the personnel is down to 708.

Cold Trailing: A method of controlling a partly dead fire edge by carefully inspecting and feeling with the hand for heat to detect any fire, and lining any live edge (Glossary of Wildland Fire Terminology).

I have never been able to resist the names of things. In fact, one of the reasons I got myself so involved with horses, and backpacking, and river running is that each pursuit came with a whole new vocabulary, a new set of words to roll over my tongue. In the last six weeks I've learned much about the ranch, and myself, and the properties of fire. I have also learned the language of firefighting, and in learning that language, I've learned yet another way to love the land.

On July 11, InciWeb reports that at 8:00 p.m. Beth Lund and the Great Basin Incident Management Team will assume command of the entire West Fork Complex as the Central Coast Team completes their assigned time over on the western side. On the Papoose Fire, scattered interior heat is being monitored, but, Beth assures us, the lines look good overall. On the East Zone of the West Fork, only minimal areas of heat remain. After three consecutive days of red flag warnings, relative humidity is back on the rise.

All evacuations have been lifted. Firefighters will continue to monitor, patrol, and start to haul back excess equipment and trash from the fire line. If any member of the public comes across some of this fire equipment that may have been missed or overlooked, please call 719 569-**** and notify us of the item and its location so it can be recovered. The equipment will be returned for rehabilitation and ready for use on the next incident.
Containment is at 25% (NFS InciWeb).

On July 12, we see another smoke plume back up valley above the 4UR Ranch. We have become expert spotters. That evening on Inci-Web, Beth Lund assures us the spot fire was located and contained by crews within a few hours. Significant rain is in the forecast every day for the next seven. The air is the clearest it's been in weeks and we take the dogs for a hike up into Shallow Creek, on the unburnt side of Highway 149.

Even in a year as dry as this one, Shallow Creek, with its reliable, rushing water, its giant beaver ponds and its steep canyon walls that provide shade most of the day, is an oasis. The dogs run and splash all the way up the creek, and in the meadow, just before the trail really starts climbing, the columbine are blooming like always.

On the evening of July 13, the InciWeb status summary reports 66 percent containment on the West Fork Complex. It confirms no threat from the fire remains to any structures. It adds that threats *do* remain from falling trees and from the possibility of sliding mud and ash. On July 14 we receive the last daily InciWeb report on the fire. The total burn area is 109,615 acres, and at least in the official literature, 66 percent containment is all we are ever going to get.

> Today will be the final day the fire information team will be posting updates at area businesses. At 6:00 pm today the Great Basin Incident Management Team 1 will hand off responsibility to manage the Papoose and West Fork Fires to Phil Daniel's Colorado Type 3 Incident Management Team. Beth Lund's Great Basin Incident Management Team 1 would like to thank all the communities for their kind support of our firefighters and the local businesses and agencies for assisting us in sharing the changing status of this incident with the visitors and residents of this beautiful area.

An interagency Burn Area Emergency Response (BAER) team will be arriving tomorrow to begin their initial assessments. The goal of a BAER team is to assess the after effects of a fire(s) and develop strategy for emergency stabilization and rehabilitation. Everything from erosion protection to what needs to be done to make trails, roads and campgrounds safe for people to reenter damaged sections of the forest (NFS InciWeb).

The horses and donkeys stay in Gunnison until late July, when the monsoon rains have been at it long enough to turn the pasture from its desiccated brown to something that resembles hope. The monsoon brings several inches of rain, enough to put the fire out everywhere but perhaps the deepest pockets of beetle-killed forest. Greg returns to California, and I start turning the sheep out again to nibble the little green shoots that are coming up along the creek corridor. I put Sheryl Crow née Manson into a box and give her to a gentleman who wants to eat her for dinner.

In August, my friend Kae comes up from Denver and we decide to walk into the burn area for the first time. We drive up Middle Creek Road to the trailhead above the Soward Ranch, the access point for Copper Ridge. For the first several hundred yards we are in an aspen and spruce mixture and the forest looks normal, but then Kae points to a burn scar, maybe ten feet in diameter.

"Spot fire," I say, and once we have seen one, we see a whole lot more.

We can smell the burn line before we can see it, though I don't know if what we are smelling is burnt trunks or scorched ground or the chemical residue of the retardant they dropped from the bambi buckets. All of the trunks of the aspens near the edge of the burn seem to have been splashed with an orange liquid. This is not the smell of the aftermath of a campfire—there's something much more toxic in it than that.

Fugitive Color: A coloring agent used in fire retardants that is designed to fade rapidly following retardant application in order to minimize visual impacts (Glossary of Wildland Fire Terminology).

Then we are walking through partially burnt aspens, some with a few leaves quaking above a half-scorched trunk. I can see here, just as Beth Lund described, how the aspens turned the fire back into the spruce. In the spruce forest every single tree is wasted. Most of the dead trees are still standing, though some have been reduced to charred stumps and others have been burned from the inside out or melted into shapes like hoodoos, like sculpture, like African masks. The ground is covered with ash and char; in many places the dirt has melted and cauterized.

Alligatoring: Char patterns formed on the paint or burned wood remains, usually in the shape of blisters (Glossary of Wildland Fire Terminology).

Angle of Char Indicators: Standing fuels that are burned at an angle that indicates the direction of the fire spread (Glossary of Wildland Fire Terminology).

Kae and I haven't spoken since we entered the burn and finally she says, "I keep thinking of the word 'church.'" There's no doubt about it, there is something holy in the burn. Something purified. Something cleansed.

It's severe in here, but not lifeless. Woodpeckers and flickers flit from tree to tree and clear water trickles down through charred stumps and standing pillars of charcoal. It's only been a few weeks and the fireweed is up already, short plants with tiny leaves and lots of purple blossoms. A few baby aspen shoots have started. We climb through the forest, awed, our boots turning black, our legs turning black, eventually our arms and faces. We put our hands on the cauterized tree stumps, spend too little time worrying about snags that might fall on us. There is something here that induces breathlessness, that threatens to stop the heart, but it is not despair.

We come to the top of a little rise and see something in all that blackness that makes us both gasp: a tiny wetland, not much bigger than a backyard pond, filled from end to end with shoots of new grass of the most exquisite green imaginable. Above the charred ground and in front of the blackened trees it looks fluorescent, even neon. We stand silently, looking at it a very long time.

"I was reading just this morning about the Great Fire of London in 1666," I finally say. "Eighty percent of the city burned to the ground, thousands of homes and churches, but only six people were injured. It took Londoners several months to realize the fire also ended the bubonic plague epidemic that had killed sixty-five thousand people because the fire killed all the rats and fleas that spread it." I don't extend the metaphor to its logical conclusion where, if climate change is our bubonic plague, that makes us the fleas and rats. But it's not lost on either of us that we are looking at some version of what might happen, what might be already happening, when the earth finally gets sad and mad enough to shake its most determined parasite off her back: a charred mountain, a million dead trees and one pool of clean water, new grass shooting through. Even this may be wishful thinking.

I try to imagine myself gone from this scene, gone from the earth—a tricky mind exercise in any circumstance. A boy I dated years ago often said, unequivocally, that he would give his life to save his mother's, even if she'd been alive, by then, an extremely long time. Would I give up my life to save the earth? Easy to say yes when the earth does not have a gun to my head, but I believe, if truly given the choice, I'd agree.

We finally turn from the wetland and head back down the trail knowing that for today, anyway, this small corner of the earth has been rejuvenated. The clutter is gone. The mountain is clean.

Ranch Almanac: Carving Rivers

Today I'll spend three hours carving rivers through ice with a pointed shovel and a maul, and by the day's end I'll have the blisters to prove it. It's to do with Deseo, who finds all manner of things scary and off-putting. Purple buckets, flapping jackets, the wind whispering through the pines.

The trough where the horses drink in winter is at the end of the pasture where all the water from the snowmelt drains toward Lime Creek. The trough is there because that's where the frost-free hydrant is, and the frost-free hydrant is there because it's the closest point to the house from which the water originates. The longer the line from the house to the frost-free hydrant, the higher the chance of the system freezing, and then we go back to hauling water again.

Unfortunately, when we get into the freeze-and-melt portion of the winter, which can last from early March to mid-May, a pond develops around the trough, which turns into a skating rink

*every time the temperature dips below 30, which is to say, every
single night. And to Deseo, a skating rink surrounding a horse
trough might be the scariest thing of all.*

*When Deseo doesn't drink, his metabolic condition gets worse.
When he refuses to cross the ice, I carry a bucket of water out to
him. Sadly, then, the bucket becomes the object of his fear. I can
leave it on the ground and walk away to prove it is neither strange
nor alive; I can float little bits of carrot on the surface of the
water to make it more enticing; I can even get on my hands and
knees and pretend to slurp some of the water up into my mouth
myself, but he simply won't have it. He feels there is only one
designated safe place to drink in this pasture and that is the water
trough, the water trough now booby-trapped by a nonnegotiable
platform of ice.*

*So I wait until the temperature crawls above freezing—about
noon—and head to the pasture with my tools. The sun has felt
truly warm all week, but this ice that formed on the bottom of
what used to be deep snow has had a good four months of subzero
to harden. I jump up and down as hard as I can and kick at it with
my steel-toed boots and about detach my arms from my shoulder
blades wielding the maul over my head to shatter the surface (this
part is fun, how it must feel to break a car's windshield). Once pits
and cracks begin to form, I dig little tributaries into the ice with
the tip of my shovel.*

*In about thirty minutes, it has warmed up a few more
degrees, and I get a satisfying little trickle to flow downhill, out
of the skating rink, around the trough and into the yard. I hack
some more, the thermometer ticks up another degree, and the
water does what water does best—gives in to gravity. I follow it,
assisting with a few hacks of my shovel all across the front of my
property. Before too long, I have the world's smallest river flowing
from the bottom of my pasture, all the way across the yard, and
into Lime Creek. I watch the creek water tumble toward the Rio*

Grande, imagine it running past the town of Creede, and then through Wagon Wheel Gap, down the canyon and across the San Luis Valley, through the Box near Taos, eventually forming the border between Texas and Mexico and flowing into the Gulf. I am filled with a completely disproportionate sense of satisfaction. For a second, I understand why those guys were crazy enough to think they could build the Panama Canal.

I return to the trough and hack my way to another tiny river, and then another one, learning quite a bit about the various properties of water and ice in the process. Once I get the little rivers started, for instance, they deepen and widen and hasten on their own, just like I learned in geology class. Two cubic feet per second turn into twenty with a little more sun and little more coaxing. In three hours I have ten outlet rivers carved into the ice surrounding the trough, and I am starting to develop blisters on my blisters. But the sun is still up and snow is in the forecast and I love my old nervous horse, so I cut five more rivers around the far edges of the ice just in case the pond gets even bigger.

PART FOUR

Elsewhere

Kindness

Junior year of college and my best friend, Mary, and I wanted to go to the Bahamas (as exotic a place as we could imagine) for spring break. Mary didn't have much money, and I had less, but I talked one of the rich kids in the dorm into letting me clean his room for a hundred dollars.

I had to do seventeen loads of laundry (all polo shirts, oxfords, and khakis) just to *get* to the floor, and the boy invited several of his friends over to "watch the maid work," but it was worth it. We put enough gas money to get home in the glove box and parked the car at the Ft. Lauderdale airport with $235 between us. In an hour we were sitting on cases of ketchup in a cargo plane high above the Atlantic on our way to Andros Island, our first mission—a free flight to the Bahamas—complete.

The pilot had been friendly, but the customs official in Andros took a much dimmer view of two American stowaways. He demanded we pay full price for our tickets, which was more money than we had. After hours of negotiating, he agreed to let us work off our debt with the crew that was paving the island's main road. We didn't even know what it meant to do roadwork, but we didn't much care. Our adventure wasn't twenty-four hours old and we were in the thick of it already.

In Andros Town we got all the grouper, peas, and rice we could handle for a twelve-dollar donation at a Baptist church dinner, and when we told the Bahamians about our deal with the customs official, the Baptists told us about the once-a-week mail boat that would be leaving for Nassau at 7:00 a.m.

"He'll be none the wiser," the man who had cooked the grouper said. "You girls don't need no black tar in your hair."

We slept under a diesel generator right near the docks so we'd be sure to hear the boat horn. Just after dawn we were awakened by a small pack of Bahamian boys who couldn't have been much over twelve, but they were brandishing switchblades and they wanted our sleeping bags.

"You see," Mary said, disguising her fear well enough to fool everyone but me, "if we gave them to *you*, then *we* wouldn't have them." She shooed the boys away and we packed up and boarded the mail boat for five dollars each. It occurred to us that if he wanted to, the Andros customs official could make our reentry into the U.S. challenging, but since we had no idea how we'd be getting back to the mainland anyway, we decided not to dwell upon it.

The men and boys that surrounded us the second we disembarked in Nassau were aggressive enough to make us hitchhike straight out of the city. We weren't at the side of the road two minutes when a Bahamian picked us up. His name was Dennis Lightbourne and he was a cadet in the Royal Bahamas Defence Force. He told us in short order we were putting ourselves in grave danger hitchhiking in Nassau, and he would take us directly to a beachfront home that had been left in his care. We could stay there for as long as we were comfortable, and, since he was on extended leave, he would fetch us each morning and show us the island, deposit us in the late afternoon to get cleaned up for dinner, and then pick us up again and take us to one of a dozen restaurants where Dennis and his closest friends always ate free.

We spent the next seven days like that—snorkeling in hidden coves, meandering through passageways of long deserted fortresses, eating more lobster and grouper and conch fritters than we thought we could hold. Any time we tried to pay, Dennis wouldn't hear of it. He was an ambassador for his country, he said, happy to do his part. We trusted him completely, and he never gave us any reason to doubt him. The only money we spent that week was on the present we gave him when we left: a necklace made of rare flamingo shells. He had told us they brought whoever wore them good luck.

My mother was still in the obstetrics wing of the hospital, and already frantic to go to a party, when she pulled Martha Washington's name off the babysitter's bulletin board, called her up and asked her if she'd come watch me for the night. The way Martha always told it, it was love at first sight, which was lucky for me, because even when they were sober, my parents were not much interested in being parents, even by the standards of the time. We met when I was two days old, and Martha died later the same year I met Dennis Lightbourne, and some overwhelming percentage of the good memories generated in the two decades between all have Martha's face in them.

Martha had a sister named Mildred whom she lived with in an old brownstone in downtown Trenton, and a brother named George who died in the war—*the first war*, Martha always said, as if there had never been any wars before that one. Martha had been married once but the only thing she ever said about it was that it "didn't take." She was stubborn and sturdy, and she did things like take my hand and step out in traffic with her arm raised to the *stop* position like a traffic cop. When the inevitable brakes started screeching and horns started blaring, she'd yell, "Don't give me that crap, I used to work for the motor vehicles!" It was the midsixties, and no one was going to run over an old lady and a little girl, no matter how much they wanted to get down the road.

Martha played card games with me: gin rummy and canasta and something called casino where the ten of diamonds was called Big Gus and the two of spades was called Little Casino, and you got a point for cards and a point for spades and a point for each ace you held when the hand was finished. She let me try on her costume jewelry—a donkey with a ruby for its eye, and a little gold Christmas tree with semiprecious stones for ornaments. We made forts out of card tables and blankets, and she'd crawl in there with me for séances and tea parties, even though she was approaching seventy. She was every bit as good as an imaginary friend, only visible, touchable. It was my mother I could never bring fully into view.

Before my father married my mother, he had won the dubious title of most eligible bachelor in Trenton, New Jersey, though it was more for his tennis-playing ability and Buick convertible than emotional stability or money in the bank. My parents were sophisticated, worldly, each brilliant in their own way, but because of the drinking the rules of behavior in my parents' house existed in a swirling vortex, the consequences of breaking them often involved violence and sometimes there was violence for no traceable reason at all.

At Martha's house I was loved even when I made mistakes, which I didn't often, because the guidelines were so clear. Be helpful, tell the truth, do unto others. It wasn't as profound as it was miraculously consistent. Take your dishes to the sink, clean up your Legos, think about the other person as often as you think of yourself.

I spent about half the nights of my childhood at Martha's, which was a good thing because I never got much sleep at home. At her house I slept so soundly that one night, when someone broke in and set off the burglar alarm and it went off for twenty-five minutes and the cops showed up with their sirens blaring and then came inside to take pictures and drink a pot of Martha's coffee, I slept like a rock through the entire thing.

"Your parents aren't bad people," Martha would always say to me. "Your mother just suffers from a lack of self-respect and your father suffers from a lack of . . ." She always paused there, as if there were too many options. Sometimes she settled on "generosity of spirit," and sometimes it was "imagination," and sometimes it was "well, maybe your father *is* a bad person after all."

On my birthday each year, Martha would make me a cake. (My

mother didn't believe in birthday cake and would go so far as to put perfume, bubble bath, and eventually apricot acne scrub in my Easter basket.) The cake was always layered, vanilla or lemon, peanut butter fudge or German chocolate. She always went out of her way to make it look just like it had come from the grocery store because I had one time spoken too enthusiastically about being at a little friend's party and being served a perfect pink IGA rose.

After we had cake, we would pool my allowance and her pillow money, go down to the grocery store, buy as much food as we could afford, and take it to the food bank. We did this on Christmas and Thanksgiving and Easter as well. She'd say "Pam, do unto others is really only the beginning." It took me a few years to understand she was telling me the big secret people like my father didn't know: that the best part about giving is not what you might get back but the actual giving itself. When I am in need of an endorphin rush, a spring in my step, a feeling of peace, a good night sleep, I can get it faster and keep it longer by giving than by any getting there has ever been. I know for most of you, this is Humanity 101, but I had to actually learn it, and were my father still alive, there would be no way I could explain it to him that would make him believe it was so.

Whenever I tell the story of Mary and me in the Bahamas, or a different story where a stranger steps in and saves me from either dire circumstances or myself, I am invariably told I trust too easily, that Dennis Lightbourne or his equivalent had ulterior motives, that Mary and I are lucky we didn't end up dead. I am often told by the people closest to me (and often in anger) that I'm more likely to trust a total stranger than someone I have known for years. I am saddened by the fact that it's true. There was little kindness in the house I grew up in, and even less trust, and I learned quickly to ask for it elsewhere—from my fifth grade teacher, a pretty lifeguard at the public pool, a stranger in a parking lot.

Martha's arrival forty-eight hours after my birth and her dedication to my well-being for the last twenty years of her life had made me understand that if I entered the world believing in the existence of a Dennis Lightbourne, it wouldn't be very long before one appeared. As often as I got myself into a tight corner, some light-borne thing appeared to bail me out, which was handy, as Mary and I would need several more such visitations to get us back to college from the Bahamas.

Martha made me French toast with maple blueberry sausages in the morning and chocolate milk with real Hershey's syrup and grilled cheese for lunch. We went to the New Jersey State Museum (could it possibly have been weekly?) and saw the same show at the Planetarium over and over again. What I looked forward to most each year was the week Martha took me to Seaside Heights, at the Jersey Shore, where a friend let her borrow a house. We'd spend every morning at the beach, come home for lunch and then go back to the boardwalk for the afternoon. Martha would buy me all the tickets I wanted to ride the rides, but usually I didn't need them because the old carnies who had the afternoon shift on the Himalaya, the Tilt-a-Whirl and the Zipper all wanted to flirt with Martha. When I climbed out of my teacup, they'd just push me back in the direction of the ride and start it up again. There was hardly anybody at the boardwalk on a weekday afternoon except for them and me and Martha, and I'd go around and around while "Honky Tonk Women" and "Maggie May" blasted from the tired old speakers. On the way back to the cottage each night, we'd stop at Dairy Queen, where I'd get a Mr. Misty Kiss, lime or raspberry, and we'd run from the mosquito truck that sent huge clouds of poison gas into the moist, salty sky.

Martha would let me swim in the ocean as long as I did it right in front of the lifeguard chair, and she'd stand there with her cotton pants rolled up, calf deep in the surf, and watch me. Whenever I tried to get her to come in with me, she'd say, "No, I can't do that, honey. Your Martha is too old and feeble." Martha didn't seem old or feeble to me, especially when she took me to the senior's aerobics class she taught at the Y, or when she was yelling at my father, "Jesus, Bev, that's not the way you treat a child." My mother had told me Martha was born in the century before our century and that our century was three-quarters over.

The house in Seaside Heights was piled high with true crime books. I was allowed to sleep on the screened-in porch where it was cooler, and some nights I'd read until Martha saw my flashlight under the covers and came out and gave me hell. I told her (politely) it was her fault because she was the one who had taught me how to read, at two and a half, by paying me a nickel every time I read a road sign, or a cereal box, or a new book meant for somebody in the first or second grade. She bought me a Dr. Seuss book called *On Beyond Zebra,* about the twenty-six letters that came after Z, and all the creatures whose names you needed those extra letters to spell, and I think that's where I first got the idea language was infinite.

She taught me to swim and dive that way too, a nickel for the length of the pool, a dime for jumping, a quarter for diving head-first. She taught me to hold the door for my elders simply by standing behind it for as long as it took me to realize I had left her on the other side. She taught me all the golden and goldenish rules my parents mostly did not subscribe to. She taught me "I'm sorry" when said sincerely can be the two most useful, most powerful words known to man. Maybe most important, she taught me love *could* be unconditional, some people *did* keep their promises and gratitude is an appropriate response to almost everything.

On lobster night in Seaside Heights, we'd go down to the fish market and Martha would buy three 1¼-pound lobsters, and she'd ask the man to cook them up. He'd give us sliced lemons wrapped in tin foil and melted butter in a plastic container and then we'd cross Highway 35 and walk home. Martha would spread about five tons of newspaper across the kitchen table and we'd dig in like Viking queens, lobster juice up to our ears. I didn't understand fixed income back then, or social security, or Medicare, but I heard my parents say the words, and I knew enough to understand our yearly lobster feast was no small thing for Martha.

After her first stroke, Martha told me she was ready to die, that she'd had eighty-six of the best years anybody could ask for and she was ready to go. She said, "You've got to promise me one thing and that's that you won't come to my funeral. I want you to remember the good times, without mucking them up with the bad." Four days later the next stroke took her voice and left her silent, scared and sad for three more years.

I made good on my promise, though my mother called me "Heartless, as cold through and through as your father," and my father said, "If I can be there when they put the old battle-axe in the ground, so can you."

After our week in Nassau, Mary and I figured we had just enough money to take the mail boat to Bimini where we'd catch the puddle jumper back to Florida, but we figured wrong. First, we didn't anticipate the hurricane that would hit, turning the twelve-hour sail to Bimini into thirty-six of the most gut churning, white-knuckled hours of our lives. Next, we didn't count on the fact that while the mail boat docked on North Bimini, the airport was on South Bimini, and the boat taxi fare between them was thirty dollars apiece. Finally, we didn't realize Bimini, in those days, was run entirely by drug money, about as safe as Central Park after dark. We wouldn't be sleeping under any diesel generators there, and if we couldn't get ourselves to South Bimini, we wouldn't be getting home.

I'll remember forever the cook on the mail boat, how he walked across the rain-slick decks, against the crazy pitch of that flat-bottomed tub, carrying plates of peas and rice to even the sickest passengers. He sang the whole time. He told us it would cure us, and either the peas and rice, or the singing did. I'll remember forever the harbormaster who broke the rules to let us hang out on Bimini's private docks so we could stay off the streets. And I'll remember the Coast Guard guy who walked past with a plate of grilled grouper, saw the way we eyed it a little hungrily and invited us to dinner. He and two friends were on a three-day pass, and we sailed with them on their twenty-seven-foot catamaran back to Miami the next morning under perfect sunshine and in front of a big following sea. They even drove us to our car in Lauderdale. We never even had to clear customs. We got back to school two days late with almost a hundred dollars to spare.

Sometimes when I tell this story I put it all down to being pretty and brave and just foolish enough to be lucky. But I'm thirty-five years older now and considerably less pretty. There's not enough luck in the world to explain all the gifts I've received since then, all the strangers who've come through for me when I trusted them with my life.

There was the couple in Botswana who ended their safari three days early to drive a seriously malarial me hundreds of miles to a hospital. There was the backcountry skier in Utah who came upon me cursing what I refused to believe was a broken tib/fib and who skied the three miles back to the road with me in his arms. There was the Parisian woman I met in the Luxembourg Gardens who took me home and fed me after my money and passport had been stolen. There was the Fijian woman who caught me crying in her garden and then, without one word (she spoke no English and I spoke no Fijian), led me by the hand onto her patio, sat me in a chair and served me tea. There was the Tibetan monk who gave me a ride on his tiny, tiny pony over a

17,000-foot pass in Bhutan because I was having chest pains that could have been just altitude or could have been a heart attack. And this is all not to mention the ranchers in Creede who've pulled their trucks out of alignment getting me out of snowdrifts, or saved one of my animals in the middle of a frigid night.

It's been thirty-five years since Martha died, and in that time I have mentored a goddaughter, a stepdaughter, and several hundred creative-writing students of all ages. I think I can say not a day has gone by when I haven't thought of Martha, when I haven't invited—sometimes effectively, sometimes less so—her patience and wisdom into my own demeanor, when I haven't stopped to think What would Martha Washington do?

And while my childhood was not what anyone would call easy, all the years I have spent holding space for my students' stories has made me aware of so many others who had it far worse than me. I had enough food to eat, teachers who cared, and good friends to lean on. I had the wherewithal and the race/class-related privilege to get myself to college, to get myself into therapy, to get myself outdoors. Before I had any of that, I had Martha Washington.

Far more than either of my parents, she is the person I have tried to become—in the way I'll roll up my sleeves and crawl under the furniture with anybody if that's what's required, in the way I have taught everyone I have even dated for five minutes to play the game casino (honestly, if you meet someone who knows how to play casino, I have probably slept with them), in the way I still know the names and location of all the stars.

Martha died more than a decade before I bought the ranch. She never saw it. She didn't even know me after I came out west and found the place in the world I was meant to live. That's the reason I kept trying to leave her out of this book. And yet her memory kept insinuating itself, demanding to be included. A voice in my head kept saying, *But you never would have* had *the ranch if not for Martha*, a statement that sounded undeniably true, though I wasn't sure in what way.

Buying this ranch for 5 percent down with no job was clear evidence of *something*: either an urge toward self-annihilation or a deep-seated belief in myself. If it was the latter—and I'd like to believe it was the latter—it was Martha Washington who made me a believer. All those nights in her house proved there *were* safe places, rooms where I could sleep through the night without fear. She taught me how to identify kindness, to recognize it when it was coming at me, and to open wide my arms.

About a decade after I bought the ranch, I went on assignment to Patagonia with a photographer and her husband for five weeks over the holidays. Overgrazed beyond repair and almost entirely alcoholic, more sparsely populated than Alaska and with wind that is never less than a gust and far more often a gale, Patagonia is not a gentle place. A magazine had sent us there to chronicle the death of the gaucho. We spent most of our days watching sheep get castrated, listening to sad stories of drunken men and riding skittish horses behind them into the mountains against 80 mph winds. Even on the estancias that still kept cooks, there was only lamb to eat and wine to drink and pantry shelves full of Kool-Aid. Most of the ranchers lived without even potatoes and lettuce, even butter and bread.

The holiday season, after all these years, is still my Achilles' heel. I'm edgy and grim from Thanksgiving until the tenth of January (the day after my birthday), and the photographer and her husband had a way of fighting that was so precisely like the way my parents fought I found myself smack in the middle of the type of holiday scenario I'd gone all the way to Patagonia to avoid. I spent Christmas Eve in my room crying and New Year's walking in a dust storm. By the time my birthday rolled around, I was trying not to think suicidally and counting the minutes (8,640) until I got home.

We were at our tenth estancia of the trip, watching our sixth mass shearing and castration. The men were high on maté and the smell of lambs' blood. The photographer snapped rolls of film and joked with the gauchos, and my poor Spanish couldn't keep up. Two old women in housedresses peeked out of the weather-beaten farmhouse windows from behind tattered lace curtains. There are so few women left in Patagonia; even the men agree their departure is both the result of and the reason for everything going to hell. It was hard not to think of Martha and Mildred in their decaying brownstone in downtown Trenton.

I couldn't watch any more sheep get their balls cut off, so I turned back toward the tents we had pitched three days before, just before the team of Uruguayan shearers rolled in. When I passed the ranch house, one of the old women, the younger of the two I thought, with still dark hair and piercing blue eyes, beckoned to me so briefly I couldn't be sure it wasn't my imagination. She didn't smile, and when she opened the door she didn't speak. She gestured toward a chair and I took it. I tried a few sentences in my pathetic Spanish, and we all looked nervously at our feet.

After a few minutes, both women disappeared into the kitchen and came back carrying a German chocolate cake between them. They sang happy birthday to me in Spanish. They apologized for having no candles. They didn't seem to mind that I cried. We had given our passports over at every place we stayed, which is the only way they could have known it was my birthday.

Martha has been gone now, many more years of my life than I had her, but she set me up to trust these strangers and to trust the feeling I had arrived safe at home, the first time I sat on the ranch's split-rail fence. Before writing this essay, I sat down and counted how many times I might have been dead if I hadn't placed my trust in the kind and divine intervention of strangers. Even being conservative, I came up with forty-six. Whether Martha actually sends these visitors, or simply gave me the means to see them, matters less to me now than how grateful I am she opened my eyes.

I can still see her standing with her arms crossed at the edge of the Atlantic Ocean, her eyes never leaving my small, bobbing frame, and I know I can trace every decent thing about myself back to her devotion, and the way she'd lock my hand inside of hers each morning, as we stepped into the path of the oncoming cars.

Ranch Almanac: Woolly Nelson

Woolly Nelson is the friendliest ram we have ever had at the ranch. He's never butted anyone and he shows no inclination to harm his own offspring and he still wags his tail whenever you pet him, just the way the babies do. He has sired three generations of healthy lambs and the ewes can't seem to get enough of him. He is black and white with such strict demarcations between the colors he looks like three different rams glued together, but his babies come out all colors, sometimes even orange or gold. Woolly's only problem is that he has a genetic defect that make his large circular horns grow in too tight a spiral, the tip pointing in toward his face rather than out. After three years of adult growth, his horns were threatening, first to block his vision, and then to forcefully close his eyes.

I waited too long to call Doc Howard because I'd read that a sheep's horns carry so much blood many animals bleed to death in the dehorning process. I was worried Doc would tell me it wasn't worth the risk and I should put Woolly down. As the horns got closer and closer to his eyes I kept hoping they would twist away from them at the last minute, and his horns had curled so strangely over the years it seemed possible they would, until it didn't seem possible anymore and I had a ram who was almost blind.

"Go ahead and bring him in, Pam," Doc said, at eleven on the Tuesday morning I finally got the nerve to call. "We'll cut those horns off and he'll probably be all right."

I hung up and my new ranchsitters, Emma and Kyle, looked at me expectantly. "Is Doc coming out?" Emma asked.

"He said to bring Woolly in," I said, and we all thought about that for a minute. One more sign I am not a real rancher is that I don't own a livestock trailer, and Doc had just had his knee replaced so I knew he wouldn't want to come out.

"The 4Runner?" Kyle said, and because it had carried dogs, cats, a baby elk and, most recently, Ingrid the yearling lamb when she came down with a bad case of bloat, there seemed no reason not to give it a try.

Except that Ingrid weighed roughly a hundred pounds less than Woolly and we had been able to lift her into the hatchback. However gentle, Woolly was still a ram; if he made up his mind to take his horns to the back window of the 4Runner, there wouldn't be any back window left.

Kyle is strong and wiry, a snowboard instructor and a

gymnast. He thought if I backed the 4Runner up to the gravel pile near the cabin, he could pull, drag and/or ride Woolly from the corral across the yard, up onto the gravel pile and into the hatch. He would sit in the back with Woolly—well, basically on Woolly—to try to keep him calm, try to keep him from bashing his way out either the back or the side windows. I would drive to Doc's, and Emma would sit in the front passenger seat, holding tight a rope we would attach to the hatchback, because we had recently discovered the locking mechanism in the backdoor had a short in it and wouldn't relatch unless we disconnected the battery at the same exact second the hatch hit the frame. Getting that timing right took an average of 200 tries, and with the nearest reliable mechanic ninety miles away, we had been avoiding opening the hatch for weeks. The dogs had no problem getting in and out the side doors but it was more than we could ask of Kyle and Woolly. Nor could we ask them to be patient for a half hour while we fiddled with the battery and the door.

It's eight miles from the ranch to Doc's and Kyle spent most of them riding Woolly the way I once upon a time rode mechanical bulls in bars, trying to keep his body between Woolly's horns and the ceiling, between Woolly's horns and the front seat, between Woolly's horns and any piece of automotive glass.

Doc's assistant, Sam, greeted me at the office door.

"You have a goat in the back of that car, Pam?" she asked.

"That's Woolly Nelson," I said. "He's an Icelandic sheep."

"And who's his sidekick?" she asked.

"That's Kyle," I said. "New housesitter. Steep learning curve."

"Bring him around to the side, Pam," Doc said, so I backed around and after checking with Kyle to see if he was ready— "more than," he said—Emma dropped the rope and we opened the hatch and Woolly and Kyle tumbled out.

"Tie him to the propane tank," Doc said to Kyle, who was wrestling Woolly to the ground by his horns.

I glanced at Doc. "He's just kidding," I said.

"No, he's not," said Sam.

"No, I'm not," Doc said, and so we tied all 200 pounds of Woolly to a half-full 120-gallon propane tank and Doc gave him a sedative that made him fall to his knees. Sam brought a veterinary wire saw strung between two hemostats and Doc went to work on Woolly's first horn, about four inches from where it met his skull plate. We could smell the horn as the metal burned into it. Doc barked out orders for Sam to fetch him various drugs I'd never heard of, but I understood from context that one was in case Woolly started to wake up, one was to restart his heart if they gave him too much of the first one, and the third was to make his blood clot if we couldn't stop the bleeding otherwise. We all leaned in and waited. Doc was about half an inch through a four-inch horn when he motioned Kyle over.

"You do this for a while," he said, and Kyle glanced once at me and then took the hemostats from Doc's hands.

"You want to do it fast," Doc said, "if you go too slow he's gonna bleed to death."

Emma caught my eye. The day the two of them arrived at the ranch, Rick Davie delivered 250 bales of hay and we had stacked them. This was only week two.

Kyle got down on his knees and bore down with the saw. "A little faster if you can manage it," Doc said, more kindly this time. After a few minutes my arms started tingling with sympathy fatigue and Kyle started emitting tiny grunts. Finally the horn fell into the dust and Sam jumped in to press gauze against the raw end of what was left, and then held the gauze up, revealing only a small spot of blood.

"Well done!" Doc said, "Take a minute, and we'll do the other horn."

The second horn bled even less than the first, and Woolly started waking up thirty seconds after Kyle finished, Doc's

estimates on the timing and amount of sedation uncannily
accurate as always.

"If you get that ram home before he wakes up all the way,"
Doc said, "Kyle will have an easier ride than he did on the way
here," so together we heaved Woolly—who looked now a little
less like a ram and a little more like Princess Leia—into the
hatchback, reattached the rope and headed back to the ranch.

Of Spirit Bears, Humpbacks, Narwhal, Manatees and Mothers

The Great Bear Rainforest is made up of approximately 1,200 square miles of the British Columbia coastline, from the Discovery Islands to the south all the way up to the Alaska-Canada border, and is part of the largest intact temperate rainforest in the world.

In October 2015, I was invited on a trip to the Great Bear by a Canadian philanthropist who is deeply invested in saving that wild place from logging and development, particularly in the form of a tar sands project and a proposed liquefied natural-gas pipeline.

Twelve writers, I was told, would spend a week on a sailboat, starting in Bella Bella, BC, and traveling the inland passages up as high as Hartley Bay before, weather permitting, coming to the outside and running back south in the Pacific. There would be humpbacks, orcas, grizzlies, wolves, and if we were very lucky, we might catch a glimpse of the all-white spirit bear. It was exactly the kind of invitation I live for.

But the day before I was to fly to Bella Bella, I noticed William was having a hard time urinating. It was taking him far longer than usual and the stream was very weak. I was in Davis at the time—the trip was during my teaching quarter—and my Davis vet told me Wil

liam most likely had a stone in his urethra. She said it would be a routine procedure to flush the stone back into his bladder, and we could
address it with diet from there. She said at 150 pounds he was too big
for her operating table, and I should take him to Vista Veterinary in
Sacramento.

"He's not in an emergency situation at present," she said, "because
he's still able to empty his bladder, but you don't want to mess around
because if that stone shifts things can change very fast."

"I can do this," Greg said, when I got home from the vet's office, "I
want to. You go on your trip." Greg always says I should trust him with
the big things in life, but trusting humans has never been my strong
suit, and in my life, there's nothing bigger than my dogs.

I wobbled but eventually capitulated. Greg dropped me at the
Sacramento airport and took William straight to Vista from there. By
the time I changed planes in Seattle, the procedure had turned out to
be not so routine after all, and by the time the wheels touched down
in Bella Bella at eight the next morning, William's condition had
worsened—the flushing procedure had not worked, and two Vista
vets were arguing over whether surgery would damage his urethra
irreversibly, making it not worth the risk.

Greg said he had it handled, but I wasn't sure that was fair to him.
And what kind of mother did this make me, that I would go gallivant-
ing off on a sailboat, leaving my boy in what were turning out to be
increasingly dire straits. If it had been a work trip, I would have told
the person in charge it was a medical emergency and I had to go home.
But this trip had been a gift—a big one—from a total stranger, which
made it trickier to know what to do. Of course, I also wanted to see the
spirit bears.

We got off the plane and stood in an awkward clump while we
waited for the single airport employee to roll our luggage over on a
handcart.

"Hi," I said, sticking out my hand to the lady I took to be the
philanthropist, "I'm Pam Houston."

"Oh . . . the writer," she said. "Nice to meet you."

"Aren't we all writers?" I said, and several people standing around me smirked.

"I'm really sorry to bother you with this," I said, "but my most beloved dog has fallen very ill in the last twenty-four hours and will probably have emergency surgery today or tomorrow. I know our letter said there'd be no connectivity, but I wondered, is there any place along the way we might get a signal, just so I can see if he made it through?"

My question was disingenuous. I had been a wilderness guide for more than a decade and knew no outfitter in the first world would run a trip like this without a radio phone—too much liability. I suspected the "no connectivity" clause was more of a preference than a condition. *My* guiding days had been mostly before cell phones, and I knew one great challenge of guiding in the cyber era was to get people to put away their devices and be where they were. I also knew the crew who'd been working on that boat all summer would know by heart every single spot on the journey, where if you climbed halfway up the mizzenmast, licked your fingers and held your arm at a forty-five-degree angle to your body, you might get one bar of 3G to buzz in.

I'd spent the whole plane ride trying not to cry. Now the look on the philanthropist's face was making it easier.

"Sorry," she said, turning her palms in the air. "That's against the rules of this trip." She made to turn away from me, then possibly thought better of it. "You know," she said, "it's always *something* when you travel. If it makes you feel any better, I got sued this morning."

It did not make me feel any better.

I watched the little plane that had deposited us in the Heiltsuk village of Bella Bella taxi to the end of the runway and considered making a run to catch it. From the air, Bella Bella had looked like a one-plane-a-day kind of town, if not three planes a week. I suddenly found myself less inclined to spend seven days shipboard with the people—writers or not—the philanthropist had assembled.

"I mean," she said, "if it were your *parent*, we could make an exception."

If it were my parent, I wanted to say, *we wouldn't need to.* "Both my parents are dead," I said, "but thanks."

We rode an old school bus into town and were told we had an hour before the boat would arrive at the dock. I introduced myself to some of my fellow passengers—a massage therapist from Vancouver and a mother of three from the Bronx. I went into the one store in town that looked open, a café that sold T-shirts that said *No Enbridge, No Tankers, No Pipeline, No Problem.* There were scarves for sale with Native designs on them that looked mass-produced in Vancouver, and some jewelry that looked less so. In the middle of the jewelry was a string of antique Venetian glass trade beads.

"Are those for sale?" I asked the girl, sounding just like the tourist I was.

"Hmmm," she said. "About those, I will have to get Charlie."

Charlie had a sweet face with eyes that smiled even when he didn't. "You are interested in the beads?" he said.

"They're beautiful," I said. "I was curious about them."

"Well," he said, "they were made in Venice, and traded in Africa. I think they are pretty old. They became popular over here with the people because, you know, they look like bear claws. But I believe the artist intended them to be flowers. You're the first person to ask about them," he said. "They have been in this case a very long time."

We eyed each other. He couldn't decide if I was a little bit interesting, and I couldn't tell if he was pulling my leg.

"They're the most beautiful thing in the store," I said.

"Were you interested in the whole string?" he said, picking up the fifty or sixty beads and running them through his fingers. "Because that would cost a lot of money."

"Maybe you don't want to sell them," I said. "Maybe you like having them here."

This made him smile. "You know," he said, "I wouldn't mind if a few of them went"—he held the string up to the sunlight—"traveling."

"I'm a traveler," I said. "Maybe the beads are in luck."

"Yes," he said, "I think it would be okay if a few of them left with you."

I grinned back at him. "What if I chose three?" I said.

"That's a good number," he said.

He cut the string and I took a lot of time choosing my three beads. He wrapped them in brown paper for me, and I paid him sixty dollars. It crossed my mind that wearing the beads might somehow help William. Convenient as it was, I went ahead and let that thought be. I walked out of the store to the sight of a large sailboat pulling into the tiny town dock and my plane-mates making their way down the gangway.

The captain's name was Neil. He had a crooked smile and wore a dirty old fisherman's sweater that seemed to have grown to his body like a pelt. He was also sick as a dog. His eyes were red and his nose was running, and it was easy to recognize his squint as the side effect of a sinus infection.

"Hi," I said, "I'm Pam."

"The writer!" he said.

"Yes," I said, "I thought we were all supposed to be writers."

"Well, in the most literal sense, I suppose." He gave me his crooked smile.

"Hey listen," I said, and told him about William's condition. "Is there some way after the surgery my boyfriend could call your office and maybe get a message to you?"

"Of course," he said, "or easier than that, you can just use the radio phone anytime you want." He picked it up off his navigation table and put it back down. "I keep it right here. You can use it whenever. Just be sure to put it back."

"Thank you so much," I said. "I mean, I know *some* people would say it's only a dog."

He squinted his already squinted-up face at me. "Well, who would ever say that?" And that's when I knew I was going to be okay.

We weren't under way thirty minutes when all traces of civilization, including power lines and cell reception, dropped completely away. The afternoon sun splashed brightly across the surface of the water, and we sat on the deck like satiated children, taking in waterfalls that tumbled down the granite walls of the surrounding islands, staring up into deep green forests that climbed the surrounding mountains as far as the eye could see.

We traveled alongside humpbacks every day. We walked up estuaries thick with dying salmon and encountered grizzlies on two occasions. We went up on deck and howled into the starry night, and most nights wolves howled back to us. One day a Gitga'at elder named Marvin led us up a small river to wait for a spirit bear, and we sat for hours, unmoving and silent on the bank, hoping one would walk by.

A spirit bear—also known as a Kermode bear—is a black bear with a double recessive gene for whiteness. It is not an albino—it is truly white; sometimes a white sow will give birth to two black cubs. The First Nation tribes in coastal British Columbia, the Tsimshian and the Gitga'ata, kept the white bear a secret for centuries, protecting it from settlers and trappers, but more recently they have come to believe raising awareness about the bear might help protect their hunting and fishing grounds from the tar sands project as well as the Enbridge pipeline.

Four hours after we arrived, when we had lost all feeling in our fingers, toes and butts, a white bear appeared a hundred yards upriver, taking her time picking through the rocks, chewing on an occasional half-dead salmon. Eventually she walked only a few feet from our breathless forms, close enough for us to see her eyelashes, the rose-colored tint of her skin through her thick white coat, the black underside of her considerable paws, which looked for all the world like the soles of well-worn bedroom slippers.

When she was out of sight, we gasped and squealed and hugged one another, broke out lunch and then resumed our positions. After a few more hours, she headed back upriver, ambling right past us again.

As it turned out, there were only two other writers on the trip—John Vaillant, who wrote, among other things, a luminous book called *The Golden Spruce*, and an important environmental blogger named Brendan DeMelle—but that didn't really matter because there were filmmakers, mediators and professional fund-raisers: twelve good people who were all doing their part for the earth. The philanthropist and I never got chummy, but it didn't make much difference. I admire her passion and commitment to the Great Bear a lot, and I'm nothing but grateful to her for giving me a week in that unspoiled place. From the very first moment, I knew I had a friend in Captain Neil.

Each night, after the philanthropist had gone to bed, Neil would crook his finger for me to come up on deck and hand me the radio phone, and each night I would point it up to the southern sky and call Greg. Sometimes, while I was waiting for a satellite, a wolf would howl, and my heart would tear, imagining my boy on the operating table, in the recovery room, wondering where I was. Sometimes the call would fail, once, twice, three times, and there would be nothing to do but surrender to the reflection of the starlight on water, to whatever would be back home. On the nights I did get through the news was never conclusive. The surgeon at Vista had eventually decided it was too risky to operate, so after $2,500 and two days worth of not much of anything, Greg took William to UC Davis, where he could have gone in the first place if his case had originally been deemed an emergency. The Davis team planned to use a supersonic blaster to try to break up the trapped stone and hopefully get it to pass. After that, they would operate to remove the other nine stones X-rays had revealed in his bladder. No one would tell Greg exactly when that would happen.

I found myself split in a way that was deeply familiar—half of me so worried about William I could barely function, the other half drunk with joy at getting to be exactly where I was. I wanted to be large enough to contain the totality of both feelings. Did their coexistence automatically make me some kind of a monster? I reached for the life lesson that was hovering close in the starry night, waiting for me to snatch it.

I was in a place both radically pristine and radically threatened, by Big Timber, by tar sands, by liquefied natural gas. The Enbridge people wanted to run multiple 400-meter tankers a day through these virgin passages, around some of the tightest turns in the shipping industry, in some of the most ferocious winter weather on earth. A 125-meter ferry, the MV *Queen of the North*, had sunk in 2006, a few miles across the water from where the spirit bears lived, because of the captain's failure to execute a simple course change. One moment of inattention, one bad decision, one corner taken too close, one jagged rock, and two million barrels of oil could poison this slice of heaven forever.

There had to be a way to know all that and still be here with my heart wide open. Could a person mourn and be joyful simultaneously? I understood it as the challenge of the twenty-first century. Maybe it was simply what being a grown-up meant.

On the second to last day of the trip we stopped at a place called CetaceaLab—a cantilevered shack a woman named Janie Wray got permission from the local Gitga'at nation to put there so she, her then husband and several volunteers could study resident and transient whales in the whales' preferred location. We rounded Whale Point at 6:00 p.m. on what had been a grey day, but now the clouds were washed pink, red and blue in an extended sunset.

We had seen the spouts from a long way off, backlit, and shooting into the air in the three-pointed shape of a scepter's crown. The humpbacks were tight in the harbor and feeding, and there were a lot of them. Neil pulled the boat in among them, and just as we dropped anchor, two whales full-breached off our starboard bow simultaneously, once, twice and then a third time—kids doing cannonballs—giving the boat and all of its passengers a serious soaking. More whales came by the boat to check us out, rolling their big eyes toward us, letting their baleened smiles come to the surface and stay there. Other whales bubble-fed in groups of three and four off the bow. A young whale practiced fin and tail slaps off the stern, in front of what was left of the sunset. No wonder Janie Wray chose this place to build CetaceaLab.

We were all so high on the show we almost didn't hear Darcy, the CetaceaLab volunteer we would be transporting back to Bella Bella, when she told us everyone at the lab was concerned because the whales were especially skinny this year.

"Do you think the warmer water is affecting their food supply?" Neil asked. The warmer water was affecting a lot of things in the Pacific. The California sea lions were dying by the thousands and the exoskeletons of the purple sea stars, found on all the coasts of British Columbia, were turning into mush.

"It's hard to know for sure," Darcy said, "but whales are staying in the area longer this year than ever before, maybe trying to bulk up a bit before their trip to Hawai'i. The difference from a year ago is really dramatic. Something is definitely wrong."

Worse for me than thinking about my own death, or even William's, was trying to reckon with this kind of information. The closer one got to the North and South poles, the more dramatic and obvious the effects of climate change. I didn't want to live in a world without polar bears. I wasn't sure an ocean without whales in it was any kind of ocean at all. My entire life I had watched, heartbroken, as individual pieces of wilderness that mattered to me got destroyed or developed, but I had believed, for reasons I am not clear on now (propaganda? denial? naïveté?), that the earth contained vast tracts of land humans had not pushed into. Now, I understood this thing we called technology had advanced to a point where no place on the planet was safe from our penchant for destruction. I found myself glad we had never colonized the moon.

It had gotten fully dark while we talked, and a young whale had come alongside the boat and started to sing. The massage therapist from Vancouver had pulled his harmonica out of his pocket and now they were playing a duet. I fingered the trade beads around my neck and closed my eyes to better hear the dissonant harmony. I reminded myself to be here now. Whatever calamity was around the corner, there was no denying it had been an afternoon of marvels.

Not even five months later, on February 1, 2016, an agreement would be reached between the provincial government, the First Nations, and the logging industry to protect 85 percent of the trees in the Great Bear. On October 16 of that same year a tugboat driver would fall asleep at the helm, running his ship and the barge he was towing hard aground just north of Bella Bella, releasing more than 110,000 gallons of diesel fuel into the pristine waters of Seaforth Channel.

But that night, surrounded by the squeak and blow of humpbacks, when I pointed the radio phone toward the southern horizon, I found out that a different sort of advanced technology had successfully exploded the stone in William's urethra, allowing him to pee normally. And after that, some relatively old-fashioned laser surgery had successfully removed nine rather large cystine stones from his bladder.

In early March 2011, Greg and I went to the Sea of Cortés, hoping to see blue whales. When we arrived, we were told the blues usually left in February and we would have to be content with fin whales and humpbacks. Because any day of seeing a whale is better than any day of not seeing a whale, I was more than content—I was ecstatic.

We stayed at a funky little tent camp run by an Italian named Antonio, who was disparaging of Americans, mostly because, he said, they didn't understand food, wine or coffee. We assured him things had gotten better in all three categories in the last decade or two, but he didn't believe us. He hadn't been across the border to the States in thirty-seven years, and he had no intention of crossing any time soon.

Antonio told big stories of his days on the sea, but when it came time to actually go boating he turned us over to his friend Pablo, who owned an open-topped blue and white fiberglass 20-footer with an outboard. We saw hundreds of whales during the week we were there, humpbacks that breached and slapped their flukes, and big pods of eighty-foot fin whales, moving nearly silent and torpedolike through the water.

On the sixth day, we went out with a small group of other tourists, including a Japanese couple named Hito and Mikiko. They were staying at Antonio's tent camp too, and we had gotten friendly, in spite of their limited English and our nonexistent Japanese.

Earlier that morning we had heard the news of the earthquake off the coast of Tohoku, Japan, and the disabled and leaking nuclear reactor. Hito and Mikiko were from the south, they said, hundreds of miles away, and had no relatives or friends close to the quake. Without the English words to express his grief, Hito kept it simple. "We are just happy to be with the whales," he said. "This is our dream."

We had seen the usual assortment of whales that morning and were currently pacing a baby hammerhead shark who'd been swimming alongside our boat for nearly five minutes, when off in the distance the captain sighted a humpback. As we raced toward it we could see the whale was slapping one flipper, over and over, loud, hard, in an exhausted but persistent rhythm. When we got close, we saw blood on the flipper it slapped. When we got even closer, we could see there was plastic fishing net wrapped around its lower body.

"Can we help it?" I asked Pablo, but he shook his head. "Too strong," he said, in Spanish. "It would kill me." He seemed sad about it. The whale continued to slap, almost mechanically. Who was she calling for? her mate? her friend? her mother? us?

I remembered a children's book I'd read on a whale watch in Provincetown, where some fishermen help a tangled whale, and not only does the whale let them help her, she comes back and circles the rescuer's boat three times before departing, then drenches them with a joyful fluke-created wave. I had been born knowing that if you held the proper measuring stick, animals would always test smarter than people, and nothing I've seen in my lifetime has disabused me of that notion. We may have more complicated language, opposable thumbs and this dangerous thing called reason, but any self-respecting llama or buffalo or spider knows enough not to destroy its own home.

In a combination of English and Spanish, Pablo let me know some local fishermen tried to help the whale a few days ago, but she dove, nearly killing one of the helpers in the process. "They wait for her to get more tired," he said, "and maybe they try again."

Mikiko and I exchanged desperate glances. I took several photos of the whale knowing that later, I would wish I didn't have them in my camera. Pablo shrugged and turned the boat toward the harbor. My mind raced in panicked circles, wishing plastic gill nets were illegal, wishing for a local chapter of Marine Mammal Rescue, wishing for my own boat, a life preserver and a reasonably sharp Swiss army knife.

It was only with my back to the whale, hearing that plaintive *slap . . . slap . . . slap* continuing as we pulled away, that a wall of grief so huge hit me it felt, honestly, unprecedented in my lifetime. I was doubled over by it, literally taken to my knees, and once I started crying, I thought I might never stop. And once I accepted the fact I might not ever stop crying, I then started to have to work very hard to keep myself from keening, or shrieking, or making some other sound that neither Greg, nor Pablo, nor Hito and Mikiko, nor anyone else on that boat wanted me to make. This was the kind of grief Cheryl Strayed was talking about, I realize now, when she talked about losing her mother.

Mikiko touched my shoulder. In her country, just hours before, more than ten thousand people had been killed, with thousands more missing or fatally contaminated by radiation. Even as that whale was slapping her flipper behind us, thousands of gallons of radioactive fluid were pouring into the sea, killing who would ever know how many whales and dolphins and fish and reefs. Maybe I was crying for the people and the animals and the sea creatures of Japan. Maybe I was crying for the havoc we wreak upon the planet every day. Maybe some part of me was crying for my mother.

But it *felt* like was I was grieving for *that very* whale, with the net around her flukes and blood on her flipper, and I knew as we sped away that some part of me would always be grieving for that whale, that she would live in me forever, and somehow, illogically, she might be the biggest grief of all. Of everything I have written in this book, including the death scene of my beloved Fenton, this scene was the hardest to write.

I cried longer and harder and more hopelessly for that whale than I did for my parents, for the three dearest friends I've lost to cancer, for my dogs or any of the other animals who have graced and left my life. Maybe I cry harder over animals because my love for them is so uncomplicated, or maybe it is because I trust an animal to always be itself. Maybe I cried hardest over that whale because I'd had no chance to brace myself for the sight of her. She was the last thing I expected to see on that glorious day of sparkling sea and sunshine and shark after whale after whale. And there she was, starving, dying and asking for help, and neither I, nor anyone else in the Sea of Cortés, could help her.

Last February, after a brief teaching stint at an arts high school in West Palm Beach, I tacked on three days to go down to the Keys. I love Florida, and am not afraid to say so, though it horrifies my staunch environmental friends when I do. I stayed in a marginally decent hotel on Islamorada because it had a paddleboard rental office in its parking lot. I went paddling every morning for four hours, came back and ordered room service, and wrote until I couldn't keep my eyes open.

Stand-up paddling is my new favorite sport. It's both aerobic and meditative, it helps my balance and, most important, it gets me out on the water, under my own power, surrounded by all that gorgeous aquamarine. Unlike most of the outdoor sports I've fallen in love with, it's hard to break a bone doing it. I've seen those gray braids out on their boards in Hawai'i, and it's my plan to take paddling all the way to the grave.

Last winter, on a downwind paddle off the coast of Moloka'i, in conditions that were a gnarly (not in a good way) combination of wind chop and swell, I fell so many times and so many different ways I lost count of them. Most falls were of the standard off-the-side-of-the-board variety, but once I went backward, ass over teakettle, and another time, when a wave I wasn't expecting swamped the board from behind, I fell forward, face planting right onto the surface of the board, before I bounced like a wooden plank and pitched off the side. I was so tired by the end of that day I could barely heave myself up on the board after what must have been fall number fifty, but the next morning, I wasn't even a little bit sore.

In Islamorada, out on my board, I saw several big spotted rays, one with a wingspan larger than mine, two reef sharks in the three-to-four-foot range, a baby sea turtle and dozens of tropical fish. In a mangrove basin in a back bay, I nearly paddled right into a four-foot alligator sunning himself on somebody's dock, and at the hotel pool the biggest iguana I've ever seen—at least four feet long—with the most complicated and colorful face armor imaginable, walked right under my lounge chair and out the other side. Later that night, a white heron, in his full mating plumage, preened himself on my balcony as I sat in a lawn chair, reading about the recent releases from Lake Okeechobee.

The dike on that giant lake is not stable, and the lake is filled with poison from central Florida's agriculture. The Everglades would clean that water right up for Florida and send it back into the ocean, as it did for millions of years before people started polluting it, but Big Sugar owns the land that would have to be reflooded to allow it to happen, and Florida's governor is in bed with Big Sugar.

So each winter, when the lake gets full to bursting and the dike threatens to break and poison all of central Florida in the process, the Army Corp of Engineers sends ten billion gallons a day of poisoned water down the St. Lucie Canal to the Atlantic, creating massive algae blooms that kill fish by the thousands, making the ocean beaches dangerous to swim in, and driving several species, including the Cape

Sable sparrow, one step closer to extinction. That very week people up the coast were posting pictures of seawater the color of black tea.

I realized, sitting on my balcony, making eyes at the white heron, that I loved Florida particularly and precisely *because* the apocalypse has already happened there, is happening daily, and yet the animals are still there, going about their business. The building of the Tamiami Trail, the damming of the Everglades, the filling of the swamps, development after development, with little or no environmental protections enforced, and the animals make the best of it, amid the beer cans, the half-finished dream homes and the Jet Skis.

In the middle of downtown Islamorada, on Highway 1, which these days sees 24/7 wall-to-wall traffic and is currently in the midst of a widening project, on top of an especially tall power pole, sits an osprey nest. Stopped by flagmen, I looked up to see the osprey couple peering over the side, watching the bulldozer and the backhoe, listening to the back-up buzzers. Nobody told *them* it was an inappropriate place to raise a family, and perhaps by these standards it isn't. Florida animals are adaptors. And something about them gives me hope.

I know there's a different way to tell this story. I could enumerate the animals lost (individuals and entire species) because of the greed and corruption that has run rampant in Florida for years. That story is here too, running right alongside the one I have going about resilience and against-all-odds survival. But sometimes, this other story is the one I need, the iguana at the hotel pool, the gator on the patio. It makes me believe that when push comes to shove, maybe the creatures of the earth will fight back.

On the final morning of my trip, I went out for one last paddle. It was 8:00 a.m. and I only had ninety minutes before I needed to leave for the airport, and because I beat the sport fishermen and the Jet Skiers and the party boaters out there, the water was as clear as glass. I paddled along the shoreline into what little wind there was, with the idea I would swing offshore some distance, ride the small swell back and see if I could find any creatures. After thirty minutes, I made my turn out to sea, and in front of me, something humped itself momentarily out of the water. A ray? a dolphin?

I paddled toward the spot where the hump appeared, right on the end of a point I had paddled around several times that week, and when I got there I saw, maybe thirty yards offshore and just below the surface, a big tan mottled rock that I had somehow missed on the other days. Coral? conglomerate?

The nose of my board was right on top of the big rock when it finally moved, unhumping its back and lifting both rounded nose and paddle tail out of the water simultaneously. The noise he made was more sigh than blow, as he slowly pushed himself out from under the shadow of my board.

Is there anything in the world more vulnerable than the manatee? Anything slower, sweeter, more deserving of our care? I paddled along beside him and he turned his gentle eye on me and rolled over on his side in a kind of greeting. We moved at the same pace for a little while, when out of nowhere, a backward-hatted frat boy and his girlfriend came roaring up in a speedboat behind me. The manatee reared up and dove as deep as he could, given the shallows we were in, which was almost no depth at all.

"No!" I screamed, and waited for the blood in the water.

The frat boy cut his engine. "Did you see it?" he asked his girlfriend who was picking her fingernails. She shook her head and with a giant surge of gasoline to his massive twin engines he spun his boat and roared off.

There it is, I thought. There is Florida.

I stood perfectly still on the water with my paddle resting on the board and waited for the manatee to resurface, which he did, after about a minute, and we began moving again. He was taking me, it seemed, into a private boat basin, one with eight or nine houses and a medium-sized sign that said Trespassers Will Be Prosecuted to the Fullest Extent of the Law. I briefly considered whether that rule applied to paddleboarding trespassers—and decided it probably did, but I could already see, in front of me, five other manatees in the boat basin, including a mother and very small calf.

I drifted in slowly and silently several yards behind my friend, barely using my paddle. I didn't have time to get arrested that morning. If anyone yelled at me, I reasoned, I would just turn around and go. The other manatees raised their heads out of the water to greet their friend. The calf was no more than a foot long; the biggest manatee, its mother, more than ten feet from tip to tail. I watched them hang and bob a few minutes, before turning and paddling, as quietly as I could, back out of the private boat basin.

During that January week I spent in Hanalei with Cheryl, she introduced me to a woman named Hob Osterlund, a writer who has dedicated much of her life to an albatross population, one that has only in recent years returned—one bird at a time—to Kaua'i. In 1971, after the species had been absent from Kaua'i for a hundred years, a single albatross flew a thousand miles past her fledgling ground on Midway to reclaim the island her ancestors had called home before tourism developed. When I was there, in 2016, there was a thriving colony, fastidiously protected by Hob and others.

Cheryl told me she and Hob had talked at length about mother loss, and the potential power of the wilderness to mitigate, if not heal it. I liked Hob instantly. She's a no-nonsense woman who can make mystery and manifestation seem as everyday as lawn care, a practical sort who isn't the least bit afraid to talk in the same sentence about science and the human soul. She told me about her "impractical" decision to move to Kaua'i twenty-two years ago, when a deceased ancestor visited her in a dream and said Hob's life's purpose was to pay attention to what the albatross was trying to tell her about living on the earth.

I told Hob about the ranch, about how even when I am away from it, my horseshoe of mountains holds me, have held me most all of my adult life. I told her how the surface of the Rio Grande turns to mercury every afternoon, an hour before sunset, and how in that roiling silver surface I have always been able to see some version of what people call God.

Hob invited me to her house for a chat and a shower, before I'd catch the red-eye back to the mainland. While she made us guacamole, I went for a walk out the back of her Princeville house onto the sprawling golf course behind it, past several signs warning me the paths are for golfers only. Since the golf paths were the only way to access the sea cliffs, I decided if somebody needed to fine me for wanting to look out on the ocean one last time before I left Hawai'i, I would gladly pay.

I looked over the edge at the waves crashing below me, and then offshore at a relatively quiet sea. Record-setting waves had hit Hanalei Bay all week, delighting the surfers, making my daily swim a bit too exciting, but now the storm had moved on.

I trained my eyes on as much sea surface as possible between me and the horizon and settled in for a wait. Finally one spout, and then quickly another. Then a few more farther out. Then a giant splash closer in, then two more in quick succession. I swallowed tears as three more spouts rounded the corner of the island. The skinny whales had made it from the Great Bear back to Hawai'i after all.

A lady walking her dogs on the golf cart path (surely an even bigger violation than mine) approached me, grinning. "Did you see them?" she asked.

"Yes!"

"It makes me so happy," she said, and I realized there were tears in her eyes too. "I've been so worried. I hadn't seen them yet this year."

"I heard they left Canada a little late," I said. "But here they are."

I walked back to Hob's house to report my sighting. We talked about the skinny humpbacks, the warming ocean and the shrinking ice cap, the methane leak poisoning a whole subdivision in Southern California, the fracking fields in North Dakota where I'd just been to write a story, the bumper sticker I saw in the man-camp there that read *I ❤ Crack Whores*.

"These are the conversations I find myself having every day," I said. "Soon no one will want to invite me over for guacamole."

"It always hurts to lose your mother," Hob says, "no matter how old you are."

I looked up at her startled, thinking she was having a senior moment, that she had somehow gotten me confused with Cheryl.

But when I met her eyes, I saw not only that she knew it was *me* in the room with her, but that she understood me better than she had any right to, given the brevity of our acquaintance.

"It does," I said. "It hurts a little every single day."

September 2014 found my friend Tami and me on a boat with an ice-enforced hull in Nunavut, Canada, on the north side of Baffin Island along with a hundred paying passengers and a thirty-person crew of scientists and researchers. The plan was to start in Resolute Bay and travel west and south, following Sir John Franklin's historic passage on a seldom-used route through the Fury and Hecla Strait—known to early explorers as the Northwest Passage—and arrive fourteen days later in Nunavut's capital, Iqaluit.

Sir John Franklin sailed from Britain in 1845 leading 129 men and two ships—HMS *Erebus* and HMS *Terror*—to try to open that route for trade. The expedition's disappearance became one of the great mysteries of Victorian exploration, leaving experts to speculate that the ships became locked in the ice near King William Island and the crews abandoned them in a desperate attempt to save themselves. The Inuit fishermen living in the area at that time reported the starving sailors resorted to cannibalism before they died. Franklin's wife used her own money to launch an unprecedented five ships from England in search of her husband, telling the sailors to leave cans of food on the ice hoping he would somehow find them.

Since 2008 the Canadian government has redoubled its efforts to find *Erebus* and *Terror* as part of a strategy to assert Canada's sovereignty over the shipping lanes that are suddenly becoming accessible due to rapidly melting sea ice. In a stroke of uncanny timing, the announcement was made that the *Erebus* was found in the waters of Victoria Strait just days before Tami and I flew to Resolute Bay, and some were calling it the biggest archaeological discovery since Tutankhamen's tomb.

I suppose, given all that, we should not have been surprised when we woke on the first morning aboard to find our boat, the *Sea Adventurer*, frozen hard into the pack ice, nor when we had to wait until almost noon for it to release us. When it happened again on the second night, our expedition leader, Alex, along with our Greek sea captain, decided that to stay the course for Fury and Hecla could lead to the same kind of trouble that found Sir John Franklin, and we therefore needed a new itinerary. We would go around Baffin Island (at nearly 200,000 square miles, the fifth largest island in the world) to the east, instead of to the west, a decision that infuriated the history buffs among the clientele, but excited the crew's geologists and biologists, for whom the east side of Baffin Island and its many deep fjords were wholly uncharted territory. Tami and I were so happy to be on the trip at all, east or west seemed equally good to us.

Because I've had the good fortune to spend a lot of time above the Arctic Circle in Alaska, I thought I knew how beguiling travel in the eastern Canadian Arctic would be. I was mistaken. Maybe it was being continuously out on the water. Maybe it was because the September light was making constant magic with the rock and the ice. Maybe it was because I was with Tami, a friend who over the years has become a true sister, and we could therefore feel, without speaking of it, every time the wild beauty made our hearts want to burst. Maybe it was because we got to watch, at close range, a couple of polar bears toss a seal carcass around like a soccer ball, or because we got to lie, one afternoon, in an open tundra meadow for an hour while a small herd of musk ox grazed toward us, or because we got to kayak every day in front of calving glaciers, sticking our paddles into the pancake ice that was threatening to close us in. Or maybe it was our visits to the Inuit villages—how the mayor of Pangnirtung came out and shook each of our hands, how the teenagers in town put on a dance for us, how a lady sold us hand-knitted hats out of her kitchen in Arctic Bay, and how we played jump rope there with three little girls whose faces shimmered with the sea salt that had dried out of the air and onto their burnished rose cheeks. Or maybe it was the way our trip leader, Alex, a very young man to be in charge of such a major expedition, infected us all with his unqualified enthusiasm. I meet a great many people who love what they do, but Alex loved his job more than anyone I have ever met in my life. I spent the whole fourteen days in something close to rapture.

Alex ran the entire expedition—including the sixty-eight-year-old Greek captain and *his* staff—with a compassionate but firm hand. I was particularly impressed with how he handled the group of older male passengers (Tami and I nicknamed them "the Captains of Industry") who couldn't get over the fact that we turned away from Fury and Hecla. I liked his no-nonsense way of stressing the importance of following the rules.

"Today we will go ashore onto Beechey Island," he began at one morning briefing. "We'll see a memorial to Franklin, as well as an Inuit archaeological site. Our entire staff is trained in firearms and whenever we are on land there will be multiple sharpshooters stationed on either side of the corridor where we will be hiking. It is imperative that the group stay together and follow every direction from the team members. We are prepared to use lethal force if necessary to stop a charging polar bear. We will shoot in front of the bear first to try to turn it around. Our company has a perfect record in that we have never had to kill a bear to protect a passenger and, I can assure you, if one of my men is forced to kill one today because one of you has not followed my directions, the trip back to Iqaluit will feel like the longest of your life."

Tami and I fell instantly in love with Alex in what I'd like to insist was an innocent, noncougarish way, although we did record his morning message on our otherwise useless iPhones. He took to us too, and we met for a beer in the library almost nightly—Tami and I playing the role of moderately hip, outdoorsy mothers. He told us the story of meeting his fiancé aboard one of these excursions. How he dressed in his formal captain's gear, knelt down in front of the girl's father and asked for her hand. He told us Verité (her real name) was already pushing him to get off the water, to move to Toronto and settle down and have children, that he was trying to get her to compromise, to let him leave the sea gradually, that he was encouraging the employment of a five-year and a ten-year plan. We listened sympathetically, told him that while we knew Verité must be very special (for how could she not be?), it had not escaped our notice that he was living a life most only dreamed of and he was spectacularly qualified for the job he had. We suggested Verité most likely fell in love with him because of the way he stood on the bridge scanning the water, because of his unending love for whatever was on the horizon, for the way his voice caught over the loudspeaker every time he'd spotted a bear, or an orca, or just wanted us to come out on deck and see the way the icy clouds were reflecting off the surface of the sea.

Like the Great Bear Rainforest, Nunavut is being heavily pressured by the oil and gas industry, and even though it is less populated, much harder to access and many times bigger than the Great Bear, the eastern Canadian Arctic is every bit as fragile. One day, on our unplanned route, we saw in front of us an island where the charts indicated no such thing. As we got closer, the captain identified what we had mistaken for a landmass as what remained of the giant hunk of the Greenland ice sheet that had famously fallen into the sea in 2012—the largest break-off ever at the time.

The berg was beautiful in the low arctic light, a blue crystal five miles square, beaten translucent by sun and waves, so massive that rivers poured off its top and into the sea on all sides of it, carving giant spouts—a whiter blue than the rest of the surface—every several hundred feet.

I was face-to-face with my familiar koan: how to be with the incandescent beauty of the iceberg without grieving the loss of polar bear habitat its appearance implied. How to grieve the polar bear without loving it any less. How to let the sight of such a strange and beautiful thing as this floating jewel make me happy, as wild and surprising things have always done, from the top of my head to the tips of my toes. How to hang on to that full-body joy I knew I was capable of and still understand it as elegy.

Each day we heard lectures on the flora, fauna, geology and history of the region. We made friends with the scientists, who were closer to Tami and me in temperament and age than most of the paying passengers, a group that seemed to spend a lot of time in their rooms. Arctic expeditions are mostly free of the nonsense that infects cruises down south but one night about halfway through the trip, Alex announced there would be a costume party where we were to come as our favorite arctic character. The most innovative costumes would receive prizes. This was especially fun, Alex went on to say, because he knew none of us would have thought to bring costumes, and we would have to make do with whatever we could find on the ship.

Once back in our room, Tami said, "Okay. If we're going to enter this thing, we are damn sure gonna win it." Which may tell you something about our sisterhood. Tami first suggested we dress as Alex's five-year plan and his ten-year plan, an idea that sent us into hysterics until we realized the only two people who would be laughing would be us. So we made a headless and armless man out of our rubber boots and personal man-overboard equipment, talked the chef out of a few ketchup and mustard bottles to hang on strings around our necks, smeared a bunch of red stage makeup we borrowed from a crew member around our mouths, carried forks and knives in our hands, and went as a couple of Franklin's cannibals. We tied for first in the costume competition with a woman who had dressed up as Sedna, the sea goddess in Inuit mythology, and more excitingly, Tami beat out a sweet British karate black belt in a game where you had to bend from the waist and pick up an ever shrinking barf bag with your teeth.

By day ten of the trip, we had made our way down the coast of Baffin Island and into the depths of Sam Ford Fjord, a place that was making the geologists nutty with excitement. Still trying to appease the Captains of Industry, Alex told us in his morning briefing that we had seen more wildlife in the fjords than we ever would have in Fury and Hecla. We'd had bears nearly every day, walrus twice, a humpback, a couple of fin whales, three pods of orcas and the musk ox.

"Now, all that's left is a narwhal!" was the running joke on the boat, because nobody *ever* saw narwhal, except for the Inuit fishermen, who, it was said, always knew where they were. Thought to be the origin of the unicorn myth, narwhal (*Monodon monoceros* from the Greek, or one-toothed unicorn) are medium-sized whales that have a large "tusk," which is actually an elongated and protruding canine tooth. Narwhal can live up to fifty years; they travel in pods and communicate in clicks, whistles and knocks. The narwhal are listed as "near endangered," but some scientists believe they are even more threatened by the rapid melt of sea ice than the polar bear, because the narwhal depend on the sea ice to provide them fishing grounds with no competition. The number of narwhal left in the world is almost impossible to confirm because they are so hard to find. Few of the scientists we had befriended had ever seen one, and they had been working in the Arctic for anywhere from seven to fifteen years.

Sam Ford Fjord was the last day for the kayaks—according to Alex we would have to make real time heading south from there on out. Only four people, besides Tami and me—all of them women—had signed up for daily kayaking at the start of the trip, though Val the guide had said she had space for twelve. Our hours kayaking were the very best of the trip, and by week's end the six of us trusted Val so completely that when she suggested, as we were being towed en masse back to the ship by one of the Zodiacs, that we all take the kayakers' polar plunge together, we were overboard and into the 33 degree water before the Zodiac driver even had time to raise his camera.

By the time we were showered and redressed in our sixteen layers plus parkas, we were nearly out of San Ford Fjord and ready to burn it south toward Iqaluit. Most of us were on deck, shooting the afternoon light on the hanging glaciers, when Alex's voice came over the loudspeaker.

"Good afternoon, ladies and gentlemen. Good afternoon." (It was Alex's habit to always greet us twice.) "The captain believes he has spotted narwhal about a mile off the bow of the boat. Get your cameras and come out on deck, and I will be back with you soon with more information."

The energy on deck crackled as if someone had sprayed a fine cocaine mist into the air. The biologists couldn't wipe the smiles off their faces. In five minutes Alex was back on the loudspeaker, "Ladies and gentlemen," and this time we could hear the heavy emotion in his voice, "the captain believes there are between six and eight hundred animals a hundred yards in front of the ship. It seems our detour has taken us directly into the path of the annual narwhal migration. Ladies and gentlemen, please be clear this is not a once-in-a-lifetime experience. This is once in a hundred lifetimes."

We spent the next five hours running into the sunset alongside six to eight hundred narwhal. If a group of narwhal is a blessing, this was a whole damn conversion. Narwhal are not showy, like humpbacks, or huge and lightning-fast, like fin whales, or finned with that improbable black blade, like orcas. They don't even show their tusks very much, especially when they are on the move, which they definitely were, having not much trouble keeping up with our powerful engines. But here they were, by the hundreds, their black bodies thick enough in places to walk across the sea, shining in the late sun, moving toward wherever they would find food next, every now and then giving us a quick glimpse of the tusk that gave them their name.

To run with them that day was as magical a thing as will happen to me in my lifetime. I watched the sun roll toward the horizon and across the glaciers of the entirely unpopulated Bylot Island, the seventy-first largest island in the world, a place the Canadian government has protected almost entirely with the designation of Sirmilik National Park.

All that day I felt perfectly cared for, rocked by the boat and the beauty and the strange-toothed tour guides surrounding us. I stayed on deck until there was only an occasional straggler in the water, well into evening, long after the cold had chased everyone else inside, some new knowledge of my place in the earth's natural order keeping me warm from within.

How many nights had the ocean rocked me to sleep? How many times had I lain on the ground and felt its sustenance? How many times had I turned my face to the sky and borrowed its power? I had been born to two humans who wanted me not at all, but maybe that didn't matter so much. I would always be a child of the wilderness.

Ranch Almanac: Almanac

It's as beautiful a thing as I have ever known, living inside the ranch's almanac. How the weather shapes and dictates our lives, not just during a blizzard but in every season. How the Leonids always follow the Perseids. How the monsoon always follows fire season. How wood follows hay, and lambs follow the draining of the pasture. How lupine follows paintbrush, which follows flox, which follows iris, which follows the arrival of the bluebirds, which follows the last day of below zero cold.

There's the way the sun warms the house, right after sunrise through the east-facing kitchen windows. There's the smell of 250 bales of fresh hay in the barn on a warm September afternoon and the colors in the sky over Bristol Head at dusk. A good bed of coals in the woodstove; a pot of Hungarian mushroom soup on the range. The fuchsia blooms of the skyrocket on either side of the driveway. A coyote pausing, one foot in the air, crossing my pasture feet deep in snow. The smell of lanolin rising off the sheep. Five elk beds near the creek in the back acreage, still holding warmth from the vacated elk. The tiny tracks of mice in the snow. Roany, impatient for carrots, staring me down through the kitchen window on a frigid January morning. Orion, so bright and close outside my bedroom window in February, it is as if he's waiting for an invitation. The barn—always the barn—and its roofline against the blue of the mountain. The Milky Way— appearing nightly, and milky above me. Moonglow on Pinckley's cabin, on the barn roof, on the snow in the pasture on a midnight cross-country ski. The screech of a redtail, the hoot of a barn owl, the high singing of a coyote, the bugle of an elk, or some other wild thing calling. A silence so big I can hear my own silence inside it. These are only a few of the ways the ranch mothers me.

PART FIVE

Deep Creek

Deep Creek

eep Creek, Shallow Creek, Middle Creek, Fern Creek. West Willow, East Willow, Antelope Park. These are the place-names that have dominated my lexicon for twenty-five years, the places that surround and abut and verge upon my 120 acres of high mountain meadow.

Miners Creek, Ivy Creek, Ute Creek, Rat Creek. The places I have walked up and down, again and again, with friends and lovers and generations of wolfhounds. I call the Shallow Creek hike Dante's favorite, because my very first wolfhound could still make it all the way to the aspen meadow at the trail's end during the last three years of his life, which he spent on three legs, after bone cancer. Coyote Rock got its name because once, when Rose was in heat, a coyote flirted with her up there for a good forty-five minutes until I finally got scared for both of them and chased him off.

San Luis Peak, Bristol Head, Red Mountain, Snow Mesa. Where I have skidded down a scree field to escape lightning bolts, and run from a cow elk who thought Dante got too close to her calf. Emily's Summit is a lesser peak, adjacent to 14,000-foot San Luis Peak, which we named for a writer named Emily Bernard, who came out to visit and took the first real hike of her life.

Copper Creek, Farmers Creek, Clear Creek Falls, Phoenix Park. Where I have picked wild raspberries and strawberries and more chanterelles than one person ought to be entitled to, and where, on several occasions, I have caught enough brook trout for a meal. Where I have encountered Basque shepherds mounted on compact, recently tamed mustangs, driving hundreds of domesticated sheep in their yearly circuit around the West.

Lime Creek, Spring Creek, the Snowshoe, Wason Park. Where mountainsides of aspen trees burst into tequila-sunrise tapestries in mid-September, and glow an almost alien green in June. Where the summer meadows uncover their treasures one at a time, first late May's wild iris, and then the blue flax in mid-June. The silvery lupine and the Indian paintbrush pop up all at once and usually together in mid-July, followed by the skyrocket and the blue penstemon, and those delicate purple harebells that, when the sun hits them from a certain angle, seem to be filled with light.

Deep Creek, Shallow Creek, Middle Creek, Fern Creek

Robert Pinckley's cabin is more than a hundred years old now. It has leaned to the west a bit ever since I've owned it, but last summer the ground underneath it seemed to be rising up from under the floorboards and if I didn't address it, the cabin was going to split in the center like an overbaked cupcake.

I have never had enough savings to restore the cabin. And even if I maxed out my credit cards to do it, I'd face difficult questions about how true to the original to be. Did I have any use for a cabin with a ceiling so low it caused the short man who built it to walk bent in half for fifty years of his life?

Creede, Colorado, is not Concord, Massachusetts. There wouldn't be a preservation society that cared how much I did or did not honor Pinckley's original plan. But *I* cared: about his memory, and about any feelings his ghost might have on the subject. If all I wanted was a dedicated writing studio, I could have knocked it down years ago and saved a bunch of money by starting from scratch.

Then I met RJ Mann, a young contractor in Creede who loves the town's old buildings and has made it his life's work to honor the spirit of the past within them, while making them functional here and now. First, RJ lifted the cabin and put a new foundation under it. He did that in trade for my 1964 Ford F-100 with three on the tree.

Belted kingfishers have always been my favorite bird, no contest. It goes back to my river-guiding days, when I interpreted the appearance of a kingfisher flitting along the banks above a particularly gnarly set of rapids as a sign that I would maneuver my raft through safely, without killing any of my passengers or myself. We have kingfishers along the Rio Grande—I see them occasionally when I'm walking the dogs there in summer, but kingfishers find me everywhere I go, from Florida to Cape Cod to the Puget Sound and Alaska. With their bright eyes, powdery blue backs, Eraserhead top-do, and jaunty white necktie, I've spent my life thinking of kingfishers as personal guardian angels whether I'm on foot, on a paddleboard, on my bike, in a car or on my raft.

In the process of pulling up the old rotted floor of the cabin, RJ found many of Bob Pinckley's belongings. Mousetraps, rat traps, pieces of a harmonica, a pipe, a pair of scissors, a pocket watch, empty tins of tobacco, newspapers so putrid with animal urine they were impossible to read. There was a well-preserved insert from a package of Super Anahist antihistamine cough syrup with vitamin C, several yellowed card stock receipts from a company in Minneapolis where Pinckley shipped the furs from his trapping business (including one for the sale of a house cat), a label from Prince Albert Crimp Cut in a can, and two beautifully rendered drawings of belted kingfishers, one that had graced a 25-yard container of Martin's Highest Quality Enameled Fishing Line (test 21 pounds), and the other a "collectible" insert from a box of Arm & Hammer baking soda. Other than the 1940s cartoon physician on the cough-syrup insert, and fat Prince Albert of "in a can" fame, the only two pieces of what one might call visual art that Pinckley intentionally saved were images of my favorite birds. After that discovery, I was determined to save his cabin, even if it meant cutting into savings I didn't exactly have.

"The first thing we want to do is raise the roof," RJ said. "We have to put a new roof on it anyhow. I mean we can make the roof *look* old—for about a thousand bucks extra we can get you a roof that'll only take one summer to rust. While we're at it we could put a sleeping loft up there so the whole downstairs could be your writing room."

"That sounds good," I said.

"I want to try to save this old window," RJ said. It was the one Pinckley shot rabbits out of and it *was* a beauty. A rectangle divided four ways, made of thick beveled glass, it opened out and downward, as if it had been designed for serving milk shakes out of. "And I think we ought to try to replace those smaller broken windows with something that resembles this one in style. None of that will be cheap." He laughed. "You have to pay big money for things that look old. I can probably use the lumber from the roof as wainscoting, depending on what shape it's in, and then we can seal the logs real good inside and out. We'll build a porch, front and back so you can listen to the creek, maybe a French door to the south for sun. I've got a beautiful piece of bristlecone pine that might make a perfect kitchen counter. . . ."

"How much money are we talking?" I asked. "Roughly, I mean. Top to bottom, to get it to the point where I can walk right in here and sit down to write."

"Thirty thousand," he said. "Could be a little less."

"And it will be rat proof?" I asked.

"If you leave food out here I can't make any promises," he said, "but they sure won't be running right in between the logs like they are now."

I wanted to do it. I wanted RJ to do it. I didn't have thirty thousand dollars, unless you counted my father's money.

In 2003, a few months after his ninetieth birthday, my mother already ten years in the ground, my father called to say, "You know, I was just getting ready to write my monthly check to the life insurance people, and it occurred to me, there's no scenario in which I'm going to benefit from the $225 I am putting into this fund every month. So if you want the thirty grand after I'm dead, you're going to have to start making the payments."

I said, "That seems a little like betting against my own team in the Super Bowl, just because I think the other guys have a better defense."

I wasn't surprised in the least by the proposition, but I was stunned that someone (my mother?) had talked my father into buying life insurance at all.

"Well, it's up to you," he said. "I've probably put about nine thousand in there already. That ought to be enough to get me in the ground."

"Let's call that good then," I said, smiling. There was a purity to my father's love of money that approached a kind of perfection. Like always, he hung up without saying goodbye.

A couple of years later, my father ran his "spend out and die plan" past me, which included several cruises he'd signed up for during what would be his ninety-third year.

"It's cleaner this way," he said, sounding for all the world like one of the Corleone brothers, though he was not even a little bit Italian. "You don't gain anything, but you also don't have to spend."

I pictured my father collapsing on the foredeck of a fifteen-story wedding cake of a boat as it pulled into Miami harbor. "If you like it, I like it," I said. The last thing I wanted was to take whatever was left of my father's money. Some part of me believed he would never actually die.

My father cruised to Italy, Turkey and the Caribbean that year and died instantly of a massive heart attack with a nice tan and about $40,000 in assets to his name. After nearly losing the ranch to Dani and her grandfather, I had made sure every dollar I put toward my mortgage I earned through writing, speaking or teaching, afraid that anything else might jinx it. I left my father's money in the investment account where he'd had it, and barely noticed when it lost half its value in 2008–09, or as it slowly gained itself back. *My* money, Drew had always insisted I call it during our therapy sessions, but I didn't, ever, at least not inside my own head.

The man in charge of the account was a friend of my father's who signed all his letters to me "Uncle Jim." The first time I called him after my father died it was to ask for a few thousand dollars because lightning had struck the ranch and fried the water pump in a month where money was tight already. But before I'd worked up the nerve to state the amount he said, "You know who went into the factories in World War II, Pam?" I said that I didn't. "It was the women. Pam, the women," and I said something like, "Yeah, I guess that's true," and hung up, and it was four more years before I gathered the courage to ask Uncle Jim for $10,000 to buy my friend Sarah's Prius, so I could save gas on my ten-hour airport round trip during the nonblizzarding months. The Prius cost fifteen thousand, but I only took ten out of my father's account, and made up the rest by taking on extra work over the summer, which sent Drew into raucous laughter. "Well," he said, wiping his eyes, "it's always nice to get your self-worth down to an exact figure."

My best friend from college, Kelly—a clinical psychologist—once wrote out a script for me, actual words to say when I called the office, including comebacks when they pressured me into leaving the money alone, and my friend Practical Karen offered to call *for* me, to just say she *was* me and get the money moved into my Creede checking account. But I still couldn't get it done. The only thing I *had* managed to do was switch it, against the broker's recommendation, into a socially responsible portfolio.

Now my father's been dead for more than a decade, and I'm older than he was when I was born. Jim has gone into some kind of semiretirement and even the woman who Jim passed me on to after that has moved on. Kurt, the new guy, sounds half my age, and still, I hesitate.

A few years ago, in the back of a car on the way to a reading, the poet Terrance Hayes and I were talking about fathers and when I told him about the money and how afraid I was to touch it he said, "I understand completely."

"You do?" I said, since none of my friends nor my therapist seemed to.

"Sure," Terrance said. "That money is the only thing your father is ever going to give you, whether he wanted to give it to you or not. The money is a kind of reparation. Once you spend it, both it and he will really be gone."

"What do you think would happen," I asked Tami on the phone, the night after RJ had given me the estimate, "if I used the rest of my father's money to restore the cabin?"

"Your money," Tami said, as she always did, when this subject came up.

"My money," I said, emptily.

"I think it's a terrific idea," Tami said.

"And even if it turns out I don't need all of it for the cabin, there's no reason I shouldn't move it all into my own account, right?" I said.

"Pam," Tami said, "I know you don't believe this, but that *is* your own account. There really isn't anybody else there."

In the end, I borrowed $20,000 from my dead father, and added nine back-to-back weeks of summer-conference teaching to make up the balance, which turned out to be another $20,000, because once RJ sent me photos and I saw how beautiful it was turning out to be, I told him not to skimp. I don't see Drew too often anymore, so I haven't gotten to tell him my self-worth has gone up in the last decade by exactly $10,000. It feels good to have busted my ass this summer toward a dedicated space for my writing. And to be perfectly honest, it feels a little strange—but not awful—to have finally let my father give me that gift.

West Willow, East Willow, Antelope Park

The last thing this book needs is another dead elk story. I know that. And yet a herd of two hundred elk live in the national forest immediately to the south of me. They come through my pasture to drink from the river in winter, en masse. Once the Soward Ranch closes up for the year, the elk are my closest neighbors, so I see a lot of them. Excluding the domesticated animals who live with me, I see more of them than I do anyone else.

More than ten years ago, on a pasture walk, the ground still muddy but not impassable, walking the fence line looking for breaks and fallen posts, I came upon an elk skeleton, caught up in the fence. Her bones had been picked clean by coyotes, but not clean enough to have disentangled her from the barbed wire that meant her end. In twenty-five years she had been the only elk who fell victim to my fences, until yesterday.

Samantha Dunn, who I teach with each summer at Esalen, was visiting. We didn't know each other all that well, if we were measuring in quantifiable, real-world terms. But we knew each other's books and could recognize each other's scars. We both had limbs partially and permanently disfigured by horses, and we were pretty sure we'd had the same mother in two different models, the New Jersey and the New Mexico. Sam needed out of Orange County for a bit, so I invited her to come back to her beloved Southwest landscape, to relax for a few days surrounded by the big blue sky, spruce trees and gamma grass.

It was late March, and in the days before Sam arrived, my pasture freed itself from the last of the snow (or, the last of the snow until the great May blizzard of 2016 would "surprise" us, as it did every spring), so we took the year's first pasture walk together. Out across the dead grass and over the still saturated ground to the first corner post of the pasture, where we saw the elk, caught in the fence, the barbed wire twisted around both her forelegs. We assumed she was dead, so there was first that sadness, but when the dogs went up to sniff her, she flailed her strangled and bleeding legs at them, which kicked the sadness up into a whole different category. I ran back to the house for the wire cutters; we cut her free, and she fell to the ground. Her eyes were opened too wide, and her stomach looked unnaturally bloated. Pregnant, we thought, because we needed one more thing that morning to tear at our hearts.

"Do you have a gun?" Sam asked, and I said I didn't.

Sam was shocked by this, and I considered for the first time in twenty-two years that it might be irresponsible of me *not* to have a gun, when—my mind flashed back to Monroe and Daphne—I'd always thought about it the other way around. This morning was the first time I actually could have used one. Even when I had to kill the chicken whose guts William had spilled all over the yard, the axe had been more than enough.

"Well," Sam said, "now that she's free, I think she'll die very quickly. It was probably just the pain and the adrenaline keeping her alive."

"Let's leave her then," I said, "to die in peace." We both told her we were sorry, called the dogs away from their sniffing and continued on the pasture walk.

When we returned from the walk, I put the dogs in the house and went to let the sheep out. I looked across the five hundred yards or so of pasture that separated the elk from me, and was pretty sure I saw her kicking. It seemed impossible she had not died during the duration of our walk. Maybe it was just a big bird of prey I had seen, rising off the carcass and it had only looked like her legs. I ran inside and grabbed the binoculars. She was definitely kicking, but in spite of her vigor, seemed unable to raise her neck and head.

Sam walked back out there to check on her. Her eyes looked better, Sam said, she was blinking, and licking the patch of snow under her head to get water and actually swallowing it down. She was breathing deeply but normally. But her forelegs were cut all the way to the tendons, and then there was the fact that she couldn't seem to move her head separately from her neck, or her neck separately from her spine.

I went back out there with Sam and we put our hands on her neck and spoke to her softly, apologizing for my barbed-wire fences, that tamer and scourge of the American West. Then I returned to the house and called Doc Howard. "I don't think there's any way she could possibly make it," I said. "But she's very much alive and I don't have a gun here."

"Fish and Game doesn't really like you to shoot anything anyway, Pam," Doc said, and I felt relief flood through me. "Give Brent a call—I know it's Sunday, but he'll have his cell phone. If you can't get a hold of him I can give you the numbers of half a dozen people in town who'll have a gun."

"Do you think somebody would want to eat her?" I asked.

"I think she's been stressed too long," Doc said. "I don't think it would be good for anybody to eat that meat."

"Except for the coyotes," I said.

"Yeah," he said. "They're not so fussy."

I left a message for Brent. I went out with my binoculars again and now the elk seemed to be lying still.

I went back inside, where Sam had made us tea. "I know she's suffering, but I don't want some random man from town to bring his gun and all his macho energy out here to the ranch and shoot her," I said and for the first time in that difficult day finally burst into tears.

Sam hugged me. "You want to save all the wild things from all the bad men," she said, and in *my* kitchen at least, no truer words had ever been spoken.

"Brent's not that way," I said. "He's super calm and decent. He's had this job for twenty-one years. He loves the elk more than anybody in the world."

"Then we wait for Brent," Sam said.

"But what if he doesn't call back and it gets dark and she gets eaten alive by coyotes?"

"Then she will be like many other elk who lived here long before you did," Sam said.

That was the right answer. But still, without my fences, this particular elk would not have had to die.

"There's always my kitchen cleaver," I said, "but we might get that all wrong too."

Brent called back within a half hour and thirty minutes after that he stood on my porch. He took one look at our faces, and rattled off a series of stories of elk who had pulled through, one that had had three legs cut all the way around by wire.

"When I started this job I used to put them down if they had a runny nose," he said, "but in twenty-one years I've learned a lot about how tough these critters are, and I've also seen lots of three-leggeds, the same animals, winter after winter. Especially the females. They're tougher than you think."

It was sweet of him to try to cheer us up, but we were all but certain that once he got out there and saw her, there was only going to be one answer.

"Should we go with him?" I asked Sam, something in me afraid I was shirking my duties if I did not. What I wanted to be least of all was one of those people who dropped the earth, or a dog, or an elk, off at the door of the vet.

"I think we already said goodbye," Sam said. "I think the fewer the people, the better for her."

From the kitchen window we watched Brent walk across the pasture, then we watched him look her over, and then take out his pistol, and then we heard the muffled report of the shot.

I had told him on the phone I was worried about how close she was to the house, worried about the coyotes and the dogs getting into the carcass. He had said he would try to take the carcass away in his truck if he could drive out there, but it was four o'clock in the afternoon, and 41 degrees, and I knew the pasture would be soup all the way. We watched him drag her carcass a few feet away from the fence. And then we watched him drag her a little farther, and then it occurred to me he was going to try to drag that elk all the way to the back of my property himself.

Sam and I threw on our boots and crossed the space between us and the elk for the fourth time that day. Brent told us the elk was last year's calf, and as soon as he said it I realized she was, in fact, quite small, and that's why she hadn't made it over my fence. This was a bad news/good news scenario—while she had only lived a year herself, she did not, at least, have a nearly viable calf in her belly.

"Sometimes when they hang up like that they destroy a vertebra," he said, which I took as his explanation for why she couldn't lift her head, why he knew so immediately she was a lost cause.

She was gone now, a pile of meat that bore little resemblance to the sweet soul who blinked her eyes at us, who tried to lick water from the top of the melting snow. We each picked up a leg and started pulling. It was, in fact, easier to have her dead than to have her in pain and living with no hope of recovery. We pulled her across the pasture and around to the back of the hill where the homesteaders are buried. This might keep her scent off the wind that blew toward the house, and keep the coyotes farther away from the sheep when they came, as they would, probably as soon as nightfall, to begin the process of breaking down the carcass.

Standing above her one minute more, I had the terrible thought that maybe this *was* Willa, who, if she lived, would now be a yearling. Maybe she had remembered the barn and gotten left behind somehow and was coming back to see us—but this was, I decided, a thought that might be too self-torturing even for me. There were at least two hundred head of elk who used my ranch in winter, and probably seventy-five calves born each year. If Willa had made it through those first weeks of her life, with or without a mother, likely she was somewhere up on the mountain right now, eating the brand-new shoots of grass that were, just in these last few days, starting to poke through in sheltered microclimates.

One day, if I could put away enough money maybe I could change my fences from barbed wire to wood. I had no idea how much that would cost for 120 acres, maybe ten thousand dollars, maybe a hundred thousand. I could be like Dona and Robert Blair and buy myself a half mile every Christmas. It would make me the laughingstock of the county, but I didn't care about that. Be the change, I thought, as I did twenty or thirty times every day during the moments I was so obviously not.

The sun was falling toward Handies Peak, washing the pasture golden as Brent, Sam and I made our way back to the house. We talked about the bighorn sheep that live up in Seepage Creek, and an extra-large coyote I had seen up there the last time I was snowshoeing. I told Brent I used to be a Dall-sheep-hunting guide in Alaska, and I knew he could not quite reconcile that information with the fifty-four-year-old grief-stricken-over-an-elk-yearling woman before him. Or perhaps he could, perhaps in his own way he was as sad about the young elk cow as I was, and perhaps that's why, the year before with Willa, when he had said, "Pam, I'm going to need you to trust me a little bit," I had.

"I had an insatiable appetite for being in the wilderness," I said. "I never killed anything myself, but on those ten-day, one-hunter-one-guide sheep hunts, I learned a lot about how to conduct myself." Some hunters were assholes. Just like some of everything are assholes. But in the years I spent guiding hunters, I met many men who had deep respect for wildlife and wilderness, and Brent reminded me of the best of them.

I gave him a mircobrewed root beer for the road along with my endless gratitude.

"This is just what I do," he said, for the third time since he arrived, though whether he was convincing me or himself I couldn't be sure.

Later that night, after I'd made Sam and me a good, comforting dinner that included my famous mashed potatoes, and we were still sad anyway, I said, "Well, here is the one thing. The one silver lining. Now you and I have been through something together. In the actual world. It's not just a hunch anymore. Now she'll always be right there between us."

Two weeks later a package came to the ranch, the return address belonging to Daniel Leslie, a jeweler in Oregon. Inside were two tiny elk prints, one for each ear, and a gift card that said, "Us orphans, it matters that we stick together."

Miners Creek, Ivy Creek, Ute Creek, Rat Creek

In the years since the sheep slaughter, I have upped my ranch time by at least 30 percent. I've missed out on a couple of big paychecks and great destinations, but it's felt good to be home enough to feel the rhythms of all the seasons, to keep a close eye on Roany as he ages, to watch each year's lambs turn into sheep.

I replaced the forty-year-old woodstove with one that doesn't leak, so now my clothes smell better. I replaced the furnace so it doesn't sound like it's walking from one side of the basement to the other during the coldest January nights. My friend Sarna bought me a gift certificate to Home Depot and I bought some tools I'm learning to use.

Every time Jeff Larson—Creede mayor, hot dog stand owner and my go-to odd-job guy—comes out to replace the furnace fan belt, or the water filter housing, or a breaker box fuse out at one of the frost-free pumps, he insists I pay very close attention.

"A woman living out here all by herself has got to know how to fix things!" he always says to me as I crane over whatever pile of parts he is craned over, trying to guess which tool he is going to ask for next and fearing I won't know it by name.

Jeff is whatever kind of genius it is that allows him to know the make and model of every propane furnace fan made since 1936 (just as one example), so I listen and watch, and try to learn. I'm more game now to take a stab at a repair job myself, even when it takes me three tries and that many trips to the hardware store. Although I still tend to use butter knives as screwdrivers, and the heel of my cowboy boot as a hammer, progress is progress. In fact, I've come to appreciate duct tape and baling wire so much I have to force myself not to sneak a little of each into my suitcase whenever I go traveling. Add a can of WD-40, a universal socket set and my Leatherman, and I can put most disasters on temporary hold until Jeff can get out here and bail me out.

I mounted a gear hammock in the mudroom to collect the hats and gloves and neck gaiters that accumulate on the countertops in winter. I fixed an ice dam in my freezer after watching a YouTube video. I reinforced the whole sheep pen with an extra layer of chicken fencing to protect them better against varmints. I solved a recently developing problem of William jumping over the four-foot fence to chase the donkeys by stringing a single white cord six inches above the fence for a half a mile to make a visual barrier. I understand none of these things is particularly impressive, but they make me feel good about how I'm living my life.

I'm still frustrated by the things I don't know, the things I do wrong, the things I can't fix. I still feel stupid and helpless out here some of the time. But another thing the ranch is teaching me—maybe something I needed to learn more than how to use a band saw—is that it's not so awful to have to sometimes rely on others. I'd be lost without the handymen, horsemen, farriers, shearers and especially Doc, continually bailing me out.

I've also gotten better at choosing ranchsitters. Jessica was one of four guides on a five-day all-women's float/writing workshop on the San Juan River where I'd been asked to guest teach. Uncowed by rapids, bad weather or the mansplainer who was her superior on the trip, Jessica was well read, deeply competent and apparently tireless, and by the second day I had already asked her what she did with her winters. That I met her on the very same river where I had guided for six years seemed like part of the magic; I couldn't shake the fact that I was being taken down the river by my twenty-five-year-old self. Jess and I spent the next three winters trading off the ranch duties and during those winters I was as close as I ever get to worry-free.

When I got home after the month and a half Josh Weil watched the ranch, I could tell all the animals were relaxed and happy.

"One thing," Josh said, "I didn't pick up your mail."

When I told him it was no problem he said, "Honestly, I never actually made it into town. In fact, I never even made it out the driveway. The dogs and I took our walks, I tended the animals—I couldn't think of a reason to go anywhere."

"What did you eat?" I asked him.

"Oh," he said, "you had lots of expired food in that pantry. I'm an excellent forager."

Last summer I traded weeks with a young man named Dustin whom I'd met on a three-day visit to the M.F.A. program at Louisana's McNeese State. Every time I came home between gigs I could feel how the ranch was getting under his skin. The way he'd get up, just after sunrise, and top off all the water troughs as an excuse to be out in the pasture in the first blush of dawn. The way Livie followed him around all day, mooning up at him like he was her boyfriend. The way he'd disappear suddenly after dinner, and thirty minutes later the moonlight would catch him standing in the driveway, listening to the coyotes, looking up at the sky.

I knew right from the beginning that, as much as I love my solitude, I was never meant to keep the ranch all to myself. Now my coming and goings make space for other people to work in this quiet beauty for a while.

Another March comes to an end and it's time to load the dogs up in the 4Runner and head out to Davis for the teaching quarter. "We get to come home in ten short weeks," I tell the dogs, by which I mean, myself. I have promised us all a weekly hike up in the Sierras. I am ready for sushi and Thai food and movie theaters. I am eager to be back in the classroom, and excited to work with the grad students on their theses. I am determined—because hope never dies—to try once more to find a place to run the dogs in the Davis area where we won't get shot at or arrested or poisoned. But I am never quite ready to leave this leashless paradise, this wild heaven, that is, at the very moment I write these words, bathed in the clearest, finest, late-in-the-day high-altitude light.

San Luis Peak, Bristol Head, Red Mountain, Snow Mesa

When I told my friends I went off to California to teach for ten weeks trusting RJ's vision for the cabin more than my own, they all said I was crazy. But my friends live mostly in cities, and have had their run-ins with urban contractors. I consoled myself by saying they didn't understand Creede and they didn't know RJ. "He really seems to care about the old buildings," I said, which turned out to be the understatement of the century.

After ten long weeks and a late-night drive home from the Denver airport, I rose after only a few hours' sleep and went out to feed the horses. Standing in the corral, my hands full of carrots and apples, was the first time I saw the renovated cabin in person, its old logs freshly caulked, its much taller roof already rusting, its new pine porches shining in the morning sun. Looking harder, I saw that the east window, the beautiful rectangle with the hinged wooden door, was throwing some kind of strange shadows. I squinted my eyes to make sense of what I was seeing: forks and spoons and combs and church keys. I gave Roany the last of the apples all in one mouthful and walked toward the cabin. Friends of RJ—John and Allie—had made me one of their signature windows, but unlike the ones I had seen at their gallery in town, everything that was embedded in the glass of *this* window came from under the floor of the cabin. Pinckley's pipe, his harmonica, a mousetrap, a bullet casing, a tin with two ladies dancing, a file, half of a safety pin, a few gears and several padlocks with the key still in the lock. I stared at it amazed for a few minutes. Then I stepped inside the cabin.

RJ did use the wood from the old roof for the wainscoting, his piece of bristlecone pine for the backsplash, a slice of redwood for the counter where the sink would eventually go, and barn wood that had been laying around my yard to trim out the windows. Jesse Albright, who grew up right on the other side of the cattle guard, made me a pair of maple French doors that look out on the creek and Red Mountain. Even the threshold beneath those doors is an art piece, a rectangle of maple, with a spiral of darker wood grain, sanded so when the sunlight hits it, it shines. Even the ladder to the sleeping loft is beautiful, a split log for the handrails, and tiger-striped pine for the steps.

I have never before had a room of my own in which to write. I understand in a world where so many are suffering, this does not make the very longest hardship list. But I have one now, still full of that cranky old homesteader's energy, but made new, made beautiful, by the hands of RJ, his sidekick Jess Biernat and my neighbor Jesse Albright.

Standing in the umber glow of 9,000-foot sunshine hitting the golden pine walls, it's easy to believe I have done the right thing, on behalf of Pinckley's ghost and on behalf of my writing. There's another part of me that believes just as strongly I ought to have given all of the money to the Wilderness Society or the NRDC. I reckon guilt is just part of the equation, here on the brink of the empire's fall. I can't drive a car, get on a plane, waste a bit of food, use a noncompostable paper plate—or even a compostable paper plate—without being acutely aware I'm part of the problem. Perhaps this is exactly how it should be. Perhaps this is how it should have been all along.

"Being in here makes me feel loved," I blurt to RJ, making him blush, later that day when he comes out to gray the porch pine. It's true, and even though I don't know RJ nearly well enough to say such a thing, there's something to this idea that makes me want to chase it. There is love in these old logs and in RJ's workmanship and I can feel it every time I walk inside. We call such a limited number of relationships love in our lives, but there is always love around us—it's as ubiquitous as oxygen. It lives in the houses where we've slept, the kitchens where we've cooked, in the food we've prepared for the people we love and in the walls we have shaped with our hands.

"I'm just glad you're happy," RJ says.

"I'm so happy," I say. "I'm so happy I haven't even caught up to how happy I am."

Copper Creek, Farmers Creek, Clear Creek Falls, Phoenix Park

I walk up into the burn today for the first time this summer. The dogs and I follow the trail as it drops off sharply into the Trout Creek drainage, and then starts to climb, gradually toward the burn. There's that not-quite-right smell again, getting stronger the closer we get to the burn line: retardant and char and seared earth. I've been walking in the burn for four years now, with enough frequency that the smell has become a part of me. I can smell it in hotel rooms in Alaska or New Jersey when I open my suitcase and pull out my hiking boots.

The year after the fire the burn was full of woodpeckers, and last summer I heard peepers in the wetland well inside the line, but today, other than flies, no wildlife is stirring. This could be a function of my timing; it is just about high noon. I round the corner where there used to be a creek crossing the dogs liked to drink from, only to find the bed dry as a bone. We've had our predictable monsoonal moisture every day for the last ten, so this stream didn't dry up due to drought. A mudslide higher up on the fire scar must have diverted the flow. I pause to listen and in the midday stillness I can hear the place where the creek has shifted: flowing water a hundred yards ahead.

We enter the burn, and I startle at the size of the new aspens. They have exploded since last summer and the entire hillside is thick with them. Trunks about the diameter of a dime, stringy limbs that reach taller than the dogs and in some places taller than me. It still looks like a burn in here: there are still the charcoaled stumps sculpted into goblin shapes, the proliferation of fuchsia-blooming fireweed, still ash on the ground. But now the dominant landscape is a miniature, wildly cluttered aspen grove, a million sets of roots entwining to form one giant root structure, reaching down into the newly replenished earth.

Many of the dead trees have fallen, and many more—the sign back at the trailhead warned me—are poised to fall: THIS IS YOUR DECISION POINT! say the giant red letters. All of the fugitive color from the retardant drops on the standing unburnt trees has washed away in the snow and rain. What was here before was mostly subalpine forest, predominantly Engelmann spruce, and there are a few young trees tucked here and there among the aspen, but this particular piece of the burn will spend the next fifty to seventy-five years of its life as an aspen grove. When the aspens get old and start to fall, the spruce will take back over. Depending on climate change. Depending on how our priorities shift.

Lime Creek, Spring Creek, the Snowshoe, Wason Park

This book has taken me nearly five years to write, a long time, even by my own molasses standards. When I started, I was attempting to express my love for a piece of land that has defined the largest portion—by far—of my life. Somewhere along the way I came to understand that to write a book about my little parcel of take-your-breath beauty, sitting up here, as it does, in one of the last valleys in North America that will go under water when the oceans start to rise in earnest, to write a book about loving this particular pristine acreage, when so many millions of acres are being destroyed at an unprecedented rate, would be a kind of heresy. Somewhere in the process I started writing toward an answer to the question I wake up with every morning and go to bed with every night. How do I find hope on a dying planet, and if there is no hope to be found, how do I live in its absence? In what state of being? Respect? Tenderness? Unmitigated love? The rich and sometimes deeply clarifying dreamscape of vast inconsolable grief?

In her book *Hope in the Dark*, Rebecca Solnit calls for us to redefine hope as "an accounting of complexities and uncertainties, with openings." Is there an opening before us big enough to save the planet? And if so, is there an opening big enough to save the planet that does not necessitate the annihilation of us? E. O. Wilson says we could take the earth all the way down to the microbes, and she would still find a way to recover. Even now, evidence of the earth's ability to heal herself is all around us, a daily astonishment. Every day the Everglades purify stream water by filtering out agricultural toxins, mycelia mushrooms filter radioactivity from the ground around Chernobyl, earthworms are *still* cleaning all that DDT we put in the soil in decades past. We won't know until the ninth inning what she'll do in her last at bat.

This book has been an effort to write my way to an understanding of how to be alive in the meantime, in the final days, if not of the earth, then at least of the earth as I've known her. Because it has only been in knowing her that I've come to know myself.

Deep Creek, Shallow Creek, Middle Creek, Fern Creek

In early October, my friends Byron and Seth come to spend the night. Byron is Diné and has that gentle Diné worldview that makes it feel as though the sun is always out around him. Seth, his husband, commands a fair amount of wonder on his own.

I offer them the cabin rather than the guest room because I am hoping a little Byron magic might rub off in there, that I might get wiser in my writing because of whatever he might leave behind in his sleep. We laugh our way through dinner, I light the cabin's brand-new pellet stove and send them to bed, telling them nothing about the cabin except that it's where the original homesteader lived.

"So who's the old guy?" Seth says to me, first thing, when they come inside for breakfast. "Little guy, skinny. Walks all bent over?"

The skin on my scalp prickles. "That's Bob Pinckley," I say. "It's his cabin."

"I wondered . . . ," Seth says. "I figured."

"What happened?" I ask.

"Oh, at first he tried to scare me a little," Seth says, "but I could tell his heart wasn't in it. I went out for a bedtime smoke and he wanted to stand on the porch with me. I think what he really wanted was to get near my cigarette. Seemed he'd been missing them kinda bad."

In the fall of 2015, Pittsburgh Kyle and her canine copilot Apacha had come to housesit, and the morning after they arrived Kyle came to breakfast with her head still full of a dream she'd had where a man, who said his name was Bob, asked her if he could get into bed with her. He was cold, he said, and lonely, but Kyle could tell there was nothing salacious about it, and he meant her no harm. She asked him flat out, if it was his intention to hurt or try to scare her, and Bob said it wasn't, so she let him cuddle up to her. The dream scared Kyle, only after waking, because she'd left a friend behind in Pittsburgh—an elderly gentleman named Bob, whom she had been looking after. After breakfast she called the assisted living home where *her* Bob lived to make sure he was okay, and he was. "This Bob didn't look like my Bob, though," Kyle said. "This guy wasn't even as big as me."

I worried, through the entire cabin renovation, that I might disturb or disappoint or enrage Bob Pinckley. It was right after RJ put the new foundation under it that Pinckley appeared to Kyle in her dream. I worried there was too much of *me* in the cabin now: the shiny red Enviro stove, the sandstone sink, the giant cushy chair perfect for writing. To say nothing of the T3-R Triple High Impact mouse brain scrambler, which had been emitting its little whirrs and beeps since August in an attempt to convince the rodents that have inhabited Pinckley's cabin since the 1960s that they needed to find another place to live.

"I don't think he has any problem with you," Seth says. "I think if he did, you would know."

I've seen five or six ghosts in my life, so I don't know whether to feel relieved or a little hurt that I have not seen Pinckley. Maybe now that I'll be spending more time in the cabin that will change.

"What do you know about the little girl who died in there?" Seth asks me later. "Terribly sick, breathless, drowning in her own blood."

"That was Ada," I say, "Bob's sister. She died when they were children. Of heart failure."

West Willow, East Willow, Antelope Park

Today I am sitting inside Bob Pinckley's restored cabin. *My* cabin, restored using *my* money. The cabin where Pinckley lived simply for fifty years and then died. The place I will finish this book.

I'm looking out the same window he did, listening to Lime Creek as it falls through the beaver ponds, watching the young aspen leaves quake in the breeze, watching this year's lambs—Hillary, Clark and Myrtle—play something that for all the world looks like red rover in their newly expanded enclosure, which runs all the way to the creek. Soon I will get Bob's kingfishers framed and put up in here, though the wood is too pretty to want to cover it with anything more than that.

Livie comes barreling into the cabin with her wet and muddy paws—she's been down at the creek—and tracks up the floors that are so glorious right now, fresh from their second coat of urethane, nobody ought to be allowed to walk on them ever.

This is a *cabin*, I remind myself, a cabin in the mountains where you live with your beloved dogs.

Greg and I parted ways last year, mostly amicably. There are a million possible expanations, but one is that he loves living in California, and I love living at the ranch. I remain grateful to him for so many things from the years we spent together, most especially how he took care of William when I was in the Great Bear Rainforest, and how he tended the ranch while the forest burned.

Half a year ago, I met a Taoist national forest ranger and landscape photographer named Mike Blakeman, a man who has loved these particular mountains, this particular river valley, for even more years than I have. Forty to be exact.

"Phoenix Peak is my stupa and the willows, wind, elk, and creeks my sangha," he wrote in one of our first emails, "I hear the voices of miners and woodsmen in the babble of the creeks in Phoenix and Wason parks." He went on to describe his day up on the mountain, letting the scree fields and the snow squalls and the willows talk to him, asking the mountain questions about our potential, listening hard for its response. "I hope you don't think I am too wacko after reading this email, but if so it is who I am and I thought you should know . . . if this doesn't scare you away, well then . . . let's just see what happens."

These days we spend a lot of time walking in these mountains together. We take every opportunity we can to sleep on the ground. We are seeing what happens. But our feelings for each other are inextricable from our feelings for these rocks and trees and rivers. In the classroom I always tell my students: trust the metaphor because it knows more than you do. I look across the river toward Bristol Head, and it tells me everything I need to know.

And one more thing about Mike Blakeman: four years before we met, he wrote the paragraph that, three years before we met, I copied from the USDA Forest Service website to serve as the epigraph for "Diary of a Fire." In that odd way that the story writes a life at the same time the life is writing the story, he was in my book years before he was in my life.

Livie leans in for a pet, while William stands in the driveway at attention. They are trying to talk me into a walk down to the river before my writing day begins, and I can find no reason not to oblige. After a quarter century, I'm starting to learn what farmers like Rick Davie know. When you give yourself wholly to a piece of ground, its goodness enters your bloodstream like an infusion. You will never be alone in the same way again, and never quite dislocated. Your heart will grow down into and back out of that ground like a tree.

After my father broke my femur, I thought he might kill me every single day. Because of that, I got pretty good at compartmentalizing my fear for the future and only being in my body part of the time. But

I've had a lot of therapy since then and now I'm ready to be whole. I will never know all the abuses my father suffered that made him need to hurt me, but for the rest of my *own* life, I want to live simultaneously inside the wonder and the grief without having to diminish one to accommodate the other. I want to be honest with myself about our condition, but also to love the damaged world and do what I can to help it thrive. In December 2018, I signed the papers to put this ranch in an environmental land trust. Maybe before too long, I'll get those smooth and safe white fences put up.

Where there is life, there is hope, a veterinarian I loved for the way he loved my dog once told me. By which he meant, as long as we are living, there is always time to expand the story.

My mother always told me, I don't even want to *see* you until dinner. And with those words she freed me to go out and love the earth.

b

Acknowledgments

Sections of these essays, or in a few cases, the entire essay, have appeared in modified form in other publications as follows:

"Some Kind of Calling," in the fortieth-anniversary issue of *Outside*, edited by Alex Heard.

About three paragraphs of the essay "The Tinnitus of Truth Telling," in an essay entitled "Ebeneezer Laughs Back," in the anthology *Double Bind: Women on Ambition*, edited by Robin Romm; "Ebeneezer Laughs Back" also appeared in *Elle*.

Approximately one-quarter of the essay "The Season of Hunkering Down," under the title "Let It Snow," in *Sunset*, edited by Nino Padova.

"Mother's Day Storm," under the title "What Has Irony Done for Us Lately," in the "Political Landscapes" issue of *About Place Journal*, edited by Taylor Brorby; the "Fenton" section of that same essay in *The Dharma of Dogs*, edited by Leslie Brown.

"A Kind of Quiet Most People Have Forgotten," in the anthology *Shades of Blue*, edited by Amy Ferris.

"The Sound of Horse Teeth on Hay," in *High Desert Journal*, edited by Joe Wilkins.

"Ranch Almanac: Donkey Chasing," in *Catamaran*, edited by Elizabeth McKensie.

Approximately half of the essay "Kindness," under the title "Every Decent Thing About Myself," in the anthology *A Matter of Being*, edited by Annie Liontas.

Thanks

This book, more than any other I have written, took a village. I am so very grateful for every one of you, I haven't even caught up to how grateful I am yet:

Emma Bogdonoff, who, in the final days and weeks of editing, was my true collaborator. No one has ever cared about a book they did not write more.

Maggie Pahos, Becky Mandelbaum, Dustin Shattuck, Greg Glazner, Cynthia Newberry Martin, Mike Blakeman, Melanie Simonich, Kyle Piatkoski and Tami Anderson, who read or listened to all of this book in various stages and gave invaluable feedback and fact-checking.

Liz Darhansoff for her sharp eye and her passion, and Michele Mortimer, who gave me the single best set of edits I have ever received.

Alane Mason and Ashley Patrick for their good and steady editorial advice and their work within W. W. Norton on my behalf.

Trent Duffy, for his thoughtful and exacting copy editing.

Tom Payne and Carl Vavak for agreeing to be interviewed.

Johanna Gray and Jan Jacobs at the Creede Historical Society for help with research.

All my writer sisters and brothers, but Samantha Dunn, Lidia Yuknavitch and Taylor Brorby in particular, who would not let me give up on myself or this book.

My students, from whom I learn more and more with every passing year.

Doc Howard, Brent Woodward, RJ Mann, Rick Davie, Connie Stobbe, Jeff Larson, Sam Arnold, Dale Pizel, John Stynchula and again, Mike Blakeman, for coming when I called.

Dona Blair Smith, for selling me the ranch for 5 percent down and a copy of *Cowboys Are My Weakness*, and for carrying the note, and for believing I would find a way to pay it.